Public Sector Innovation

Governments around the world are under pressure to do more with less. Dispelling the conventional wisdom that government is the enemy of innovation, this book argues that the promise of innovation addressing the most compelling societal problems will only come to fruition if governments become full partners and participants in innovation. The authors provide a systematic overview, analysis, framework, research agenda, and strategic directions for the study of public sector innovation, examining drivers, sources, barriers, typologies, and outcomes of innovation along with ethics. They suggest that innovation in government requires a new approach to public sector strategy, organization, human resources, and culture. Featuring large data analyses and poignant case studies drawn from best practices across the globe, Demircioglu and Audretsch identify what works and what doesn't in transforming governments from the periphery to the very heart of the most profound innovations driving societal change and development.

MEHMET AKIF DEMIRCIOGLU is Faculty Member in the School of Public Policy and Administration at Carleton University. He is also affiliated with the Executive Education program at the National University of Singapore, the Institute for Future Government at Yonsei University, the Institute for Development Strategies at Indiana University, and Arizona State University. He was ranked among the top 2% of the world's top scientists released by Standard University (2023), and received three research excellence awards (National University of Singapore) and a teaching award (Indiana University).

DAVID B. AUDRETSCH is Distinguished Professor in the O'Neill School of Public & Environmental Affairs at Indiana University. He was recognized as a Clarivate Citation Laureate in 2021 and awarded the Global Award for Entrepreneurship Research by the Swedish Foundation for Entrepreneurship. He has received honorary doctorate degrees from the University of Augsburg, Jonköping University, and the University of Siegen, and has been awarded the Schumpeter Prize from the University of Wuppertal.

Public Sector Innovation

MEHMET AKIF DEMIRCIOGLU
Carleton University

DAVID B. AUDRETSCH
Indiana University

Shaftesbury Road, Cambridge CB2 8EA, United Kingdom

One Liberty Plaza, 20th Floor, New York, NY 10006, USA

477 Williamstown Road, Port Melbourne, VIC 3207, Australia

314–321, 3rd Floor, Plot 3, Splendor Forum, Jasola District Centre,
New Delhi – 110025, India

103 Penang Road, #05–06/07, Visioncrest Commercial, Singapore 238467

Cambridge University Press is part of Cambridge University Press & Assessment,
a department of the University of Cambridge.

We share the University's mission to contribute to society through the pursuit of
education, learning and research at the highest international levels of excellence.

www.cambridge.org
Information on this title: www.cambridge.org/9781009279239

DOI: 10.1017/9781009279277

First published 2024

A catalogue record for this publication is available from the British Library

Library of Congress Cataloging-in-Publication Data
Names: Demircioglu, Mehmet Akif, author. | Audretsch, David B., author.
Title: Public sector innovation / Mehmet Akif Demircioglu, Carleton
University, David B. Audretsch, Indiana University.
Description: New York, NY : Cambridge University Press, 2024. | Includes
bibliographical references and index.
Identifiers: LCCN 2023047139 | ISBN 9781009279239 (hardback) |
ISBN 9781009279277 (ebook)
Subjects: LCSH: Public administration. | Organizational change. | Public
policy. | Industrial management – Philosophy. | Public
administration – Economic aspects.
Classification: LCC JF1321 .D46 2024 | DDC 351–dc23/eng/20240111
LC record available at https://lccn.loc.gov/2023047139

ISBN 978-1-009-27923-9 Hardback
ISBN 978-1-009-27924-6 Paperback

*This book is dedicated to the public sector champions
of innovation, who prove through example and leadership
that government is part of the solution, not the problem.*

Contents

Figures

Tables

Acknowledgments

We started this book project when the first author (Mehmet) approached the second author (David) in early 2017 regarding research gaps in the public sector innovation literature. Mehmet thanks David for encouraging him to write a book about these ideas. Since then, we have met in several places, including Bloomington, Munich, and Singapore, to finish the book. Similarly, David is grateful to Mehmet for leading the project.

We are thankful to the many people who played an essential role in the process of writing this book. First, Senior Commissioning Editor Valerie Appleby and Editorial Assistant Carrie Parkinson have been fantastic support from the beginning to the end. In particular, we are grateful to Carrie because Carrie is patient, supportive, accommodating, and helpful despite our project being delayed several times. We want to thank Chloe Quinn and Ranjith Kumar for their support and guidance during the production stage. We are also thankful to our institutions: The National University of Singapore's Lee Kuan Yew (LKY) School of Public Policy, Carleton University's School of Public Policy, and Indiana University's O'Neill School of Public and Environmental Affairs. Mehmet received financial support from both LKY School and Carleton University's Faculty of Public Affairs to complete the book. He is thankful for this financial and institutional support.

We are grateful to our research assistants, including Roberto Vivona, Aarthi Raghavan, Kidjie Saguin, Ola El Taliawi, Burra Naga Trinadh (B. N. T.), Shaleen Khanal, and Lin Zhu, as well as our editors Molly Hamer, Brian Case, and Daniel Bingul. Mamta Jha did a tremendous job for indexing, so we are thankful to her. We are also grateful to Katie O'Shea for her outstanding assistance, particularly during the production stage of the book.

Mehmet is also thankful for his dissertation chair and PhD advisor Sergio Fernandez, his dissertation committee members – Claudia

Avellaneda, Barry Rubin, and Lois R. Wise – his other professors from Indiana University, and most specifically to Roy W. Shin, Michael McGinnis, James L. Perry, Maureen Pirog, Edwardo L. Rhodes, Robert (Bob) Agranoff (RIP), Randell Baker (RIP), Patricia McManus, Jeffrey G. Covin, Dean Shepherd, Chuck Bonser, and Scott Long.

In addition, he is grateful to be an active member of the LKY School's Executive Education program since 2017. He appreciates support from Vice-Dean for Executive Education Francesco Mancini and his outstanding former or current Executive Education team members, including Sheila Kwek, Alvyn Lim, Jie Lin Cheong, Jasper Tan, Mei Mei Chen, Wai Linn Aye, Farisha Binte Ishak, Jessica Lim Yuan Chern, Janna Abdikyerim, Nurul Huda Binte Abdul Jalil, Nishalini Santharasagaran (Nisha Santhar), Muhammad Rusyaidi Bin Muhammad Radzi, Hui Won Lim, and several others. These opportunities allow Mehmet to merge theory and practice, thus adding important insights and examples to the book. Furthermore, LKY School's former and current Research Support Unit members are always helpful and available. Hence, we are grateful for their support: Thomas Chan Hean Boon, Ong Bee Leng, Sharon Ho, Diana Endang, Beiqi Chen, Evelyn Lee, Er Siew Ming, and Grace Lim.

Finally, we are also thankful to our colleagues, coauthors, and friends, such as Emre Cinar, Kohei Suzuki, Ali Asker Guenduez, Zeger van der Wal, Eduardo Araral, M. Ramesh, Evan Berman, Alfred Muluan Wu, Siong Guan Lim, Yong Soon Tan, Taha Hameduddin, Araz Taeihagh, Kanti Bajpai, Ben Cashore, Yuen Foong Khong, Weng Tat Hui, Vu Minh Khuong, Tommy Clausen, Petter Gullmark, Assel Mussagulova, Kim Moloney, Albert Link, M. Di (Manuel) Loreto, Yousueng Han, Hyesong Ha, Chung-An Chen, Farzana Chowdhury, Albert Meijer, Paul Trott, Christopher Simms, Serik Orazgaliyev, Mete Yildiz, Pablo Sanabria Pulido, Cenay Babaoglu, Aleksey Kolpakov, John Kamensky, Yuhao Ba, Ishani Mukherjee, Sreeja Nair, and many others, from whom Mehmet learned a lot while collaborating or interacting with them.

1 | Introduction

Can public sector organizations and public sector employees be innovative? If your answer to these questions is no, we encourage you to think again. For example, how would you explain the fact that some countries are more innovative than others? We believe that the answer to this question lies in the government: the public sector. If you are absolutely convinced that public organizations and public sector employees cannot be innovative (or that they should not be innovative), then you do not need this book.

However, if you are open to the possibility that public sector organizations and employees *can* be innovative – regardless of whether you are a public sector manager or employee, an employee of a private firm, an academic, a student, or simply a reader interested in understanding under what circumstances public organizations and employees can innovate – then this book is for you.

Although public organizations and employees can be innovative, admittedly, there *are* many challenges facing public organizations. Therefore, understanding innovative activities requires systematic thinking and a comprehensive approach. That would be our main message and contribution to the literature and practice in the book. This book will provide you with case studies, real-world examples, lessons, and implications from the practice of innovation. At the same time, however, this book aims to provide a systematic and comprehensive overview of public sector innovation, so that it will become apparent how these innovative activities are linked.

Many studies across the globe observe that public sector innovation has long been considered an "oxymoron" (Arundel & Huber, 2013; Bommert, 2010; Borins, 2002; Earl, 2003; Stewart-Weeks & Kastelle, 2015). The Cambridge dictionary defines an oxymoron as "two words or phrases used together that have, or seem to have, opposite meanings." In other words, it has commonly been assumed the public sector and innovation are incompatible. However, the same

1

studies also find evidence that "public sector innovation" is not an oxymoron, as it turns out that innovation is not rare in the public sector. On the contrary, public organizations are constantly innovating (though the intensity and frequency of innovations differ based on the specific national, socio-economic, technological, organizational, and demographic contexts).

For example, one study shows that more than four out of five public managers in the Australian government have reported at least one innovation within the last two years (Arundel & Huber, 2013). Surveys conducted in Europe (Arundel et al., 2015; Bloch & Bugge, 2013; Bugge & Bloch, 2016; Clausen et al., 2020), Australia (Demircioglu, 2019, 2020), South Korea (Cho & Song, 2021; Oh & Yi, 2022), and elsewhere support these findings (Raghavan et al., 2021). Many case studies and innovation awards report that not only the United States and Commonwealth countries (Borins, 2001, 2014) but also other countries such as Japan, Italy, and Turkey have reported many innovations despite challenges in their bureaucratic system (Cinar et al., 2021, 2022a, 2022b). Another study finds that the "Canadian public sector, based on rates of organisational and technological change, is not staid and unchanging. Rather it is innovative and adaptive. The public sector is leading the way in both organisational and technological change" (Earl, 2003, p. 21). These studies suggest that we should be optimistic about prospects for public sector innovation.

Chapters 1–3 are introductory but not elementary, meaning that those chapters are relevant to those without previous knowledge of public organizations, innovation, or public sector innovation. However, this information is fundamental to understanding public sector innovation, as in these early chapters we define what actually constitutes public sector innovation.

This book further provides a systematic overview, analysis, framework, and strategic directions for studying public sector innovation. This book is likely one of the first (if not the first) attempts to write a systematic overview of public sector innovation that can also be used as a classroom textbook. This text addresses an issue of considerable interest that has typically been underresearched: innovation within public administration and management. This book covers what scholars have discovered so far and what remains to be done in the study of public sector innovation. Reasons for the analysis of public sector innovation include but are not limited to: (1) the need for more efficient, effective, and responsive bureaucracies in the context of globalization; (2) the need for greater utilization of information technologies, such as social media; (3) enhancing the legitimacy of government; (4) increased expectations for governments among citizens and other stakeholders; (5) the need for solutions to socio-economic problems and grand challenges; and (6) the need to select and train public sector employees to be more innovative.

Despite a growing interest in public sector innovation, no systematic book exists on public sector innovation. Unfortunately, existing studies focus on only one or a few aspects of public sector innovation, overlooking the bigger picture of how these various concepts are related. In addition, scholars (and particularly students and young academics) may not be familiar with the subfields of public sector innovation or possible future research directions. As Demircioglu (2017, p. 804) points out: "there is no comprehensive and systematic textbook on public sector innovation [other than with a compilation of chapters on innovation]. This seems unfortunate given the importance of innovation in public organizations. Although similar books exist in the field of public management reforms (e.g., Lægreid & Christensen, 2013; Pollitt & Bouckaert, 2011), no such books exist for public sector innovation."

In addition to the theoretical and academic need for a book on public sector innovation, there is considerable interest in this topic among decision-makers and policymakers in public, private, and non-profit organizations, and universities and research centers. Due to the increasing importance of innovative activity, public sector employees are expected to be innovative (Bason, 2010; Bugge & Bloch, 2016; Damanpour et al., 2009; Demircioglu & Audretsch, 2017, 2020; Serrat, 2017; van der Wal, 2017). This book provides a systematic approach to understanding innovative activities in the public sector that should be of great interest to practitioners. Many existing studies on public sector innovation focus on innovation only at the government/national level using a national level of analysis (e.g., Altshuler & Behn, 1997; Borins, 2009), and most studies treat public sector innovation as a policy strategy and goal rather than as a management tool and technique (e.g., Fagerberg et al., 2006; Leyden & Link, 1992; Link & Siegel, 2007). This book, in contrast, analyzes innovation at every level – from the individual to the national and international – and considers management tools and techniques in the public sector.

This book also offers insights into how organizational and political leaders can encourage innovation in public organizations.

Studies of public sector innovation claim that public sector innovation is still undertheorized despite increasing research (Chen et al., 2021). Thus, this study also offers theoretical advancements in the study of innovation by developing concepts such as innovation context, typologies, rationales, conditions, sources, and outcomes. Likewise, despite the importance of innovation for public organizations, Vigoda-Gadot et al. (2005, p. 58) argues that "it is quite surprising to find that the topic of innovation has played only a minor role in the discussion about the renewal of public administration. Moreover, the vast body of knowledge about innovation, entrepreneurship, and proactiveness in business management has never been used extensively in public management," suggesting that researchers should further investigate public sector innovation.

In a similar vein, Stewart-Weeks and Kastelle observe: "Many leaders and others in the public sector want innovation but fear its impact on settled patterns of control, power, and authority; the contest between persistence and disruption is never easy and has to be waged anew for each project and, often, within and across projects" (2015, p. 65). We agree with this statement. In fact, while writing this book, we have engaged in many conversations with public managers worldwide, particularly in the Asia-Pacific region. We have learned from their experiences that there are often barriers to implementing innovations in public organizations. Innovation often requires changing mindsets and motivating employees, among other requirements. However, there are many other dimensions of innovative activities. This book examines these many dimensions, including such topics as where innovative ideas come from, the government's role in innovation, and the ethics of innovations.

Target Audience

The target audience for this book includes academics, policymakers, and practitioners. First, this book will be highly relevant to scholars, including professors, postdocs, researchers, graduate students interested in public sector innovation, and those writing research papers and dissertations on public sector innovation. In addition, this book will be relevant to advanced undergraduate students interested in learning about public sector innovation more systematically. Instructors of public management and public sector innovation may assign several chapters of this book, such as Chapter 2, "What Is Public Sector Innovation?," and Chapter 6, "Why Public Sector Innovation?," as required or optional reading.

A second target audience includes policymakers and practitioners who are interested in or have a mandate to engage in public sector innovation and need to understand the basics of public sector innovation, such as how the relevant concepts correlate and interact (e.g., the relationship between sources of innovation and the benefits of innovation). These include public officials in federal, state, and local governments, employees in international organizations (e.g., the Organisation for Economic Co-operation and Development [OECD] and the United Nations), employees of businesses and consulting firms, community leaders, and concerned citizens interested in learning about innovative activities in the public sector. This book provides some guidelines and lessons for students and practitioners through the case studies presented throughout the book.

Although public sector innovation has generated tremendous interest among scholars, graduate students, and practitioners in recent years, there has been little effort to study the essential aspects of public sector innovation in a systematic, holistic, and integrated analysis. Other books typically focus on one or (at most) several aspects of public sector innovation, such as collaborative innovation (e.g., Torfing & Triantafillou, 2016) and the effects of leadership and capacity on public sector innovation (Bekkers et al., 2011). What sets this book apart is that it provides a systematic way of thinking about important and novel questions regarding public sector innovation. Current or future public management scholars and students will find this book relevant and vital because it identifies and articulates the most critical and compelling themes and topics, research gaps, and future directions in the field. Thus, this book identifies and provides some guidelines and potential research topics for those interested in contributing to the scholarly literature in the form of articles, book chapters, and books, as well as for thought leaders and decision-makers in public policy and business fields.

To sum up, this book is written with the target audience of (1) academics with either a broad or specific interest in public sector innovation, (2) scholars or students who are interested in developing a research agenda about public sector innovation and writing research papers on public sector innovation, (3) instructors who teach or would like to teach a course or a section of a course about public sector innovation, and (4) the policy and practitioner community. This book may be considered an academic book but it avoids jargon; each chapter links to the scholarly literature (e.g., to show some important underlying frameworks) and practical implications. Our goal is for the book to be scholarly, relevant, lively, and interesting to a broad audience of readers as well as to the specific audience engaged in the study of public sector innovation. This book is primarily scholarly but is written in a manner that speaks to a broad audience of nonspecialists. The book aims to translate insights from scholarly literature and experience and synthesize those ideas into a coherent framework that is accessible and compelling to policymakers and practitioners.

Organization

The book is organized into thirteen chapters, as detailed in the accompanying book outline. The introductory chapter, Chapter 1, has explained why this book is essential and timely, why we should care about public sector innovation, and why innovation matters for the public sector. Chapter 2, "What Is Public Sector Innovation?," defines innovation and the public sector. This chapter also differentiates innovation from similar concepts, such as public management reforms, organizational change, invention, creativity, entrepreneurship, and improvement. Chapter 3, "Public versus Private," explores similarities and differences between public and private sector innovation, along with the potential implications of innovative activities. Understanding the difference between the public and private sector is crucial and has implications for market and government failure, which we explore further in Chapter 10.

Chapter 4, "The Context of Public Sector Innovation," discusses the importance of contexts, such as national, political, social, organizational, and demographic, and how context has potential implications for innovative activities. Chapter 5, "Innovation Typologies," analyzes the heterogeneity inherent in innovative activity and provides a typology distinguishing different types of innovations. This chapter draws on fundamental concepts from the innovation literature to define innovation types and explain innovation typology, including radical, incremental, complex, and open innovations. Chapter 6, "Why Public Sector Innovation?," explains the importance and necessity of innovative activity in the public sector. Some examples and real-world insights, such as the role of governments in innovative activities, are given in this chapter.

Chapter 7, "Drivers and Conditions for Innovation," analyzes why some individuals, groups, organizations, and nations engage in innovative activities while others do not. Based on the context and involvement of actors, there may be different conditions conducive to public sector innovation. Chapter 8, "Sources of Knowledge and Collaborative Innovation," first identifies sources for innovative activity in the public sector. Significant sources of innovation include top down (such as from government and organizational leaders), bottom up (such as from employee work groups), and external (such as from industry, business stakeholders, universities, and members of the public). Chapter 9, "Barriers to Public Sector Innovation," explores major barriers to public sector innovation and how and why barriers exist in the public sector context. We also discuss the relationship between barriers to innovation and other innovative activities, such as implementing public sector innovations. For instance, we compare two types of barriers: deterrent versus revealing. We discuss under what circumstances barriers are negatively associated with innovation and under what circumstances barriers are positively associated with public sector innovation.

Chapter 10, "National Systems of Innovation and Market and Government Failure," focuses on the government's role in spurring innovative activity, how and why market failure occurs, and how the government's role is crucial in dealing with market failure. Likewise, we explore how and why government failure occurs, such as when governments lead innovation. Chapter 11, "Outcomes of Public Sector Innovation," explains how particular public sector innovations positively or negatively affect organizations and individuals, such as organizational performance and individual job satisfaction. This chapter also explains how and why analyzing innovation outcomes is crucial. Without analysis of the impact of innovative activity, we cannot assess whether a particular innovation is worthwhile. Chapter 12, "Ethics and Public Sector Innovation," deals with a relatively unexplored question: How are public sector innovations associated with ethics? There is little work that examines the ethics of innovative activities in the public sector.

Chapter 13, "Conclusions," summarizes the most salient findings, main insights, and critical "takeaways" from the book. In addition, this chapter offers some guidelines about innovative activities in the public sector. Thus, this chapter offers potentially fruitful themes and topics for researchers interested in undertaking future research on public sector innovation. Overall, the main point of this chapter is that innovative activities matter for numerous reasons, particularly given the complex problems confronting contemporary society, which emanate at least partially from a high degree of globalization and technological change and have increased the extent to which countries, organizations, and employees are interrelated.

Conclusion

At least five disparate academic fields have emerged that contribute to the study of public sector innovation: public administration and management (which focuses on the management, operationalization, and big questions of government), innovation (which focuses on the role of innovation and research for public policy), business administration (which focuses on organization theory and behavior), economics (which focuses on the actions of human beings and organizations), and public policy (which focuses on what and how governments do or not do). As there is a paucity of knowledge about the intersection of these fields, we believe that this book will pioneer the intersection of these five essential fields at their most relevant and compelling point: the role of innovation in the management of public organizations. As readers will see throughout the book, we provide examples of innovations and their roles in the private sector context as well as in the public sector context. Although people realized that innovation was crucial for the United States, particularly in the private sector, in the 1970s and 1980s, there was little analysis of other national and geographic contexts, such as in the Asia-Pacific. However, over the next four decades, research on innovative activity increased, and we can now provide examples from virtually every national and cultural context. This contemporary work focuses on the role of nationally and regionally specific institutions and contexts in innovative activity. This introductory chapter has provided a coherent road map and synopsis of the substantive chapters and contents of the book, how each chapter is related, and the main lessons and takeaways concerning public sector innovation.

There is an early argument that there is no playbook for public sector innovation (Roessner, 1977) because which strategies for public sector innovation will prove to be effective and those that should be avoided remain vague and uncertain. Still, the empirical evidence, particularly in recent decades, flies in the face of skeptics and doubters rejecting the reality and potential of public sector innovation. In this regard, this book can be a playbook for public sector innovation.

2 | *What Is Public Sector Innovation?*

Introduction and Definitions

Public sector, public organizations, or government refers to the general government organizations owned and funded by the government. While some studies consider state-owned enterprises as public organizations, they may include or exclude state-owned enterprises (Christensen et al., 2007). However, almost all public sector definitions exclude privately owned companies aiming to make profits from the concept of the public sector. Therefore, government ministries or departments and agencies that are not privately owned are public organizations. Public schools, universities funded by states, and public hospitals can also be considered as public organizations.

However, public services and the public sector are not the same, as private, nonprofit organizations can provide public services without being public organizations. Thus, "public service" is broader than the public sector. Perry and Wise (1990, p. 368) state: "Public service is often used as a synonym for government service embracing all those who work in the public sector. But public service signifies much more than one's locus of employment." According to many studies, public service is an attitude and feeling of duty, so employees in nonprofit and even private organizations can contribute to society and citizens even if they are not working in public organizations (Denhardt & Denhardt, 2015; Perry, 2020; Perry & Wise, 1990; Piatak et al., 2020). In other words, the public service is broader than the public sector (or organizations) and does not refer to sectoral differences.

However, a website from the Office of the Prime Minister in Malta defines public service and public organizations differently:

The Public Service is not the same as the public sector. The term "public sector" refers to all government organisations and their employees, as distinct from the private sector (private companies, non-government organisations, and their employees). The Public Service consists of ministries and departments of Government. The Public Service is the core of the Government's administrative machinery, but this machinery has other components. These include statutory authorities and agencies, Government foundations, and companies with a government majority shareholding. These entities are part of the public sector but not the Public Service ... Public Service employees are referred to also as public officers and as Government employees. The latter term reflects the fact that Public Service employees work in ministries and departments, which are integral components of the Government of Malta. By contrast, entities in the wider public sector have their own legal personality which is separate from that of the Government – meaning that while such entities belong to the Government, they are not part of the Government. Accordingly, their employees are not Government employees. (publicservice.gov.mt, n.d., paras. 1–3)

In other words, this definition considers public service to be narrower than is the public sector.

To avoid confusion, we intentionally use the term public sector innovation rather than public service innovation although both can be used interchangeably (Chen et al., 2021). Our definition of the public sector or public organization is consistent with the definition of Hartley, Sørensen, and Torfing (2013, p. 822): "a collective effort to produce and deliver public value that is authorized or sponsored by federal, state, provincial, or local government." In other words, public sector innovation is an innovative activity by public organizations (Demircioglu, 2021; Vivona et al., 2021).

The second concept, "innovation," is difficult to define as there is no single, universally agreed-upon definition of innovation. In this regard, we need to define innovation and understand what it is and what it is not. Without a clear definition, it will have different understandings and implications. There is no established definition of public sector innovation, and it is often used synonymously with reform and organizational change (Kattel et al., 2013; Sørensen & Torfing, 2011).

So, what is public sector innovation? Public sector innovation can be defined as a novel idea, practice, or object created, developed, or implemented by a public organization that is not necessarily new to the public service but is at least new to a particular organization (Brown & Osborne, 2012; Bysted & Hansen, 2015; Damanpour & Schneider, 2009; Fernandez & Wise, 2010; Walker, 2008, 2014; Wegrich, 2019). Similarly, Bartos (2003, p. 10) defines innovation as "a change in policy or management practice that leads to a lasting improvement in level of service or quantity or quality of output by an organization." Bekkers et al. (2011b, p. 14), on the other hand, define innovation as "a necessary condition for the modernization of government in order to meet new societal challenges." While the first definition is concerned about the implementation and the novelty, the last two definitions have the additional concern for a potential output or outcome, such as meeting new challenges and improving services. Indeed, innovation is a "complex and iterative process through which problems are defined; new ideas are developed and combined; prototypes and pilots are designed, tested, and redesigned; and new solutions are implemented, diffused, and problematized" (Hartley et al., 2013, p. 822).

Most of the innovations in public organizations are adopted from elsewhere instead of being newly created (Borins, 2001, 2014; Fernandez & Wise, 2010); therefore, we need to understand how and why public organizations adopt or fail to adopt particular innovations in a particular context. Similarly, most innovations in the public sector are incremental (Bugge & Bloch, 2016) although radical or breakthrough innovations also exist in the public sector (Albury, 2011; Osborne & Brown, 2011; Sahni et al., 2013; Sandor, 2018). We explore these concepts further in the chapter on innovation typologies (Chapter 5).

Although Becker and Whisler (1967) argue that innovation is an individual or a group action, organizations and nations can also innovate, as many organizations and countries have implemented innovations. For example, public organizations are already innovative and need to be so due to complex and substantial long-term problems (e.g., aging populations and social security), financial constraints, and citizens' expectations of the government (Albury, 2011; Bloch & Bugge, 2013; Bugge & Bloch, 2016). Likewise:

Organizations innovate because of pressure from the external environment, such as competition, deregulation, isomorphism, resource scarcity, and customer demands, or because of an internal organizational choice, such as gaining distinctive competencies, reaching a higher level of aspiration, and increasing the extent and quality of services. Either way, the adoption of innovation is intended to ensure adaptive behaviour, changing the organization to maintain or improve its performance. (Damanpour et al., 2009, pp. 653–654)

In this regard, many innovations occur at the organizational and national levels as well.

Public sector innovation differs from private sector innovation in several fundamental ways. First, the secrecy or protection of innovation is neither expected nor a goal in the public sector context; instead, when a public organization has implemented an innovation that has a positive effect, the government encourages other public organizations to adopt it because doing so may bring benefits to citizens (APSC, 2011; Arundel et al., 2019; Bysted & Hansen, 2015; Demircioglu & Audretsch, 2020; Potts & Kastelle, 2010). In contrast, the protection and secrecy of innovation are generally prerequisites for innovative activity in the private sector because, without the protection of intellectual property, the ability of private companies to appropriate the returns accruing from innovations may be limited. In addition, while radical innovations that are technologically and organizationally disruptive are coveted in the private sector, incremental innovations are more prevalent in the public sector. Similarly, while product innovations are typical in private organizations, service innovations are more common in the public sector.

In addition, as can be seen in Joseph Schumpeter's work, business innovations are historically linked with outputs or outcomes, such as producing a new product or service for the market (Hansen & Wakonen, 1997; Zahoor & Al-Tabbaa, 2020). However, there is no requirement that innovation should be linked with outputs or outcomes. In fact, as we discuss in the following chapters, most innovations in the public sector are process innovations, which typically are not related to any outputs. Furthermore, many innovative activities may focus on changing the culture and climate of organizations to make them more innovative. For instance, organizations may encourage creativity and risk-taking, but these activities may not necessarily be linked with an innovation's implementation and outputs. Thus, we can differentiate between innovation and innovative activities. While the former concerns implementation, the latter could be more generic, including all dimensions of innovation such as sources, barriers, conditions, culture, and climate for innovation, in the public sector. However, we use these terms interchangeably (innovation versus innovative activities). In other words, what we mean by "public sector innovation" does not necessarily refer to just the implementation of an innovation but to a broader concept of innovative activities.

Furthermore, as we discuss in the following chapters (primarily Chapter 3), public organizations' external environments differ from private organizations' external environments. For instance, a public manager's decision-making capacity is minimal due to external regulations, different accountability mechanisms, and check-and-balance mechanisms in the public sector, which can reduce their capacity for innovation and risk-taking (Bozeman & Kingsley, 1998; Rainey, 2009; Wilson, 2000). This does not mean that the public sector cannot innovate, or that public employees are not innovative. Instead, research shows that while public organizations and public sector employees can be innovative (Alsos et al., 2016; Barrutia & Echebarria, 2019; Demircioglu & Audretsch, 2017; E&Y, 2017; Leman, 2002; Mulgan, 2014; Sahni et al., 2013), their innovativeness may be different from innovativeness in the private sector. While public sector innovation resembles private sector innovation, it differs significantly in terms of the context, ideas, conditions, sources, types, and measurements specific to the public sector. Thus, it is vital to understand innovative activities in the public sector.

The crucial components of innovation in the public sector are that innovations need to be novel and have positive outcomes, such as improving processes, increasing quality, and reducing costs in the public sector (Arundel & Huber, 2013). We discuss innovation typologies in Chapter 5 and cover innovation outcomes in Chapter 11. Political, social, and managerial challenges cannot be solved by simply cutting costs; thus, innovations are necessary for public organizations (Torfing & Triantafillou, 2016). In this regard, we need an understanding of how innovation occurs in the public sector (Chapter 7), who engages in innovative activities (Chapter 8), and what constitutes the outcomes of public sector innovation (Chapters 11 and 12).

What Public Sector Innovation Is Not

One of the most influential theoretical articles in the social sciences about general management, and business management in particular, was written by Sutton and Staw (1995), titled "What Theory Is Not." The authors claim that because there is no consensus on what theory is, "it is so difficult to develop strong theory in the behavioral sciences. Reviewers, editors, and other audiences may hold inconsistent beliefs about what constitutes theory and what constitutes strong versus weak theory" (Sutton & Staw, 1995, p. 372). They continue: "Though there is conflict about what theory is and should be, there is more consensus about what theory is not" (Sutton & Staw, 1995, p. 372). They have stated that "references," "data," "lists of variables or constructs," "diagrams," and "hypotheses (or predictions)" can help to develop a theory, but they are not theory. Thus, to better understand what innovation is, we follow the same logic Sutton and Staw (1995) have used to define what theory is. That is, we discuss what innovation is not because defining innovation is not an easy task as there is no established definition. When we identify what innovation is not, we will better understand what could be considered innovation. Thus, this section explains what innovation is not while comparing innovation with public management reforms, organizational change, invention, creativity, entrepreneurship, and improvement.

Public Management Reform Is Not (Necessarily) an Innovation

In their classic and highly praised work, Pollitt and Bouckaert (2011, p. 2) define public management reform as "deliberate changes to the structures and processes of public sector organizations with the objective of getting them (in some sense) to run better." Public management reforms (or public sector reforms, government reforms, or governance reforms) can be an innovation only if the reform is a novel practice for the government or a specific department or agency. As can be clearly seen here, the central unit of analysis of public sector reforms is typically at the national or agency level. However, most innovations occur at the individual, group, and agency levels, though innovations at the national level also exist (see Chapter 10).

In addition, as seen from this definition, what matters for public management reform is running public organizations better; thus, novelty is not a requirement for reforms. Suppose similar reform practices have been previously implemented in the same context, so that there is essentially no novelty. We, therefore, cannot call it innovation. In fact, research demonstrates that many reforms are considered "new bottles" with the "same drink" (Chan & Gao, 2008; Durant, 2008; Lynn, 2006; Page, 2005; Wise, 2002); hence, we cannot count them as constituting an innovation. More specifically, many New Public Management (NPM) reforms that prioritize efficiency and business-like government have been adopted by countries since the 1980s without much novelty. Thus, although some early novel practices of

NPM reforms could be considered innovation, the NPM itself or the repeated innovation attempts such as privatizing new public services cannot be an innovation.

In addition to NPM, there are also other reform practices, such as the Reinventing Government Movement or National Performance Review in the United States during the Clinton administration in the 1990s applying Total Quality Management (TQM) ideas to the public sector (Breul & Kamensky, 2008; Borins, 2000; Kamensky, 1996; Osborne & Gaebler, 1992; Osborne & Plastrik, 1997). These reform attempts are not innovations, although they reinforced and encouraged innovations in the United States government (Kelman, 2005, 2021). For instance, Kelman (2021, p. 24) states that the reinventing government movement "did promote a specific vision of an approach to innovation, i.e., reducing rules and increasing freedom for frontline employees." This means that through "a specific vision of an approach to innovation," these visions and policies positively affected public sector innovation.

Organizational Change Is Not (Necessarily) Innovation

Similar to public management reforms, we need to understand the features of organizational change. Organizational change is simply implementing new behavior, such as changing organizational structures, technologies, people, and culture (Daft & Marcic, 2019). It also includes operating new structures, operations, and cultures (Suddary & Foster, 2017). In this regard, organizational change and innovation have similarities (Palumbo & Manna, 2018). However, there are also significant differences.

First, as the name suggests, the primary unit of analysis of organizational change is at the organizational level (Fernandez & Rainey, 2006; Hage, 1999). However, innovation can occur at the national level, such as the National Innovation System (Acs et al., 2017; Demircioglu, 2019; Nelson & Rosenberg, 1993), organizational level (Daft, 1978; Sapprasert & Clausen, 2012), work group level (Anderson & West, 1998; Shim et al., 2021; Torugsa & Arundel, 2016b), and individual level (e.g., innovative work behavior; see Demircioglu et al., 2023; Palumbo, 2021; Suseno et al., 2020). Additionally, a standard organizational change in the public sector is reorganization (Agranoff, 1991; Wise, 2006). However, organizational change or reorganization cannot be an innovation unless it involves novelty. In fact, research finds significant evidence that many of the organizational changes in the public sector and international public organizations (such as organizational changes in the European Commission) are not innovative (Bauer, 2012; Durant, 2008; Kassim et al., 2013). They are simply repeating a past reform or changing practices without novelty.

According to Brown and Osborne (2012), the main difference between organizational change and innovation is that while the former continues from past practices, the latter discontinues and is distinct from past practices. In addition, while innovations are typically novel, change and reforms are not necessarily novel (Sandor, 2018).

Regarding scope and density, reforms and organizational changes primarily focus on the macro level (Pollitt & Bouckaert, 2004). For example, the creation of the Department of Homeland Security to deal with terrorism and disasters (Kapucu & van Wart, 2006; Wise, 2006), the reorganization of federal agencies to increase performance (Durant, 2008), and the reorganization of supranational organizations such as the European Commission to increase efficiency and effectiveness (Bauer, 2008; Kassim et al., 2013) are examples of public management reforms and organizational change. However, the scope of innovations is usually smaller, such as implementing smaller-scale but novel innovations in public organizations (Bloch & Bugge, 2013; Bugge & Bloch, 2016; Torugsa & Arundel, 2016a, 2016b).

Thus, particular types of reforms (e.g., NPM, reinventing government, and TQM) and organizational change have noninnovative patterns in the same context that repeat from time to time, such as simply reverting to previous ideas and practices (Kaufman, 1981; Wise, 2002). Likewise, many of the reorganizations in public organizations are not innovations (Durant, 2008). While reform implies an active agenda (Wise, 2002), organizational change may occur because of more passive forces and in response to management demands, such as changes in performance standards (Fernandez & Rainey, 2006).

As a further note, public management reforms and organizational changes in public organizations are typically political and ideological (Montgomery, 1967; Peters, 2019). However, innovations are typically instrumental (e.g., solving a management problem) and make primarily novel changes such as "a new IT solution for joint login to public services, which enabled switching between services without new logins for each service; and self-service in the personnel and payroll system" (Bugge & Bloch, 2016, p. 286).

Invention Is Not (Necessarily) Innovation

Inventions are typically associated with business products, specifically patents (Acs & Audretsch, 2003; Guerzoni et al., 2014; H. Jung & J. Lee, 2016). However, most public organizations do not produce products, let alone patents. Thus, the scope of inventions is narrower than innovations, as most innovations are not inventions, particularly for the public sector.

There is another big difference between innovations and inventions. Not all inventions are innovations because innovation is considered to be the outcome of an invention (Gault & Soete, 2022; Taques et al., 2021). Acs and Audretsch (2003, p. 58) express this distinction cleverly from their insights and findings in the private sector: "Only those inventions which have been successfully introduced in the market can claim that they are innovations ... many, if not most, patented inventions do not result in an innovation. ... In fact, many inventions which result in innovations are not patented." Gault and Soete (2022) state that invention without innovation was typical in the UK in the 1960s and later in other European countries. In other words, because many inventions are not novel, we cannot call these inventions innovations.

Creativity Is Not (Necessarily) Innovation

Both creativity and innovation refer to newness, originality, and the ability of public organizations and employees to be innovative (Denhardt & Denhardt, 2015). Additionally, both creativity and innovation can be dependent variables, such that there are certain conditions or factors affecting creativity or innovation (e.g., doing more with less and psychological and leadership support can increase both creativity and innovation) (Dudau et al., 2018; Gumusluoglu & Ilsev, 2009).

However, a major difference between creativity and innovation is that while the former does not mean implementation, the latter does (Amabile et al., 1996; McLean, 2005). In other words, creativity itself does not mean innovation unless the creative process results in an action, such as a new product, service, process, policy, marketing, or communication. It is true that innovative behavior resembles creativity, as neither requires the implementation of an innovation. However, innovation and innovative work behavior are different. The former refers to an actual product or service while the latter refers to the individual's attitudes and activities (see Demircioglu et al., 2023; Suseno et al., 2020). Studies also find that many creative ideas are not implemented by organizations (Vigoda-Gadot et al., 2005).

Furthermore, another significant difference is the unit of analysis. Most innovation studies have focused on meso (e.g., organizational) and macro levels (such as innovations in organizations and nations) while creativity research has typically focused on the micro or individual level (such as studying individual creativity) (McLean, 2005; Zhou & Rouse, 2021). In a public sector setting, Kapucu and Ustun (2018, p. 552) differentiate innovation from creativity: "creativity occurs at the individual level, while innovation occurs at the organizational level. The inputs of organizational innovation are comprised of individual characteristics of the persons who created the organization as well as features of teams and the organization. To transform these inputs to innovative behaviors and innovative products, it requires a culture and environment that supports innovation."

Entrepreneurship Is Not (Necessarily) Innovation

Public sector entrepreneurship is defined as "the pursuit of opportunity, exploration, and exploitation activities in the public sector" (Demircioglu et al., 2020, p. 2). Therefore, this definition and other definitions (e.g., Bernier & Hafsi, 2007; Demircioglu & Chowdhury, 2021; Hayter et al., 2018; Ostrom, 1965) mirrors the view of entrepreneurship in the private sector in that it revolves around opportunity. The focus is on opportunity and not necessarily innovation per se. It is certainly possible for organizations to be entrepreneurial without engaging in innovation and for them to be innovative without being entrepreneurial. In other words, individuals and organizations can be entrepreneurial (such as being proactive and going the extra mile) without implementing any innovations.

The scholarly literature on entrepreneurship, as well as thought leaders in policy and business, have generally focused on entrepreneurship from three disparate perspectives. The first is organizational, in that the concept of entrepreneurship is operationalized by the type of organization. The organizational types considered to be entrepreneurial have ranged from organizational age (startup) to size (in terms of employees or sales) and ownership status (self-employed or family owned). A very different view of entrepreneurship shifts the focus to behavior. Behavior that creates or discovers new opportunities and acts on or implements those opportunities constitutes entrepreneurship, according to this second perspective. The third view is again very different from the first two, with a focus on performance and outcomes. A stronger performance is considered to constitute entrepreneurship (Audretsch, Siegel, & Terjesen, 2020; for examples of the public sector, see also Berman et al., 2017; Kearney et al., 2008; Kim, 2010; Leyden, 2016; Moon, 1999; Moon et al., 2020). Some studies directly consider measures of innovation to reflect entrepreneurship while others focus on performance measures such as growth or survival.

Thus, the concept of entrepreneurship is operationalized by the scholars in the public discourse via three very different perspectives regarding what actually reflects entrepreneurial activity. Ultimately it may be the context that influences how and why certain types of activities are considered to be entrepreneurial. Since contexts vary considerably, so too does the actual view of what constitutes entrepreneurship.

Improvement Is Not (Necessarily) Innovation

The concepts of innovation and improvement are similar in the sense that there are some positive changes. However, there is a crucial difference between them. That is, there is no novelty in a simple improvement (Demircioglu, 2021; Hartley, 2005; Osborne & Brown, 2011). Improvements do not necessarily lead to a new product, process, or other types of innovations. For example, while TQM ideas are part of organizational improvements, they are not innovations (Hartley, 2005). Similarly, many NPM ideas and practices have improved public organizations, although these ideas and practices are not novel (and thus not innovations).

Furthermore, some innovations may not lead to any improvements in the public sector. Hartley (2005) provides several scenarios, such as increasing the choice of products and services (i.e., new innovations) that citizens have no desire for. Many innovations result in a reduction in performance because of operational costs. In other words, innovation and improvement are different concepts.

Summary of What Public Sector Innovation Is Not

To sum up, many scholars use "reform," "organizational change," and "innovation" interchangeably, as these terms all have similar connotations of making or adopting something new (e.g., Fernandez & Wise, 2010; Pierce & Delbecq, 1977; Wise, 1999; Wise & Szucs, 1996). However, what makes something an innovation is twofold. First, "something" should be new or novel to an organization, such as a policy, a management practice, an organizational process, or a method (Bartos, 2003; Borins, 2000; Demircioglu, 2017; Hartley, 2005; Pierce & Delbecq, 1977; Wettenhall, 1988). Damanpour et al. (2009, p. 653) define "innovation" as something "new to the adopting organization." Second, "something" should be implemented (OECD, 2017). Thus, we cannot call a policy or a novelty an innovation if the organization does not implement it. Furthermore, innovation differs from improvement because improvement does not necessarily include novelty (Hartley, 2014; Osborne & Brown, 2011). Innovation is also different from invention (Mohr, 1969) as most innovations in the public sector are not inventions (Fernandez & Wise, 2010).

As explained in this section, the Oslo Manual (OECD/Eurostat, 2018, pp. 78–80) also explains what innovation is not. As "innovation must have been implemented and must be significantly different from the firm's previous products or business processes" (OECD/Eurostat, 2018, p. 78), the following changes are not innovations: "routine changes or updates" (including software updates), "simple capital replacement or extension," "minor aesthetic changes," "custom production," "advertised concept, prototype or model of a product that does not yet exist" (as it is not implemented yet), "outputs of creative and professional service firms, such as reports for clients, books, or films," "the range of products handled or offered to customers," "activities of newly created firms," "mergers or the acquisition of other firms," "ceasing to use a business process, ceasing to outsource a business process, or withdrawing a product from the market," "a change due to externally determined factor prices," and "the formulation of a new corporate or managerial strategy is not an innovation if it is not implemented."

Conclusion

In conclusion, we have defined innovations as novel practices implemented by a unit such as a public organization. We have also pointed out that although innovation, reform, organizational change, entrepreneurship, and improvement are similar, they are not the same. Most innovations in the public sector are incremental or absorptive (Demircioglu & Vivona, 2021) rather than "invented innovation" (Fernandez & Wise, 2010) (or radical [Demircioglu & Vivona, 2021]). Like entrepreneurs, innovators also look for opportunities to innovate (Stewart-Weeks & Kastelle, 2015). The focus of this book is restricted to public organizations, although these typologies, models, and insights are relevant to private, nonprofit, and other organizations.

3 | *Public versus Private*

Introduction and Sectoral Differences

The works of early scholars of management – such as Taylor's (1911) scientific management, Fayol's (2013) general principles and elements of management, and Weber's (1968) theory of bureaucratic organization – did not differentiate between public and private organizations. Additionally, Gulick's (2015) POSDCORB principle (which stands for planning, organizing, staffing, directing, coordinating, reporting, and budgeting) applies to any formal organization, regardless of whether it is public or private (Allison, 1980). Similarly, the major functions of management are similar in any organization, which include strategy (e.g., establishing missions, objectives, and plans), managing internal parts (e.g., directing personnel management system), and managing external system (e.g., dealing with external authorities and stakeholders) (Allison, 1980). In other words, the generic approaches of management and managerial principles are very similar among different organizations (Bozeman, 2004). As Bozeman (2004, p. 5) observes: "Private organizations are increasingly being penetrated by government policy, and public organizations are increasingly becoming attracted to quasi-market approaches." Recently, with COVID-19, we have seen that governments' control over organizations has increased, and governments have made many regulations affecting organizations and individuals.

Different disciplines explain the difference between public and private organizations differently:

Economists begin with theories of market efficiency; organization theorists begin with analyses of bureaucratic behavior; and political scientists begin with the ways citizen demands for democratic accountability are translated into institutional arrangements and legal constraints, which in turn affect the behavior of government officials. Each approach leads, via tortuous, deductive links weakened by questionable assumptions about relationships among organizational efficiency, productivity, and innovativeness, to a consistent conclusion: public organizations are less efficient, and probably less innovative, than private organizations. What empirical evidence exists to confirm or disconfirm these predictions? (Roessner, 1977, p. 350)

Roessner (1977) does not find substantial evidence that the private sector is more innovative than the public sector.

Public organizations are defined as organizations owned and funded by the government (Arundel et al., 2019; Christensen et al., 2007; Perry & Rainey, 1988; Wamsley & Zald, 1973) and may exclude state-owned enterprises (Arundel et al., 2019). There are several dimensions along which to compare public and nonpublic organizations. The first difference between public and nonpublic organizations (private and nonprofit) is ownership. Public organizations are owned by the government (public) while private and nonprofit organizations are owned by individuals who do not represent government authority. The second difference is funding, which is whether the organization is funded by the public (e.g., taxes or government contracts) or through private means (e.g., sales, market revenue, and donations by citizens) (Perry & Rainey, 1988; Rainey, 2009). The third dimension is the mode of social control, which is whether the organization represents a polyarchy ("a politically constituted hierarchy … in advanced industrial democracies") or a market system ("relatively decentralized autonomous organizational forms controlled primarily by the price system in economic markets") (Perry & Rainey, 1988, p. 190). If it is the former, then it is a public organization. If it is the latter, then it is a private organization. Thus, these three factors (ownership, funding, and control) are the primary distinctions between public and private organizations (Boyne, 2002).

A fourth distinction is the personnel management system, which is whether the personnel system is regulated or controlled by the government (if so, it is a public organization) or controlled by individual private firms (if so, it is a private organization) (Christensen et al., 2007). Therefore, if an organization is owned, funded, and controlled by the government, and the government also controls its personnel management system, we can say that this organization is a purely public organization. In other words, public organizations are "public law bodies," "formally under at least some control by ministers and departments" (Lœgreid et al., 2011, p. 1323), and they have their own financial resources and personnel talent (Lœgreid et al., 2011). As Scott and Davis (2015, p. 14) observe: "Public agencies differ from private firms, even when they carry on the same kind of work, because they function in different institutional contexts. It matters considerably whether you operate to satisfy the demands of many decentralized customers or one centralized oversight bureau or multiple political constituencies." Typical examples of public organizations are ministries (or departments) and government agencies.

On the contrary, if an organization is not owned, funded, and controlled by the government, and a government authority does not control personnel management, then we can call these organizations purely private organizations. In other words, "(a) companies and corporations with a commercial focus, which have to closely observe the laws regulating private companies or which are registered under company law as a company; and (b) governmental foundations, trusts, and charities" are private organizations (Lœgreid et al., 2011, p. 1324). Typical examples of these types of organizations are firms such as Amazon, Pepsi, Microsoft, and Apple. However, if the institutions operate between these definitions, we can call these organizations semi- or quasi-public organizations (such as in the case of state-owned enterprises).

In his classic work "The Study of Administration," Woodrow Wilson (1887, p. 210) argues that "administration lies outside the proper sphere of politics. Administrative questions are not political questions. Although politics sets the tasks for administration, it should not be suffered to manipulate its offices," suggesting that politics should not involve itself in managing public organizations. Nevertheless, separating politics from public administration is impossible, so the political context always affects innovations in the public sector. However, the involvement of politics in business is minimal, so businesses can often be more innovative as they have more freedom from government and political influence.

Businesses may also be less innovative if they lack resources (e.g., financial or human talent) compared to public organizations. One advantage of public organizations is that governments may allocate significant money for implementing an innovation, which may not always be the case in a business organization. While the former's primary focus is public service, the latter's main goal is making profits. Thus, private organizations may avoid investing in innovations if they do not result in profits. We discuss the government's role in promoting innovation in Chapter 10.

Public and private organizations are different in many respects, and those differences impact innovation differently. As Rainey (2009, p. 62) argues:

[I]f there is no real difference between public and private organizations, can we nationalize all industrial firms, or privatize all government agencies? Private executives earn massively higher pay than their government counterparts. The financial press regularly lambastes corporate executive compensation practices as absurd and claims these compensation policies squander many billions of dollars. Can we simply put these business executives on the federal executive compensation schedule and save a lot of money for these corporations and their customers? Such questions make it clear that there are some important differences in the administration of public and private organizations.

In other words, there are intrinsic differences between public and private organizations.

Public and private organizations have different values. For public organizations, what matters includes not only efficiency and effectiveness but also responsiveness, neutrality, legitimacy, transparency, equity, state interests, and bureaucracy's interests (Heper & Berkman, 1979; Rainey, 2009). Van der Wal et al. (2008, p. 473) surveyed managers in both public sector (n ‗ 231) and private sector (n = 151) in the Netherlands and asked them extensive questions about what values were dominant in their organizations and ranked their findings. They found that:

Clear traditional differences exist between both rankings. "Lawfulness," "impartiality" and "incorruptibility" were considered most important public sector values and were absent from the business top values. "Profitability" and "innovativeness" were present at the top of the business values and absent from the public sector's top values. "Profitability" according to this measure could even be considered the least important public sector value.

The same study also finds some similarities between public and private organizations in terms of values:

Four of the most important values, "accountability," "expertise," "reliability" and "effectiveness" appear in both sectors. These four values can be considered to be the common core of shared organizational values.

Nevertheless, "expertise" and, especially, "accountability" are considered more important in the public sector (share 1.5 and 1.8 respectively) than in the private sector (share 1.4 and 1.3 respectively). In addition, when it comes to less important or relatively unimportant values, the similarities by far exceed the differences: "responsiveness," "obedience," "self-fulfillment," "social justice," and "sustainability" are ranked as relatively unimportant in both sectors. (Van der Wal et al., 2008, p. 474)

However, perhaps things have changed since then. Currently, both public and private organizations value innovation more than ever although private organizations are more concerned with innovation in order to survive and flourish.

The 2020 Australian Public Service Employee Census questioned employees working in the Australian public service about public values. One question asked: "In the last month, which APS [Australian Public Service] value did you apply most to your work?" This question had five options: impartial, committed to service, accountable, respectful, and ethical. Of the respondents, 52.63 percent (53,975 out of 102,564 employees) stated "committed to service" followed by "accountable" (17.39 percent, or 17,840 employees), "respectful" (13.79 percent, or 14,142 employees), "ethical" (8.74 percent 8,963 employees), and finally "impartial" (7.45 percent, or 7,644 employees) (APSC, 2020). The findings reveal that during COVID-19, what mattered most for public sector employees was their commitment to public service. Although none of the values indicate innovation, innovation can be strongly related to a commitment to public service as public organizations and employees may discover factors, strategies, or innovations to strengthen public service. In other words, these public service values do not conflict with innovation; on the contrary, they can support innovation.

Why Do Sectoral Differences Matter?

So far, we have discussed the differences between the public and the private sector, but we have not discussed the implications of these differences for innovation, which is particularly essential to policymakers and practitioners. The critical question is, so what? Why should we care about these differences?

In their classic work, Wamsley and Zald (1973, p. 63) explain why this difference matters: "If we seek to understand public agencies and treat some aspect of them as dependent variables, we find that they are subject to a different set of constraints and pressures than private ones." They also continue that if public agencies are "independent variables affecting political effectiveness and legitimacy, [one] will need an understanding of public organizations quite different from that necessary to understand the effectiveness and legitimacy of private organizations." In other words, the distinction matters for both independent and dependent variables. For example, the features of public organizations can affect (independent variable) innovation or be affected (dependent variable) by innovation.

Additionally, with the NPM reforms, the distinction between public and private organizations is lessened because the main idea of NPM is that public organizations should be businesslike and apply managerial principles and behavior from the private sector (e.g., performance-related pay and TQM) (Barzelay, 2000, 2001; Boyne, 2002; Hood, 1991). Furthermore, as van der Voet and Steijn (2021, p. 1275) have recently argued, "the public sector is increasingly characterized by hybrid organizational forms that blur the traditional distinction between the public and private sector [and] span organizational boundaries." In recent years, there have been shifts away from traditional bureaucratic structures in the education, social welfare, and health sectors, and there has been increasing collaboration among different actors to deliver services in these areas (van der Voet & Steijn, 2021). Therefore, the nature of innovation has changed because organizations are also changing.

Finally, Herbert Simon (1998, pp. 8–9) suggests that the boundary between public and private organizations is fluid and that they coexist:

Modern industrial societies make important use of both private and public organizations, and here, too, the boundary is very fluid. State highway departments contract much of their design work (perhaps most, nowadays) to private civil engineering firms. The U.S. Corps of Engineers, I believe, does most of its engineering in house. Some kinds of information are transported by private carriers, some by the U.S. Post Office, itself a hybrid, not-quite-governmental, organization that contracts most of the actual carrying to private airlines and trucking firms. Nor, in spite of recent trends, are private corporations free from regulation by public bodies. The answers to questions of socialization or privatization of particular industries are neither univocal nor simple, and different societies in our day have maintained different balances and have shifted those balances frequently.

Now we examine how these sectoral differences affect public sector innovation.

Sectoral Differences and Public Sector Innovation

Interest in comparing public and private organizations in terms of organizational structure, design, and decision making (e.g., Rainey, 2009) has expanded to comparing innovations in public and private organizations (Bysted & Hansen, 2015; Hartley, 2005; Lapuente et al., 2020; Torfing & Triantafillou, 2016; van der Wal, 2017; Wise, 1999). Despite these studies, Torfing and Triantafillou (2016, p. 19) argue that "the research on public innovation is still in its infancy, and more work needs to be done in this area" (see also Demircioglu & Audretsch, 2017).

Early scholars of innovation such as Schumpeter and organization theorists such as Thompson (1965) did not differentiate between public and private organizations when they analyzed the innovative activities of organizations or countries. Schumpeter most notably introduced the concept of the entrepreneur, who serves as an agent of change in society. Schumpeter viewed the entrepreneur as the catalyst for innovative activity. Schumpeter (1942, p. 13) gives the distinguishing feature of the entrepreneur as follows: "The function of entrepreneurs is to reform or revolutionize the pattern of production by exploiting an invention, or more generally, an untried technological possibility for producing a new commodity or producing an old one in a new way." After Schumpeter, the famous "A Case Study of Innovation" by Morison in 1950 analyzed technological innovation in the US Navy. There were further contributions to innovation studies in the 1960s. Some pioneering works include Burns and Stalker (1961), Thompson (1965), Wilson (1966), Lawrence and Lorsch (1967), Mansfield (1968), and Mohr (1969).

Even though the number of studies on innovation increased in the 1970s (e.g., Aiken & Hage, 1971; Baldridge & Burnham, 1975; Corwin, 1972; Daft, 1978; Downs & Mohr, 1979; Kimberly, 1979; Nelson & Winter, 1977; Pierce & Delbecq, 1977; Rowe & Boise, 1974), most of these early studies did not focus on specific features of public organizations or on how public organizations could be (more) innovative. This is true even for those studies published by public administration scholars or in public administration journals such as

Administration & Society (Downs & Mohr, 1979; Rowe & Boise, 1974). Important exceptions include Mohr's (1969) "Determinants of Innovation in Organizations." Mohr (1969, p. 111) starts his article with the following sentence: "The present study is an attempt to identify the determinants of innovation in public agencies, i.e., the degree to which they adopt and emphasize programs that depart from traditional concerns." Feller and Menzel's (1977) "Diffusion Milieus as a Focus of Research on Innovation in the Public Sector" and Perry and Kraemer's (1978) "Innovation Attributes, Policy Intervention, and the Diffusion of Computer Applications among Local Governments" are other pioneering studies of public sector innovation.

Boyne (2002) summarizes four significant differences between public and private management to keep in mind when examining innovation: environment, goals, structures, and values. According to Boyne (2002, p. 103), public managers "face less intense competitive pressures" (environment), "are required to pursue a larger number of goals" (goals), "have less autonomy from superiors" (structures), and "are less materialistic" compared to the private sector managers. We believe that these differences affect innovation differently. For instance, public organizations may have less motivation and incentive to innovate when they face less intense competitive pressures. When public managers pursue multiple goals simultaneously, they may not focus on particular innovations, so they may not be able to innovate. When public managers have less autonomy, they have less freedom to experiment and try out new ideas. When public managers are less materialistic, their innovativeness may focus on contributing to society.

Nevertheless, despite increasing interest and recent studies of public sector innovation, most studies on innovation examine only the business sector. There are several reasons for this. One reason why we see relatively less discussion of public sector innovation is that "public managers must cope with the paradox of meeting demands for innovation and requirements for bureaucratic restraints [and] public sector dynamics are more complex and nuanced" (Shim et al., 2021, p. 2). Additionally, business scholars have long studied these topics because innovative and entrepreneurship activities are typically linked with profits (and public organizations do not aspire to make profits) (Audretsch et al., 2020).

While entrepreneurship seems to be inextricably linked to the search for profits in both the scholarly literature of entrepreneurship as well as in the public discourse, a closer analysis of what is known about entrepreneurs from research reveals that the lust for profit is not the major motivation driving them and may not even be among the most important. Entrepreneurs are, of course, people too. And just as for other groups of people, they are heterogeneous and diverse and reflect a broad spectrum of motivations, beliefs, aspirations, and goals. The research on entrepreneurial motivation reflects this diversity of entrepreneurs and has found them to be motivated by the desire for autonomy, for independence, for the actualization of personal values, to contribute to societal goals and values, and to maintain control over their own situation. And yes, for personal wealth as well.

The public sector provides a context for many or most, or even all, of these underlying motivations for entrepreneurship. Even profitability may be relevant in the public sector, if entrepreneurship is viewed as leading to subsequent income and wealth garnered in the future. Careers and work experience typically consist of multiple and punctuated employment episodes, so that entrepreneurs often evolve in their work context, moving across the public and private sectors.

Bekkers et al. (2011b, p. 17) state two major differences between why public and private sector innovations occur. First, what matters most for public organizations is to achieve legitimacy. Second, public and private organizations have different contexts: "How decisive is the context? Although competition is viewed as a necessary condition for innovation which, according to scholars, leads to a hardly innovative public sector, it is argued here that the public sector can also be perceived as an innovative sector." Some studies also suggest that private sector employees and private organizations are more innovative because they are driven by competition. Competition is a primary reason for an organization to innovate regardless of the sector (Bysted & Hansen, 2015; Lewis et al., 2018). However, too much competition may reduce innovation because organizations will not share information and resources when organizations compete too much. In this regard, when public organizations encourage each other to adopt best practices, they can be more innovative. In fact, when organizations and employees share ideas and resources, the sum of an innovation may be greater than its parts, suggesting that competition may not necessarily lead to innovation (Bysted & Hansen, 2015; Hartley, 2005). These findings are consistent with Alsos et al.'s (2016, p. 85) observation that "although competition is an important driving force for innovation in the private sector, most public sector organisations do not compete in a market that rewards the 'winners' with superior economic performance. The survival of public organisations relies more on political processes and/or bureaucratic decisions, and they compete against each other for scarce resources in this setting."

Because private sector organizations have a clear bottom line and public sector organizations have more vaguely defined goals (e.g., Rainey, 2009), it is less clear for public organizations whether innovations have been successful (Potts & Kastelle, 2010). Because of equity concerns, a reluctance to take risks, and opposition monitoring, public sector organizations seek to avoid failure (Rainey, 2009). In this regard, "success through innovation" is not vital for public sector organizations (Potts & Kastelle, 2010, p. 125). Furthermore, a public sector bureaucracy that encourages formalization and centralization, the ownership and funding of public organizations, and a lack of incentive and salary systems to reward innovation are major barriers to public sector innovation (Bysted & Hansen, 2015; Vigoda-Gadot et al., 2005).

Because there is a weak relationship between performance and salary in the public sector and innovating requires taking (unrewarded) risks (Rainey, 2009), public sector employees have less incentive to innovate. For example, empirical findings demonstrate that "[b]oth entrepreneurial and conservative respondents, unlike their private sector counterparts, revealed significant risk-aversion tendencies. The public sector spends public monies, is accountable to representatives who themselves are risk averse given their need for periodic re-election or reappointment and public sector risks attract significant media attention" (Sadler, 2000, p. 38). Therefore, since public organizations have societal objectives and aim to correct market failures, the incentives, conditions, sources, and barriers of innovation are different in the public sector (Bloch & Bugge, 2013).

One of the most significant differences between public and private sector innovation is that while the former encourages other organizations to adopt successful ideas and practices, the latter aims to prevent their diffusion by protecting intellectual property via patents or other measures (Cinar, 2020). For example, Bloch and Bugge (2013, p. 136) state that: "Whereas innovation in the private sector is sought to be protected from copying by others in order to increase the benefits of temporary rents from monopoly, for the public sector it may be the opposite. Here diffusion of innovation across the public (and private) sector may ensure a better use of public resources." Likewise, time horizons in the public sector are typically short due to so many actors' involvement in decisions and different demands, concerns, and pressures from different stakeholders (Serrat, 2017)

While private sector innovation is a means to survive, flourish, make profits, and gain competitive advantages (Daft, 1978; OECD/Eurostat, 2018; Tan & Cha, 2021), public sector innovation is a means to improve governance, public services, and public service delivery, and contribute to society (Demircioglu, 2017; Moore & Hartley, 2008; Torfing & Triantafillou, 2016; van der Voet & Steijn, 2021). Therefore, the primary purpose of innovation in public and private organizations is quite different. Additionally, the organizational structure of public organizations impacts potential innovations differently and the longer-term importance, applicability, and practicality of innovations may change in the future: "What is regarded as a useful innovation today might be the subject of a public enquiry or an electoral backlash tomorrow" (Hartley & Knell, 2022, p. 41).

The main sources of innovation in public and private organizations are also different. For example, Moore (2005) states that the majority of innovative ideas implemented in public organizations arrive from external sources such as private and nonprofit organizations. Most innovative ideas are created, developed, and implemented within private organizations. According to Moore, this difference demonstrates a crucial difference between public and private organizations and their innovativeness. Therefore, while public organizations encourage top-down and more ambitious innovation, private organizations value bottom-up innovation, such as innovations emanating from frontline employees who interact with customers on a daily basis while also encouraging less ambitious and more modest changes emphasizing constant improvement (Moore, 2005). Likewise, for public organizations, "innovation is justifiable only where it increases public value in the quality, efficiency or fitness for purpose of governance or services" (Hartley, 2005, p. 30). However, for private organizations, innovation is "a virtue in itself, as a means to ensure competitiveness in new markets or to revive flagging markets" (Hartley, 2005, p. 30).

When we talk about the public sector or public organizations, some people may assume that all public sector organizations are the same in every country. In fact, there are significant differences in public organizations across different countries and even between public organizations within the same country. For instance, employees working with specialist, regulatory, and operational agencies may differ in their innovative activities (Demircioglu, 2021). Employees working in IT-related organizations may be more innovative than employees working in human services. Chapter 4 discusses why context matters for innovation.

Therefore, among public organizations, some can be more innovative than others. For instance, Roessner (1977) argues that quasi-public organizations such as the United States Postal Service are more efficient and "businesslike" than pure public agencies because they are closer to the market and must compete with private organizations. However, little empirical work exists on this topic; therefore, it is important to understand and further test how public and private organizations differ in innovative activities. For example, there are conflicting studies on the relationship between state-owned enterprises (SOEs) and innovation. On the one hand, compared to the private sector, states are long-term oriented, and SOEs are part of the National Innovation System, including building innovative capacities and capabilities (Jia et al., 2019). On the other hand, SOEs have less incentive and motivation to innovate and appreciate innovation less, as argued by public choice scholars (Niskanen, 2017; Tullock et al., 2002). Roessner (1977, p. 344) observes that "comparative studies of innovation in public and private organizations may produce useful insights into the incentive systems that induce organization members to generate, adopt, and implement innovations, thus improving our understanding of how innovation occurs."

There is another important difference between public and private organizations: public organizations are typically larger than private organizations. For example, one study in Canada finds that while only 10 percent of private organizations have more than twenty employees, only 10 percent of public organizations have fewer than twenty employees (Earl, 2003). Additionally, while only 0.4 percent of private organizations employ more than 500 employees, about 43 percent of public organizations employ more than 500 employees (Earl, 2003). These findings suggest a dramatic difference between public and private organizations, which can affect innovation. Larger organizations have been criticized for being less efficient due to rules, procedures, divisions of labor, and paperwork (see the libertarian critique by Von Mises, 1944), particularly from the public choice perspective (Niskanen, 2017). In his influential book *Bureaucracy and Representative Government*, Niskanen (2017) states that even if bureaucrats do not necessarily have bad intentions, they aim to maximize their power and their organizations' budget and authority. Therefore, a different approach to examining innovation could be to compare bigger and smaller organizations rather than public and private organizations. Another critique of larger organizations comes from population ecology theory. According to this theory, larger organizations are not innovative and adaptive to change due to inertia (Hannan & Freeman, 1984). From this view, since public organizations are larger, and larger organizations tend to be less adaptable (e.g., have fewer incentives to change), public organizations could be less innovative.

Thus, both public and private organizations can be innovative. However, large organizations may be less innovative due to their structures, regardless of whether they are public or private. Similarly, employees in social services may be more innovative than employees in technical or authoritative service areas, regardless of whether they belong to public or private sector organizations. Therefore, the difference in innovativeness between public and private organizations should not be exaggerated (Demircioglu, 2020; Rainey, 2009; Torfing and Triantafillou, 2016). These findings coincide with Scott and Davis's (2015, p. 13) observation: "Size, however, should not be equated with success. Perhaps for a time in the industrial age, size, as measured by employees or productive capacity, was instrumental to success (survival, profitability), but such an association is ill-suited to the postindustrial era ... most productive and innovative businesses are often small or intermediate in size." Of course, we do not advocate large public organizations laying off employees in order to be smaller. Instead, our goal is to determine how public sector organizations and public sector employees can innovate most effectively while operating within a bureaucratic system.

Innovations carry risks that may not be compatible with public organizations. As Albury (2005) observes: "Innovations in the public sector are exposed to higher levels of public scrutiny, and often earlier – before they have had a chance to be fully developed – than is the case for the private or voluntary sectors" (Albury, 2005, p. 54). Additionally, employees in public organizations typically have less autonomy than their counterparts in the private sector, so the former tend to be less innovative (Bysted & Hansen, 2015). In this regard, when there is too much scrutiny and too little autonomy, public managers and public sector employees may be risk-avoiders and thus less innovative. However, as we have discussed and will demonstrate further, public organizations *can* be innovative and constantly innovate. One problem is that, as Bysted and Hansen (2015) note, there are few studies empirically testing the effects of sectoral differences on innovation.

One study comparing public and private sector employees in Norway, Sweden, and Denmark finds that public sector employees are more innovative than private sector employees (Bysted & Hansen, 2015). They find that in public organizations, product innovation includes certain sections of the organization with a limited number of employees. In contrast, service innovation encompasses a wider scope of innovation with more employees involved (Bysted & Hansen, 2015). In this regard, because public organizations typically implement more service innovations than product innovations, public organizations may seem more innovative (e.g., more employees report innovation).

In addition, public organizations have the essential capacity to innovate. Because professionalism, expertise, knowledge, and power are important elements of bureaucracy (Lewis, 1988; Wilson, 2000), "professionalized public bureaucrats have a capacity to initiate and innovate that is unparalleled in the political system" (O'Leary, 2010, p. 10). Therefore, public organizations can be highly innovative with the right conditions and motivators. We discuss these conditions and drivers for innovation in Chapter 7.

Additionally, the public and private sectors can learn from each other, particularly in the case of innovation. As evidenced in Chapters 1 and 2, since the 1980s, governments worldwide have emphasized learning from the business sector. However, there are also many techniques that businesses can learn from the public sector. For example, Heracleous and Johnston (2009) analyzed Singapore Airlines and the National Library Board of Singapore and interviewed key stakeholders in both organizations over many years. They found that private organizations can learn from public organizations about how to better engage with technology to renew themselves, update their practices, be proactive, and reduce groupthink.

Although both public and private organizations can be innovative, the tools or instruments to make them innovative are different

(Potts & Kastelle, 2010). Furthermore, innovation diffusion may differ between public and private organizations. For example, Albury (2011) concludes that while manufacturing organizations, such as car industry has implemented so many innovations in the last century, the diffusion of innovations in public organizations, such as education services, are slow due to political, cultural, and isomorphic reasons.

Furthermore, while public organizations implement innovations to increase their legitimacy, private organizations implement innovations to make profits (Demircioglu, 2018). Demircioglu (2018, p. 2) points out in his work on organizational innovation that "[a]s long as these organizations are considered legitimate by government, stakeholders, and citizens, these [public] organizations can survive and prosper (e.g., receive higher budget, increase their staff, and can be praised by media)." While private sector innovation focuses on product development and profits, public sector innovation focuses on public benefit (Potts & Kastelle, 2010). Additionally, public organizations focus on interaction, communication, and negotiation among stakeholders (Lee et al., 2012), while most private sector managers are power and profit motivated (Andersen, 2010). Furthermore, the objectives of the public and private sectors are different: While profit or market share is the main objective for the private sector, solving public problems and grand challenges are main reasons for public sector innovation (OECD, 2015, p. 14).

In an early study, Roessner (1977) did not find a strong case that private organizations are more innovative than public organizations. In the Swiss public sector context, Neuroni et al. (2021) find that over 90 percent of public managers are aware of innovative activities in the public sector. Most of these managers indicated that the public sector and its employees could be even more innovative. In his well-known book *The Case for Bureaucracy*, Goodsell (1985) provides evidence that it is wrong to argue that public organizations are less innovative than private organizations, particularly in terms of public service delivery and hospitals. Goodsell (1985, p. 54) finds "[a]vailable comparative data on the efficiency, costs, and quality of services in refuse collection, hospitals, transportation, utilities, and insurance show that whereas at some times business seems superior, at other times government appears to perform better." He also finds evidence that some public organizations are more innovative than private organizations. Thus, even evidence from before and during

Table 3.1 *Innovation between public and private organizations*

Nature of innovation	Private sector (mostly product dominant)	Public sector (mostly service dominant)
Why innovate?	Competitive advantage and survival	Changing needs and problems
How to innovate?	R&D, patents, open innovation	Transfer–collaboration–procurement
Criteria for success	Profit	Public value
How to measure innovation?	Return on investment/R&D	Number of innovations introduced
Accountability	Accountability to the shareholders	Accountability to the public
The organizational climate for innovation	Flexible organizations	Bureaucracy
Transfer of innovations	Restrict transfer (patents)	Extend transfer (scale up)

Source: Adapted from Cinar, E. (2020). Chapter 3: Public Sector Innovation. In P. Trott (Ed.), *Innovation Management and New Product Development, 7th edition.* Reprinted by permission of Pearson Education Limited.

the NPM era demonstrates that public organizations are not behind the private sector in terms of innovative activities.

Finally, Cinar (2020, p. 87) explains how public and private sector innovations are different in the following way:

Public sector innovation is service dominant and occurs within public services. These are for all members of society such as the emergency services: ambulance, fire rescue and police. Second, the motivation for innovation is quite different: whilst private firms innovate to gain competitive advantage and to survive in changing market conditions, public sector organisations innovate to find solutions to organisational and social problems. Third, the methods used to innovate vary between the two sectors. Private firms invest in R&D [research and development], obtain patents and seek open innovation opportunities. On the other hand, public sector innovation depends on transferring best practices from other governments or collaborating with a wide variety of enterprises to access technology. These firms then become suppliers to exploit new technology. Fourth, the innovativeness in the private sector is measured using R&D spending ratios, return on investment, the number of patents issued, etc. Whereas, in the public sector, it is mainly measured through the number of innovations introduced. For these indicators, companies have to be accountable to their shareholders while public sector organisations are held accountable to the public. Thus, the nature of innovation risk is different in public sector as the ex-mayor of London described on the first day of the London Congestion Charge in 2003: "Other Mayors around the world have said to me that if it works, and you get re-elected, then I will do it."

Table 3.1 summarizes the nature of innovation while comparing public and private organizations.

Conclusion

Overall, significant differences between public and private organizations exist, and these differences affect innovative activities and outcomes of innovation. The critical and interesting question is not the differences between public and private organizations but how these differences affect outputs and outcomes, such as for innovation. Additionally, how can public organizations be more innovative despite constraints and barriers to innovation in the public sector is a vital question for academics and practitioners. Due to accountability mechanisms, innovation is discouraged in the public sector because innovation includes risk-taking (through experimentation). However, public organizations do adopt innovations. For example, NASA and the US military have adopted many breakthrough innovations (Mazzucato, 2015). Public sector innovations are necessarily more complex than those in private organizations, and coalition building is more important to achieve innovation in the public sector (Cunningham & Kempling, 2009). Thus, it is essential to understand the similarities and differences between public and private organizations in order to discover what public and private organizations can learn from one another, increase innovative activities, and solve social and other problems.

4 | *The Context of Public Sector Innovation*

Introduction

"Context" refers to the surroundings of individuals and organizations, and these surroundings can affect innovativeness. More specifically, context can be defined as "broader social or normative environments [work group climate, organizational and national culture] ... industry-, sector-, or economy-wide characteristics, as well as other normative and institutional structures and regimes ... [and provide] insights into how particular environmental factors may serve as temporal and/or spatial boundary conditions governing observed phenomena" (Bamberger, 2008, p. 840). In this regard, the external environment of an organization is a part of its context. Still, context has broader meanings in terms of both embeddedness and the unit of analysis.

Context theories "specify how surrounding phenomena or temporal conditions directly influence lower-level phenomena" (Bamberger, 2008, p. 841). Context is also essential to understanding how environmental, organizational, and demographic contexts affect "lower-level phenomena" such as employee engagement, commitment, performance, and turnover (Bamberger, 2008). In other words, context also represents the "systems, processes, and beliefs that shape employees' behaviours" (Ali et al., 2022, p. 2). Thus, studies of public sector innovation should consider the effects of national, socio-economic, political, organizational, and demographic contexts on innovative activities, including creativity, innovative work behavior, and the implementation of innovations in public organizations. Ideas that are effective in one organization may not be effective in other settings (Goffin & Mitchell, 2010), demonstrating that context matters. Furthermore, considering that many administrative innovation attempts fail (Bezes & Jeannot, 2018; Drechsler & Randma-Liiv, 2016; Haque, 1996; Peters, 2010), studies may focus on understanding which contexts are more suitable for different types of public sector innovations.

Torfing and Triantafillou (2016, p. 3) claim that "political, socio-economic and administrative context will affect the forms and content of governance reform, which in turn will help to spur innovation that may lead to better outcomes." Autio et al. (2014, p. 1099) similarly observe that context "play a central role in our understanding of the origins, forms, micro-processes, functioning, and diverse outcomes of entrepreneurial activities." Demircioglu (2020, p. 1869) suggests that "context always matters, and ... future studies [should] delve into the effects of the national context on innovation, including analysing reasons for differences between countries in terms of public sector innovation." Thus, different contextual factors have vital importance to innovative activities.

National Context

The national context, which is affected by historical developments, national policies, geography, religion, language, and many other factors, can affect innovative activities in the public sector. National context includes the political sphere, such as separation of powers (unitary vs. shared), federalism (e.g., one level of government vs. multiple levels), and process (e.g., corporatist vs. adversarial) (Meier et al., 2017; O'Toole & Meier, 2015). Likewise, state structure (e.g., federal vs. unitary), executive government (e.g., majoritarian vs. consensual), minister–mandarin relations (separate vs. integrated), administrative culture (e.g., public interest vs. Rechtsstaat), and diversity of policy advice (e.g., consultants, universities, and political advisers) are part of the national context (Pollitt & Bouckaert, 2017). Cinar et al. (2022b) have described the influence of the national context on public sector innovation in terms of five levels: the political context (e.g., the political parties and international political relations), the administrative context (e.g., the machinery of governments, coordination mechanisms, bureaucracy, and the rule of law), the social context (e.g., aging population, urbanization, and migration trends), the economic and technological context (e.g., macroeconomic structures and technological capabilities of nations), and the temporal context (e.g., before and after financial crises and natural disasters). Cinar et al. (2022b) find that these contextual factors have affected the innovation types and typologies in different countries. For instance, as Japan has an increasingly aging population, many innovations in Japan have focused on social innovations to deal with demographic changes (see also Suzuki et al., 2020). Temporal context has been less examined because most studies of innovation (in both the private and public sectors) employ a cross-sectional analysis of one point in time, so they are not able to capture the effects of innovation over time (Cinar et al., 2022b; Pollitt, 2007).

The national context significantly affects not only innovation and innovation types but also the different dimensions and sources of innovation. For instance, the speed of reforms is faster in majoritarian and centralized (unitary) governments such as New Zealand and the UK. However, the speed of reforms is typically slower in consensual countries such as the Netherlands (Pollitt & Bouckaert, 2017). In this regard, we could expect more radical innovations in New Zealand and the UK than in the Netherlands.

Furthermore, top-down innovations are more common in authoritarian regimes (Demircioglu, 2021). As a specific example, analyzing innovative activities in China, Zhang and Zhu (2020) observe that Chinese government officials and the central government have more power over middle managers and frontline employees because the central authority controls and can manipulate resources, promotion, and even performance evaluation, so lower-level governments have less autonomy. However, the US government has a federal system based on checks and balances, so authority is distributed (Agranoff & McGuire, 2004; Kettl, 2008). Therefore, context matters in terms of whether countries are unitary or federal systems.

Additionally, innovations are not the same in Norway and Sweden though they have similar characteristics and are geographic neighbors (Wise, 2002). Similarly, there are major differences between Germany and the United Kingdom in terms of their innovations. For instance, in Germany, innovation patterns are typically incremental, and the political influence of the bureaucracy is high; in the UK, the political influence of the bureaucracy is low (Knill, 1999). As we discuss in Chapter 10, these contextual variables affect the overall innovation systems in nations. Thus, we can predict whether certain types of innovation are incremental or persistent, and whether the source for an innovation is high or low.

National culture is another important contextual variable that can affect innovations. More specifically, Hofstede et al. (2010) have analyzed countries based on power distance, individualism, masculinity, uncertainty avoidance, long-term orientation, and indulgence. Studies suggest that countries with higher individualism, low power distance, and low uncertainty avoidance are more innovative than countries with low individualism, high power distance, and high uncertainty avoidance (Demircioglu, 2020; Rinne et al., 2012). Furthermore, femininity cultures may encourage more collaborative innovation, while masculinity cultures may encourage more top-down innovations.

National management agendas shape innovation discourse. For example, in many countries, particularly within Europe, governments have focused on making large-scale cutbacks since the 1980s (Pollitt, 2013). However, there are variations across European countries because of contextual variables that affect policies. For instance, Pollitt (2013, p. 3) concludes that "the Netherlands and Sweden are more willing to experiment than, say, France, Germany or Norway. The Nordic group is particularly interesting – they all have big state apparatuses, and relatively generous welfare states. They also have extremely low corruption, relatively limited income inequalities, and high levels of public trust in government" (Pollitt, 2013, p. 3). This suggests that the national context and countries' management agendas and priorities shape innovations, innovation types, and innovation outcomes, and a larger and more intrusive government context may be conducive to public sector innovation.

A national, social, organizational, and group culture can affect innovative activities. In some cultures, risk-taking may be allowed to some degree, but in other countries, risk-taking may not be an issue. For example, employees in former Soviet Union countries may have different mindsets and understandings of innovation compared to employees in other settings (Baker, 1994). Furthermore, although Singapore is highly innovative, particularly in terms of the implementation of ideas, when it comes to being innovative, risk-taking, and entrepreneurial, public sector employees in Singapore do not apply their innovativeness outside of their job descriptions (Carney & Zheng, 2009).

An OECD document provides recent and concrete examples of how public sector innovations are developed in different countries:

[I]n Finland, socially excluded people are getting free medical checks in bars or on the street through a new mobile health check system ... [I]n Mexico, people living in rural areas do not need to travel long distances to get public services and can get social transfer and other payment services at the nearest gas station or village store ... [I]n France, families are helping old people with no family connections to live autonomously in a caring environment by sharing housing facilities and common space. (OECD, 2017, p. 14)

Due to differences across contexts, innovation or innovative activities that work well in one country may not work in another, particularly in developing nations. For example, a liberal and democratic nation contains a representative bureaucracy, and policies are based on compromise as different political, administrative, and cultural values must be considered before making a decision (Bekkers et al., 2011b). Thus, many policies are naturally incremental in these societies (Bekkers et al., 2011b; Lindblom, 1959, 1979). Therefore, understanding and evaluating the innovative activities of developing countries from a liberal, Western, and democratic lens is problematic but (unfortunately) typical. As Alatas (2021, p. 14) observes, "the non-West was seen as underdeveloped or backward and had to adopt the 'universal' definition and criteria of development as well as the political-economic, social and cultural policies that would allow them to realise such development." This poses a significant problem to academic and practical knowledge. Likewise, Haque (1996, p. 324) defines this problem in the context of management scholarship: "the administrative reforms undertaken in most Asian, African, and Latin American countries have been detached from their own social realities, including the economic forces, political power structures and cultural patterns ... it is essential to take into account the various contextual factors of Third World societies in suggesting policy alternatives to overcome problems resulting from contextless administrative systems." Not considering contextual differences across countries will result in policy failures or a lack of innovation.

Other Contexts

Other contexts include institutional, cognitive, technological, and social contexts (Audretsch et al., 2022). Regarding institutional context, it can include both formal (e.g., the rule of law, property rights, and regulations) and informal (norms and values) policies (Hall & Thelen, 2009; Ostrom, 2005; Thelen, 2009; Weyland, 2008). An additional and often overlooked aspect of the institutional context involves culture. Culture, along with the more formal aspects of context, such as laws, shape the behavior of individuals and organizations. Thus, one reason for the observed spatial variation in innovation is simply that culture also varies across geographic space. Some cultural contexts are more conducive to innovation, while others tend to inhibit innovative activity. For example, the context of common law provides a very different legal basis than does the context of codified law. Similarly, some contexts for public administration, such as in Sweden, provide deep protection and independence, while the public administration context elsewhere, such as Turkey and Hungary, is considerably less protected and independent. Therefore, it is not surprising that Turkey and Hungary have been less innovative since the 2010s due to diminishing rule of law, property rights, and meritocracy.

Cognitive context refers to how a public sector employee perceives their organizational environment and the opportunities for innovation (Audretsch et al., 2022). For example, some employees may consider challenges or threats (e.g., COVID-19) as opportunities for further creativity and innovation in the organizational process. The same employee will respond very differently depending upon the organizational context. Organizations, just like the societies in which they operate, also have an element of culture. Some organizational cultures are clearly more conducive to innovation, while their counterparts have an organizational culture inhibiting innovation. In some organizational contexts, creativity, along with its inherent risk and failure, are not just tolerated but actually celebrated. However, in other organizational contexts, the priority is on avoiding failure at all costs, with the attendant result of discouraging creativity and innovation.

New technology is not only a product of innovation; using technologies in public services may also enhance service and process innovations in the public sector. Therefore, the technological context shapes how innovators implement and attempt to increase the efficiency and quality of public services. The technological context characterizes the extent to which opportunities abound for new technological advances. In some contexts, technological advancement is limited. This may be attributable to a technology that has matured and perhaps become increasingly irrelevant. Other contexts are rife with the potential for new technological innovations. Such contexts tend to be in the early stage of a new technology, which offers a plethora of opportunities for new innovation.

Audretsch et al. (2022) define "social context" as the relationship and communications between innovators and other stakeholders within a social network. As most innovations are collaborative in nature (Cinar et al., 2022a; Demircioglu et al., 2021), networks are vital to increasing public sector innovation. Some contexts are replete with social interactions, interfaces, and linkages. These are typically characterized by a rich and thick social network. By contrast, other contexts suffer from only a paucity of social interactions and interfaces. Such contexts are typically characterized as having a weak social network. Knowledge spillovers are facilitated by the context of rich social networks more than by weak social networks.

Other public sector contexts include environmental characteristics, such as urbanization, population growth, poverty, and wealth in communities and societies (Damanpour et al., 2021). In a federal context, such as the United States, citizens in wealthier communities can push for a higher quality of services for their local governments (Damanpour et al., 2021), so there may be divergence not only between wealthier and deprived communities in terms of the quality of public services (Suzuki & Demircioglu, 2021). However, the level of innovation may differ because public managers have fewer resources, incentives, and motivations to improve performance in deprived communities. In terms of organizational leadership, there are also differences between political (or elected) and professional leaders, as political leaders tend to focus on less risky and more popular short-term policies while professional leaders may focus on long-term goals (Damanpour et al., 2021).

Crises or perceptions of crises are other contextual variables affecting innovation (Pillai & Meindl, 1998). For example: "People in crisis seek proxy control. They find it in their 'savior,' i.e., the leader to whom they attribute extraordinary abilities. Crises provide leaders with opportunities to take bold purposeful action, which is then interpreted by followers in charismatic terms and may increase their willingness to follow" (Pillai & Meindl, 1998, p. 649). Therefore, crises may not only lead to changes but also increase the use of power by leaders (regardless of whether or not that use of power is ethical).

Other contextual variables include labor unions (Pillai & Meindl, 1998), social capital (O'Toole & Meier, 2015), complexity, munificence, and the turbulence of the external environment (O'Toole & Meier, 2015). These variables may affect public sector innovations differently. For example, union membership may reduce innovation because unions may reinforce norms not related to innovative policies

(Wise, 1999). Additionally, working in a complex external environment may increase innovation in the public sector because working in a complex environment encourages public sector employees to be innovative, efficient, and effective (Demircioglu & Audretsch, 2020).

No man is an island, and so too it is with people and organizations. Global events and crises can therefore constitute at least part of the context at the worldwide level: "Context is also shaped by macro-economic events, such as the COVID-19 global pandemic, which is largely perceived as the world's greatest public health challenge in over a century" (Audretsch, 2020, p. 470). An important aspect of context that remains relatively unexplored in the literature is massive and widespread societal shocks. Most notably, Audretsch et al. (2020) point to the pandemic as triggering a different and unprecedented societal context. Such global or macro contextual influences tend to impact everyone. For example, everyone throughout the world was impacted by the COVID-19 pandemic, either directly or indirectly. Similarly, almost everyone is impacted by global warming in one way or another. Such global contexts are a contrast to more local contexts, where only a limited population or group of stakeholders is impacted, such as a hurricane in Florida.

Time is another contextual variable that may affect innovation (Cinar et al., 2022b). For instance, while a particular innovation may have been only incremental when it is first introduced, it may subsequently prove to be disruptive and radical. For instance, Hage (1999) observes that most innovations were considered incremental in the 1960s and 1970s, but they were considered radical in the 1980s and 1990s by both public and private organizations. Additionally, the same public organization may be more innovative in one period than in another. Why is this the case? Organizational leadership, group dynamics, and socio-economic dynamics may influence such outcomes.

Organizational Context

Because larger organizations tend to have more resources, and resources are typically needed for innovations (particularly radical innovations), early scholars, such as Joseph Schumpeter, Alfred Chandler, and John Kenneth Galbraith, typically concluded that larger organizations tend to be more innovative (Acs & Audretsch, 2003). Innovation is also positively associated with organizational size as larger organizations have larger R&D laboratories (Acs & Audretsch, 1990). Another advantage of larger organizations is their involvement in university research, although there is evidence that smaller organizations can also take part in such research (Link & Rees, 1990).

However, evidence collected since the 1980s shows that smaller organizations are, in fact, more innovative than their larger counterparts (Acs & Audretsch, 1988, 1990). These findings are consistent with population ecology theories suggesting that small organizations are less bureaucratic and thus more adaptable and flexible (Hannan & Freeman, 1984). Likewise, from the perspective of public choice theory, public organizations (and particularly large ones) tend to be monopolies and budget maximizers, and do not concern themselves much with efficiency, resulting in less innovative activity (Dunleavy, 2014). In fact, smaller organizations not only have fewer bureaucratic constraints but empirical data from the United States show that they are also more innovative in terms of technical knowledge and the adoption of new products and technologies (Link & Bozeman, 1991).

What is less clear is how organizational size in the public sector affects public sector innovation. Since most public organizations are larger, there are few small organizations in the public sector. Larger municipal governments have more diverse and complex environments than smaller ones (Damanpour et al., 2021), so diversity and complexity may affect innovative activities differently. Demircioglu (2020) finds that employees working in smaller organizations (organizations with fewer than 250 employees) report more innovation than employees working in larger organizations in the APS. These findings for the public sector mirror Acs and Audretsch's (1988, 1990) findings that smaller organizations in the private sector are more innovative.

Other than the size of organizations, the sector and type of organization makes a difference. Acs and Audretsch (2003, p. 61) state that there are differences in terms of sectors for innovative activities:

[T]he most innovative industries also tend to be characterized by considerable investments in R&D and new economic knowledge. Not only are industries such as computers, pharmaceuticals and instruments high in R&D inputs that generate new economic knowledge, but also in terms of innovative outputs... industries with little R&D, such as wood products, textiles and paper, also tend to produce only a negligible amount of innovative output.

They conclude that smaller organizations are more innovative in ICT-related fields while larger organizations are more innovative in pharmaceutical and aircraft firms (Acs & Audretsch, 2003).

Referring to public organizations, Arundel et al. (2019) find that while agencies related to legal affairs and the judiciary tend to emphasize stability and integrity, which therefore reflect less innovative activity, those agencies related to agriculture and infrastructure have more flexibility to experiment and initiate risky innovations. Therefore, rather than size, the sector can determine an organization's innovativeness. Furthermore, different organizational cultures – such as production, bureaucratic, and professional cultures (Jones, 1983), process vs. results-oriented cultures, and employee vs. job-oriented cultures (Hofstede et al., 1990; Hofstede, 1998) – may affect innovations differently.

Geographic context or location also needs to be taken into account, particularly because localized knowledge spillovers can drive innovation adoptions (Aryal et al., 2018; Mann & Loveridge, 2020). For example, analyzing private organizations' innovative activities in the United States, Aryal et al. (2018, p. 371) find that urban firms are more innovative than rural firms "due to their proximity to other innovative firms or based on the degree/intensity of accessing broader markets (such as via exports and ecommerce)." Acs and Audretsch (2003, p. 69) find that "new economic knowledge may spill over but the geographic extent of such knowledge spillovers is limited." Knowledge created in one organizational context can be used for innovative activity in a different organizational context. However, geographic proximity is conducive to accessing and absorbing such knowledge. Because it is highly tacit, face-to-face communication facilitates overcoming the high uncertainty, asymmetries, and transaction costs inherent in new ideas. Thus, in the absence of local proximity, the costs of accessing and absorbing such knowledge become prohibitively high in some cases. Although knowledge spills over, it is spatially bounded and therefore difficult to access and absorb in the absence of geographic proximity. The theory of knowledge spillover entrepreneurship combined with theory of spatial localization of those spillovers accounts for the high propensity for innovative activity and entrepreneurship to cluster spatially within close geographic proximity of the knowledge source. The result has been the emergence of clusters of innovation, such as Silicon Valley in California and the Research Triangle in North Carolina.

In sum, ideas can spread, but the theory of localization by Audretsch and Feldman (1996) posits that spatial proximity is needed to access and absorb external knowledge. Thus, new ideas spill over from the organization in which they are created to be used as an input for subsequent innovative activity by other organizations, but the primacy of face-to-face communication required to access and absorb that knowledge suggests that such knowledge spillovers tend to be spatially clustered within close geographic proximity to the organization creating that knowledge. Thus, in the domain of public organizations, some innovations may not spill over to other states or local governments, particularly when states or local governments are geographically distant from one another and when there is no mandate or a regulation by a government.

Other contextual factors within organizations affecting innovation include goals (clear and consistent vs. multiple and conflicting), centralization, and professionalization (O'Toole & Meier, 2015). For example, centralization and lack of professionalization may reduce innovations (Damanpour, 1991). Although too much conflict increases political divisiveness, reduces trust, and diminishes innovation, it can ultimately moderate the amount of conflict emanating from diversity and innovation (De Dreu, 2006). In fact, analyzing the company Amazon, Kantor and Streitfeld (2015) find that it encourages conflict in order to increase innovation within the company. In the context of public organizations, Lee (2021) finds that conflicting demands and tensions among network actors have increased innovative activities in South Korean public organizations.

There are also differences in local governments' contexts, such as cultural differences among organizations and individuals, or factors such as existing innovation champions (Bartlett & Dibben, 2002). For instance, "while local authorities are good at coming up with innovative ideas and solutions to the problems generated by fiscal pressure, they are less good at seeing these ideas through and this highlights both the importance of positive cultural factors and the crucial relationship between champions and sponsors in the innovation process" (Bartlett & Dibben, 2002, p. 114).

Demographic Context

Demographic context includes gender, education, age, work experience, and occupation. These factors may affect innovation or types of innovations differently. For instance, while both men and women can be innovative, men might be more assertive and able to take risks, and women might be motivated to pursue less competitive and more collaborative innovations (Demircioglu & van der Wal, 2022; Lapuente & Suzuki, 2021; Suzuki & Avellaneda, 2018).

Regarding education, Demircioglu (2020, p. 1858) argues that: "As innovative activities include the creation of new ideas in the form of new or improved products, services, processes and/or policies, education can provide knowledge and skills for innovation. Therefore, more educated employees are more knowledgeable and may understand innovative activities and processes better than employees with less education." In particular, product, service, and technological innovations may require more education and training.

Types of education or training also impact innovations. For instance, analyzing innovative attitudes in nineteen European countries, Lapuente and Suzuki (2020) find that public sector managers with law backgrounds tend to have weaker pro-innovation attitudes. The main reasons for these findings are that pro-innovation attitudes are mostly compatible with managerial values, not legal ones. Likewise, "at law school, students learn that arguments need to be supported by case references. This predisposes them to behave conservatively when joining the labor market. Law degree holders are thus more inclined to prefer every task and process to be as predictable as possible, and be skeptical of initiatives that have not been exhaustively tested" (Lapuente & Suzuki, 2020, p. 457).

Age and experience are positively related because older employees tend to have more working experience. Age can have an impact on innovation, albeit in a complicated and nuanced manner. On the one hand, older workers have accumulated more experience and knowledge, so they can be more innovative. On the other hand, they tend to get set in their ways, which impedes their ability to discern new opportunities to do something differently that would be of value. Therefore, younger employees may be more willing to experiment and adopt new technologies. However, older employees may be more risk averse and less willing to experiment and implement technologies and product innovations, as these innovations require employees to learn new skills and knowledge.

Regarding work experience, employees working in their organizations for some time tend to be more knowledgeable and experienced, so they can understand and evaluate the innovation process (such as recognizing barriers and conditions for innovations) (Demircioglu, 2021). However, very experienced employees may also resist new innovations, particularly as they age. Furthermore, more experienced employees may not be as willing to experiment and take risks.

Finally, regarding occupation, employees working in some sectors may be more innovative, such as those working in IT sectors. This is because technological opportunities vary systematically across sectors. Those sectors that are more knowledge intensive provide a greater potential for innovation. By contrast, those industries that are not knowledge intensive provide less of an opportunity for innovation. By definition, an industry context with a paucity of knowledge does not generate much innovation, and thus employees will not exhibit a strong propensity to be innovative. An important caveat is that this distinction reflects more the concept of knowledge than the operationalized measure. All of the measures of knowledge are inherently flawed and limited. Thus, in the real world, an industry context may involve more knowledge than is actually suggested by the imperfect measures of knowledge. Thus, the sectoral and industry contexts play an important role in shaping innovative activity.

There are also individual factors such as emotions, personality, and mood that affect individual and organizational outcomes in terms of performance (Judge & Bono, 2001; Lahat & Ofek, 2022; Levitats et al., 2019). Thus, these factors can also affect public sector innovations. Furthermore, many government decisions are implemented based on the perceptions, attitudes, and acts of individuals rather than through systematic or rational analysis (Hall, 1983; Howlett et al., 2009; Simon, 1976, 1986). Thus, understanding and evaluating innovative activities in the public sector is complex due to the many different contextual and dispositional variables (Demircioglu, 2021).

Additional factors include both demographic and locational dimensions of context. Diversity has been found to be conducive to innovation. While diversity matters at the organizational level, it also matters at the geographic or spatial levels. Cities, states, and regions characterized by greater diversity tend to generate more variety in response to any given set of information challenge. There is a robust literature linking the extent of diversity at the spatial or geographic unit of analysis to innovative activity. For example, Feldman and Audretsch (1999) and Glaeser et al. (1992) find compelling evidence that those cities with a greater degree of diversity also tend to exhibit more innovative activity. Finally, immigrants to a country have long been observed to have a higher propensity to be innovative (Demircioglu & Vivona, 2021). This is because of the fact that their different experiences and background enable them to perceive opportunities that are often overlooked by the indigenous population.

Conclusion

After defining what context refers to, this chapter discussed contextual differences at social, regional, and national levels. Each country has a different context affecting innovation activities in the public sector, and some countries are more innovative than others (Nelson, 1993; OECD, 1999; Suzuki & Demircioglu, 2019; WIPO, 2021). One reason for different levels of innovation across different countries is that innovation is considered to be necessary for some countries such as Australia, due to its isolation and vast territory (Demircioglu, 2019) but not for others. Singapore, South Korea, Taiwan, and Hong Kong are all innovative because these places lack natural resources and must instead focus on human talent and development. Other countries have higher globalization rates and increasing institutional and isomorphic effects and pressures, leading to more government innovation. Thus, the national context always matters for innovation.

In addition, cultural, socio-economic, political, organizational, and demographic contexts impact innovative activities (Anderson et al., 2014; Boon et al., 2021; Demircioglu, 2020). Even within the same country, different public organizations encounter different contextual factors, suggesting that innovations are not homogeneous as some organizations are more innovative than others (Dosi, 1988; H. Jung & J. Lee, 2016; Sahni et al., 2013; Pavitt, 1984). For instance, typically treasuries and departments of human services operate under very different contexts; while the former aims to reduce expenditures, the latter aims to increase expenditures (Peters, 2010). Nevertheless, both contribute to creating public value (Moore, 1995). Thus, contextual differences impact innovation and innovative activities. Related to this point, types of innovation may differ across different agencies. For instance, while process innovations may be more common in a department of human services, product innovations are more common in IT agencies. Thus, context affects the types and outcomes of innovations.

Scholars claim that market-based reforms, such as NPM reforms, have failed in many countries because politicians and decision-makers did not consider the specific context and assumed that an innovative tool that worked in one setting would work in every setting (e.g., Drechsler, 2009, 2015; Haque, 1996; Pollitt & Bouckaert, 2011). Similarly, some countries have adopted innovations from the private sector without considering whether those innovations – which worked well in a business context – would work as effectively in a public sector context. Hence, it is crucial to understand the importance of context in analyzing innovative activities.

5 | *Innovation Typologies*

Introduction and Innovation Types

Process and product (or service) innovations are the two most common types of innovation. There is also more consensus about these types of innovation across different studies. The main difference between process and product or service innovations is that while the former focuses on the inside of the organization, the latter focuses primarily on the outside of the organization (such as providing novel products or services to service users). Additionally, while a process innovation typically does not involve creating any product or service, product or service innovations typically involve producing a product or service. Thus, the second set of innovations are typically more visible to people outside of the organization while the former are not visible to people other than employees. Walker (2014, p. 23) distinguished these innovations: "Product [or service] innovations can be understood as what is produced or, more appropriately in public sector settings, what service is delivered. Processes innovations pertain to how a service is rendered." An example of a product or a service innovation is "delivering tailored elderly care solutions 'at home' and 'real time' using online consultations and mobile teams of health-care professionals," and an example of a process innovation is "merging and automating inter-departmental authorization cycles to cut down decision layers from five to just two, reducing approval time by 80 per cent" (van der Wal, 2017, p. 170). Other examples of process innovations include digital appraisal of taxes (Bekkers et al., 2011b) and establishing one-stop shops to deliver public services (Cinar, 2020; Janenova & Kim, 2016).

Research suggests that most innovations in the private sector are product innovations (Hansen & Wakonen, 1997; Leckel et al., 2020), while most innovations in the public sector are process innovations (Torugsa & Arundel, 2016a). Studies also find that process innovation is related to organizations' sustainability (Zahoor & Al-Tabbaa, 2020), such that organizations implementing process innovations can survive and flourish. The effects of product and process innovations on organizations and nations may differ. For example, while product innovations may increase employment in the economy, process innovations may reduce employment because of the efficiency gains emanating from greater organizational size (Hage, 1999).

In addition to process, product, and service innovations, there are other innovation types. Chen et al. (2021) offer a typology with six innovation types: mission, policy, management, partner, service, and citizen innovations. These six types of public sector innovation are based on innovation focus (strategy, capacity, and operation) and innovation locus (internal and external). According to their typology, strategy focus and internal locus bring about mission innovation, capacity focus and internal locus bring about management innovation, operation focus and internal locus bring about service innovation, strategy focus and external locus bring about policy innovation, capacity focus and external locus bring about partner innovation, and operation focus and external locus bring about citizen innovation (Chen et al., 2021).

Their conceptualization and examples of management innovation are very similar to process innovations, and their service innovation is the same as the product or service innovation described earlier. Therefore, we do not discuss management and service innovations. However, we do provide information about the other four types of innovations: mission, policy, partner, and citizen.

First, mission innovation is "the introduction of new worldview, mission or purpose for the organization" (Chen et al., 2021, p. 1684). Sending people to the moon and returning them safely is a well-known example of a mission (or mission-oriented) innovation in the public sector (Kattel & Mazzucato, 2018; Mazzucato, 2018). As Kattel and Mazzucato (2018, p. 790) argue, successful mission-oriented policies mobilize "a wide variety of technological and innovation efforts under a single challenge – get to the moon – and itemize it into a variety of missions." Eventually, mission-oriented innovations have positive spillover effects on the private sector.

Second, policy innovations are "introducing to the stakeholders of new benefits and obligations for the organization as a whole to solve societal problems" (Chen et al., 2021, p. 1684). Innovations (e.g., using new methods) in energy, climate policy, education, and health are examples of policy innovations (Carley, 2011).

Third, partner innovation is "the establishment of new partnerships to improve the organization's ability to further organizational goals" (Chen et al., 2021, p. 1684). Examples of partner innovation include connecting public services with private organizations, nonprofit organizations, and community groups (Chen et al., 2021).

Finally, citizen innovation is "the establishment of new platforms to facilitate citizen collaboration to achieve organizational goals" (Chen et al., 2021, p. 1684). Examples of citizen innovations include citizens' involvement in codesigning parts of cities, such as parks and urban spaces (Chen et al., 2021; Cinar et al., 2022b). All six types of innovation support each other in spite of their differences.

Chen et al. (2021) explain the differences between these innovations and how they are related:

When an organization directs its activities toward strategic questions concerning its purpose, it begins by developing its values internally by engaging in mission innovation … Policy innovation [aims to] better reflect its political mandate and increase its ability to offer benefits to its citizens … The organization may then direct its strategic activities to the ecosystem by introducing new benefits, regulations, and obligations to its clients and its partners, which may result in new problem-solving strategies, policy tools, and governance structures … [W]hen an organization develops its capacity externally, it is engaging in partner innovation … Rather than adding an administrative function, an organization can collaborate with another organization that already has that function in place. To ensure mission effectiveness, an organization must seek to improve its operations, which include service and citizen innovation. Service innovation is the concrete way an organization applies all other innovations, from mission to partner innovation, or to a particular benefit experienced by its clients … Citizen innovation involves collaboration between citizens and public sector managers, including outreach channels to promote public-sector activity and platforms designed by managers to facilitate citizen co-creation … While service innovation is directed inward, citizen innovation is directed outward because it provides a way for that same mission statement to be influenced by the people it is designed to serve. (Chen et al., 2021, pp. 1683–1685)

Multiple studies have used this framework. For example, Cinar et al., 2022b; Suchitwarasan et al., 2023 have tested this framework in the context of Singapore. They found that citizen and partner innovations are more common in Singapore compared to the United States.

Bloch and Bugge (2013) and Windrum (2008) use a similar typology, proposing the following six types of public sector innovations: "service innovation," "service delivery innovation," "administrative and organizational innovation," "conceptual innovation," "policy innovation," and "systemic innovation." We have already discussed service innovation, administrative and organizational innovation (e.g., management innovation), and policy innovation. Service delivery innovation is defined as "new ways of delivering services to and interacting with the users," and conceptual innovation is defined as the "development of new world views that challenge assumptions that underpin existing service products, processes and organisational forms." Systemic innovation is defined as "new or improved ways of interacting with other organisations and knowledge bases" (Bloch & Bugge, 2013, p. 137; see also Windrum, 2008). The 2011 APS Commission dataset uses the typology developed by Windrum (2008) and applied by Bloch and Bugge (2013), although these innovation types are not well studied. The last two types of innovation – partner and citizen – are part of collaborative innovation.

We can also add other innovation types, such as technological innovation, although this innovation is highly related to product, service, and process innovations. In fact, according to Rogers (2003), innovation and technology have been used interchangeably, and technology has two aspects: hardware and software. Therefore, both the hardware and software sides of technology can constitute product innovation (Rogers, 2003). Cinar et al. (2022b) consider that process innovations often emerge as either administrative process innovations or technological process innovations, suggesting that technological innovations can be a part of process innovations.

Examples of technological innovation include "the use of text messaging devices and cell broadcasting to warn citizens in case of an emergency" (Bekkers et al., 2011b, p. 15) and a new online car registration system (Cinar, 2020). Technological innovation is essential in public organizations, particularly for local governments, because many public services can be handled online (Feller & Menzel, 1977). According to this view, technological innovations are typically responses to institutional pressures from outside the organization. Other studies have analyzed technological innovations such as computerization in local governments in the late 1970s and early 1980s (Perry & Danzinger, 1980; Perry & Kraemer, 1978, 1980), and, more recently, automated decision making by public organizations to deliver public services (Cinar, 2020; Ranerup & Henriksen, 2019).

Other innovation types include social innovation, governance innovation, marketing innovation, and rhetoric innovation. "Social innovation" can have two different meanings. The first definition is that social innovations are innovations developed by nonpublic and nonprivate organizations. In other words, they are developed by nonprofit organizations and community groups, excluding public sector involvement. In the second definition of social innovation, governments are the ones that develop or implement innovations or collaborate with private organizations to develop them. Examples of social innovations developed by public organizations in different settings include welfare innovations in the United States (Agranoff, 1991), ICT-driven innovations in EU countries (Nasi et al., 2015), creating the Housing Development Board (HDB) to provide affordable housing to Singaporeans (Sherraden, 2017), and providing resources to disadvantaged groups and targeting social problems (Cinar et al., 2022b).

Governance innovation typically involves collaboration across different sectors while aiming to solve social issues. For example, "combining public, private, and civic capacity to police unsafe neighbourhoods, using local stakeholder expertise while providing technology and incentives" could be considered governance innovation (van der Wal, 2017, p. 171). Examples of such innovations include citizen participation apps in smartphones and initiatives for open data (Cinar, 2020). Moore and Hartley (2008) have analyzed four innovation cases related to governance innovation: (1) the Child Protection Services program in the Department of Social Services in Massachusetts, (2) the New York Park system partnering with citizens and other groups, (3) congestion charging in the city of London, and (4) elder care in Singapore. They find that governance innovations are significantly different than product, service, and process innovations.

Marketing or communication innovations can be defined as "the implementation of a new marketing method involving significant changes in product design ... product placement, product promotion or pricing" (OECD/Eurostat, 2005, p. 49). Marketing innovations allow organizations to acquire user information more effectively and efficiently or reduce transaction costs to deliver services (Chen, 2006). Innovation in product packaging in German enterprises is an example of marketing innovations in the private sector (D'Attoma & Ieva, 2020).

Table 5.1 *Types of innovations*

Types of innovation	Example
Product and/or service innovation	Online consultation with health professionals
Process innovation	One-stop-shops by governments
Mission innovation	Get to the moon
Policy innovation	Using new methods in energy, housing, environment, health, and education
Partner innovation	Collaborating with business and nonprofit organizations to deliver public services in Europe
Citizen innovation	Codesigning parks in Singapore
Technological innovation	New online car registration
Social innovation	Creating the HDB to provide affordable housing to Singaporeans
Governance innovation	Citizen participation apps
Marketing or communication innovation	Promotion of certain public services
Rhetorical innovation	Providing a new logo and website for an organization without making any changes to the organizational structure or offering any new training

Marketing innovations are not only vital for private organizations (Fuglsang & Pedersen, 2011); they are also important for governments and particularly for small states as their economic policies and capacities can be positively influenced by marketing strategies such as promotion of their openness and innovativeness (Kattel et al., 2011). Local governments can also implement marketing innovations by promoting themselves to attract more tourists, as seen in Singapore.

Finally, rhetoric innovation refers to symbolic changes such as "rebranding a ministry of environmental affairs into 'the green department,' with accompanying new logos and websites, while the core functions and bureaucratic routines stay exactly the same" (van der Wal, 2017, p. 171). An example from the Canadian context would be "Global Affairs Canada," which has undergone some name changes after it was established as the "Department of External Affairs." However, rhetoric innovation may be a strategic and valuable innovation type in public organizations as it is a "powerful instrument" for building coalitions, advocating new policies, and affecting decisions (Bekkers et al., 2011b). Considering that our definition of innovation includes both novelty and implementation, we do not consider rhetoric innovation to be an actual innovation unless the innovation brings about new products, services, or processes. Table 5.1 provides a summary of these innovation types along with examples.

Although all of these types of innovation exist in the public sector, some innovations are more common than others. Neuroni et al. (2021) have conducted surveys of public sector leaders in Switzerland. They find that the most common types of innovation in the public sector are (internal) process innovations (23 percent), followed by product or service innovations and organizational innovations (both 20 percent). They find that around 9 percent of innovations are communication innovations. Thus, the findings are consistent with the existing studies that most innovations in the public sector are process innovations.

Radical, Incremental, Complex, and Open Innovations

In addition to the main types of innovation defined earlier, there are other innovation typologies. Not all innovations are the same; some innovations are more critical, novel, radical, or complex than others. "Breakthrough," "radical," and "transformative" are terms that can be used interchangeably to describe major innovations (Capponi et al., 2022; Demircioglu & Audretsch, 2020; Zambrano-Gutiérrez & Puppim de Oliveira, 2021). Taques et al. (2021, p. 13) compare radical innovation and incremental innovation as follows: "radical innovation" is "something actually new, while the changes usually associated with incremental innovation are defined as an improvement over previously-existing elements, i.e., a continuous process over the course of time."

Incremental innovations are a "combinatory process within a previously established technological domain … [and] supported by an absorptive capacity consisting of specialized knowledge." Therefore, because incremental innovations do not require much risk-taking (e.g., no drastic and unpredictable changes), it is easier to implement incremental innovations than radical innovations (Taques et al., 2021). Similarly, using insights from previous studies (e.g., Ettlie et al., 1984; Hultman et al., 2012; Stojčić, 2020), Demircioglu and Vivona

(2021) conceptualize innovations as "radical" or "absorptive," with the latter referring to incremental innovations. They define absorptive (or incremental) innovations as occurring when "innovators' efforts are directed at adapting existing innovations to a new setting; the innovations are still new, novel, and successful policies to the organization or context." In contrast, radical innovations occur as "innovators recognize that there are no replicable successful polices and create new, original, and ad-hoc innovations" (Demircioglu & Vivona, 2021, p. 4). In public organizations, as evidenced by successful case studies such as the Ford award winners and the Kennedy School's Innovations in American Government Awards, most innovations are "iterative, incremental, and adaptive" (Sanger & Levin, 1992, p. 104; see also Borins, 2001, 2014). An example of incremental innovation includes a program called "Welcome to Utrecht" in the Netherlands to integrate refugees into society (Demircioglu & Vivona, 2021). Community and citizen groups' involvement in this innovation is novel but not a breakthrough because many public agencies had already collaborated with citizens and other actors.

Radical innovations transform the existing conditions; they are also discontinuous, disruptive, and rare (Capponi et al., 2022; OECD/Eurostat, 2018). Therefore, radical innovations are typically technical innovations and associated with patents (Capponi et al., 2022). As Capponi et al. (2022, p. 1) state, while incremental innovations focus on improvement, radical innovations are "ruptures along specific technological trajectories, possibly leading to shifts or transformations … [and] they play a crucial role in the 'creative destruction' process that characterizes the long-run dynamics." A good example of radical innovation is the establishment of the Open University in the UK (Albury, 2005). According to H. Jung and J. Lee (2016, p. 1728), radical innovations "play a critical role in promoting entrepreneurial activities, increasing welfare … [and] organizations' growth and new business development." Because public organizations typically do not produce products or services, public sector employees and managers typically "engage in small, targeted, sometimes temporary interventions and improvements to make government 'smarter' and keep it 'up to date' alongside more fundamental reforms and overhauls" (van der Wal, 2017, p. 169).

This distinction is important because the factors affecting radical and incremental innovations as well as their outcomes may be different.

For example, Kobarg et al. (2019) find that while radical innovations benefit from search breadth ("broader collaborative activities"), incremental innovations benefit from search depth ("deep interactions with partners)." Likewise, Jia et al. (2019) state that organizations developing breakthrough innovations can become leaders in the sector in which they operate. However, because it is more costly and riskier to develop breakthrough innovations, organizations should develop both incremental and breakthrough innovations; while the former provide shorter-term benefits, the latter provide longer-term benefits.

As Albury highlights an important question relevant to both academics and practitioners is how to develop radical or breakthrough innovations:

[We need] radical innovation that can produce significantly better outcomes for significantly lower costs. That is the real challenge that we are all now facing. It involves a quantum leap in thinking. How do we equip children with 21st century skills, not just the basics of literacy and numeracy but about problem-solving, about team collaboration, about critical thinking and so forth? How do we embrace the fact that health services in the Western world were developed to deal with infectious and acute diseases (emergencies) but yet the vast majority of their expenditure now is on chronic conditions and long-term illnesses? Hospitals are antiquated institutions that bear little relation to most of the needs of most of the population. I suggest we need radical and compelling innovation to generate significantly better outcomes at significantly lower costs. This is the real challenge. (Albury, 2011, p. 228)

Additionally, significant budget cuts can trigger radical innovation (OECD, 2017, p. 127):

[A] 35% cut in resources for the Netherlands education ministry prompted a shift in the delivery of higher education assistance from grants to loans. This enabled reduced spending by distributing some of the financial burden from the general taxpayer to the beneficiary receiving the lifetime income enhancements provided by university education... The combination of new technologies, fiscal pressures and strong leadership created the space to mount major innovations in health care delivery networks in Denmark.

Moreover, to develop radical innovations, public organizations can collaborate with universities and other organizations (Demircioglu & Vivona, 2021; Walsh et al., 2016). While incremental innovations require cumulative learning (Carney & Zheng, 2009), radical innovations encourage employee empowerment and more incentives for employees and managers (Carney & Zheng, 2009). Radical innovation is based on tacit knowledge and is often more ambiguous than incremental innovation (Carney & Zheng, 2009).

Another dimension of an innovation is its complexity, which is different from whether it is an incremental or radical innovation (Demircioglu & Audretsch, 2020; Torugsa & Arundel, 2016a). According to Demircioglu and Audretsch (2020, p. 822), "complex innovation refers to innovations that demonstrate multidimensionality, or a number of different dimensions affected by a single innovation," such as whether the same innovation affected services, processes, and employee policy thinking. They differentiate complex innovations from radical innovations as follows: radical innovations are disruptive and significantly impact organizations and the external environment. However, it may impact only a few dimensions or types of innovation, such as education-related outputs. Thus, radical innovations may not be complex. However, charging a fee to enter a central business district in a city such as Singapore or London is not a radical innovation (e.g., it is not disruptive and does not transform the sector or the way the work handled, and many cities already adopted this practice). Nevertheless, "this innovation may impact more dimensions, such as employees' policy thinking, the way they provide services, the way they interact with stakeholders, and administrative and organizational processes" (Demircioglu & Audretsch, 2020, p. 823).

Understanding and evaluating these different aspects of innovation (e.g., radical, incremental, and complex) are essential because there may be specific conditions for specific types of innovation and that determine the complexity of innovations. Drivers, actors, and outcomes for complex innovations may differ from radical or single innovations. For instance, Demircioglu (2017b) has found that while budget changes are not associated with a single innovation, increasing the budget is positively associated with implementing complex innovations. Furthermore, since radical innovations are typically more expensive and difficult, incremental innovations may have advantages in many cases.

What is important for radical or breakthrough innovations in the public sector is whether those innovations are accepted by the citizens or service users. For example, open education in the United Kingdom was a radical innovation, as it transformed the entire higher education system:

The Open University, given birth to by the 1960s Labour Government under the inspiration of Michael Young, used a new mode of delivery – a combination of established technologies of radio and television with high-quality learning materials and tutorial support – to bring higher education within reach of new markets: adult, part-time, nonqualified students. In its conception and planning the OU [Open University] was met with a mixture of resistance, scepticism and ridicule from the media and incumbent higher education interests. It is now the UK's largest provider of higher education, and an acknowledged world leader in distance learning. A "top-down," national innovation driven by the determination of Ministers, officials and an enthusiastic group of academic leaders. (Albury, 2005, p. 52)

Although this radical innovation was a top-down initiative, it was accepted by the people. However, not all innovations are accepted by the users. Hargadon and Douglas (2001, p. 495) support this claim: "When innovations are designed to succeed only within a narrow set of understandings and patterns of use, the price is often failure. Even the most radical innovations, in terms of their impact on our understandings and our lives, may require humble origins to gain the public's acceptance."

Another type of innovation is open innovation (Bogers et al., 2018; De Coninck et al., 2021; Hameduddin et al., 2020; Leckel et al., 2020; Mergel & Desouza, 2013; Palumbo et al., 2021). Open innovation focuses on "leveraging external knowledge to improve internal innovation processes" (Leckel et al., 2020, p. 2), or – more concretely – innovation is cocreated or codeveloped with the involvement of many actors while sharing knowledge and expertise among these actors (Bekkers et al., 2011b; Wynn et al., 2015). Crowdsourcing, challenges and contests, and civic hackathons are three major types of open innovation (Yuan & Gascó-Hernandez, 2021). With open innovations, governments facilitate technology and knowledge transfer from businesses and other public organizations while businesses also provide innovative ideas to public organizations (Ho et al., 2016).

Open innovation is "a means to helping solution-seeking firms open up their boundaries, to bring them together with problem-solvers from research and industry in local face-to-face problem-solving events" (Leckel et al., 2020, p. 10). Examples of open innovations include establishing civic hackathons to engage members of the public and receive ideas in the United States (Yuan & Gascó-Hernandez, 2021). Another example comes from the United States Department of Veteran

Table 5.2 *Innovation typologies*

Innovation typologies	Definition	Example
Radical or breakthrough innovations	Transforming the existing conditions and disruptive innovations	Open University in the United Kingdom
Incremental innovations	Novel improvement without transforming the existing conditions	"Welcome to Utrecht," which is first designed by citizens
Complex innovations	The number of dimensions or types affected by a single innovation	Introducing a toll charge for a busy road in Singapore
Open innovations	Innovation is cocreated or developed by external actors	Civic hackathons to engage members of the public in the United States

Affairs. Wynn et al. (2015, p. 16) describe this open innovation as follows: "OSEHRA [the Open Source Electronic Health Record Alliance] was tasked with creating a climate that is conducive to interaction and collaboration among the various stakeholders, including the VA [Department of Veteran Affairs]." This open platform provides opportunities to incorporate innovations and improvements from other participants within the ecosystem (Wynen et al., 2015).

Table 5.2 illustrates these innovation typologies along with simple definitions and examples.

Conclusion

In this chapter, first we defined the most critical and prevalent types of innovation, including product, process, marketing, governance, and organizational innovation, and offered some suggestions as to how and why different types of innovations are necessary for public organizations (Arundel et al., 2019; Gault, 2018; OECD/Eurostat, 2005, 2018). We also discussed mission innovation, policy innovation, partner innovation, citizen innovation, technological innovation, social innovation, governance innovation, and rhetoric innovation. Types of innovation are not mutually exclusive; for example, a policy innovation can also be a citizen innovation and a service innovation. Because not all innovations are the same or have an equivalent impact, we discussed how and why some innovations are radical (or breakthrough), incremental, complex, or open. As Albury (2011, p. 228) suggests, "we need radical and compelling innovation to generate significantly better outcomes at significantly lower costs" in the public sector.

An important conclusion from this chapter is that not all innovations are created equal. There are a number of different dimensions of innovation, including how the innovation is breakthrough (radical). Radical innovations have the greatest impact in that they are transformative, both to wider society as well as to their organization of origin. By contrast, incremental innovations generally enhance the value of an existing product, process, or service, but in such a way that leaves the underlying society and organization unchanged. Other key dimensions of innovation include their degree of complexity and their openness. The latter has a particular focus on the process by which they are created and how they can be extended. It may take a village to innovate, but in the case of open innovation an entire community of users is typically involved. Thus, while innovation is an important force in the public as well as the private sector context, it is difficult to generalize regarding what exactly is the nature of innovation. This is because of the multidimensionality of innovations. While innovations may be crucial, they are also slippery and often escape categorization.

6 | *Why Public Sector Innovation?*

Introduction and Background for Public Sector Innovation

In his well-known paper "The Study of Administration," Woodrow Wilson (1887, p. 197) stated that "the object of administrative study [is] to discover, first, what government can properly and successfully do, and, secondly, how it can do these proper things with the utmost possible efficiency and at the least possible cost either of money or of energy." How governments can become more efficient is an important question. One way for governments to become more efficient is to innovate. Nevertheless, a generation ago, very little was known about innovation and its role and impact on the economy and society in the private sector, let alone in the public sector. As Kuznets (1962) pointed out, the paucity of understanding about the vital role played by innovation in the process of economic growth seemed to pose an obstacle to investing in the collection of the requisite data to analyze innovative inputs and outputs. However, as innovation emerged as the central driver of economic growth (Lucas, 1988, 1993; Romer, 1986, 1990), a new field of research exploded, with innovation as the central focus. Virtually all of that research focused on innovation in the private sector in the last generation.

In particular, Griliches (1979) provided a framework linking the inputs of the innovation process, such as R&D and human capital, to innovative outputs, which became known as the model of the knowledge production function. According to the knowledge production function model, innovative activity responds positively to greater knowledge inputs. The link between knowledge inputs, such as R&D, human capital, and university research, and various measures of innovative outputs has been found to be generally positive and hold across all levels of analysis, ranging from firms and industries to regions and countries (Acs & Audretsch, 1988, 1990).

In the private sector, innovation is seen to increase company profit and competitive advantage (Sally, 2013; Vigoda-Gadot et al., 2005).

However, innovation also contributes substantially to the economic development of cities, states, regions, and entire nations. For instance, innovations, particularly technological innovations, are key drivers for many sectors, including computers, electronics, medical instruments, semiconductors, and chemical companies, which directly impact national-level economic developments (Sally, 2013). As the United States was confronted by economic stagnation in the late 1980s from the loss of competitiveness in traditional manufacturing industries such as steel and automobiles, it was the innovations in newly emerging industries such as software, computers, biotechnology, and information technologies that reignited economic growth in the 1990s in what the Nobel Prize laureate Joseph Stiglitz (2004) characterized as "the most prosperous decade" in the history of the world. A plethora of research has found that those countries with greater innovative activity also exhibit higher rates of economic development, typically measured by per capita gross domestic product (Griliches, 1987).

In addition, the innovation of the smartphone by Apple created not just a rich competitive advantage for the company but also a compelling source of competitiveness for the region of Silicon Valley and beyond in the United States. Employment in the tech industry surged as global sales skyrocketed, creating hundreds of thousands of high-paying jobs for software engineers and other tech workers. Similarly, the entire region in Seattle enjoyed an increase in the standard of living thanks to the innovations emanating from Amazon and Microsoft, as did the region around Heidelberg and Mannheim in the Baden-Württemberg region in Germany from innovations by the software company SAP.

Rationales for Public Sector Innovation

Despite a vast amount of research on private sector innovation, less research has analyzed innovative activity in the public sector context. This has partly been due to a lack of focus on the public sector as an important source of innovative activity, but it is also due to the lack of data and measurement of innovative inputs and outputs in the public sector (Arundel et al., 2019; Demircioglu & Audretsch, 2020). Perhaps the two most important reasons why there was a paucity of interest in public sector innovations was practical: Governments worldwide did not prioritize innovations until the 1980s, and there were no clear metrics or measurements for public sector innovations.

As Bernier (2001, p. 18) argues, "[b]udget cuts, early retirements, technological changes, among other things, have made the work of public servants much more difficult. More than ever, innovations were becoming necessary," suggesting that necessities cause innovations in the public sector. Similarly, Sahni et al. (2013) point out that governments in developed nations face a paradoxical dilemma of stimulating economic growth while concurrently cutting expenses. This can only be achieved by innovative solutions to problems that we have traditionally depended on the government to resolve. In particular, since the early 1980s, governments around the world have been under pressure "to do more with less," which is consistent with NPM reform agendas (Alsos et al., 2016; Hood, 1991; Hood & Dixon, 2015; Kettl, 2005; Pollitt & Bouckaert, 2011; van der Voet, 2019). NPM can be defined as "the transfer of business and market principles and management techniques from the private into the public sector, symbiotic with and based on a neo-liberal understanding of state and economy" (Drechsler, 2009, p. 8).

With the NPM reforms, most governments worldwide have aimed to make the public sector more innovative, which can contribute to solving fiscal, administrative, and social problems since the 1980s (Barzelay, 2001; Kettl, 2005; Peters, 2010). NPM reforms also aim to increase managerial skills and professionalism over the politicization of bureaucracy (Vigoda-Gadot et al., 2005). Thus, it is not surprising that there have been increasing calls for innovation in the public sector since then (e.g., Albury, 2005, 2011; ANAO, 2009; Bason, 2010; Bloch & Bugge, 2013; de Lancer & Gibson, 2016; E&Y, 2017; Kattel et al., 2013; Mulgan, 2014; Osborne & Brown, 2005; Windrum & Koch, 2008). For example, Fernandez and Pitts (2011, p. 202) argue that "[e]mphasis on innovation in government agencies has perhaps never been stronger," suggesting that public sector innovation has become more critical in recent years. Post-NPM reforms also aim to increase innovation via a changing bureaucratic culture, increasing global partnership, learning, and emulation (Vigoda-Gadot et al., 2005).

However, the important question is: Why public sector innovation? Why do nations want to be innovative? As Sanger and Levin (1992, p. 89) suggest, increasing effectiveness in the public sector seems to be the primary motivation for innovation:

Routine public management responses have not proven adequate to improve effectively the well-being of people and environments within the public sphere. Indeed, it is commonly the failure of routine treatments (e.g., the market, the family) that creates the public sector's work. Practitioners and students of public management need to look for new and innovative solutions. They seek inspirational stories of innovations to provide incentives to continue the good fight. Increasingly, good public management must be innovative management.

Potts and Kastelle (2010) provided five reasons why innovation in the public sector is necessary: (1) the large size of the public service, and innovation in the public sector is associated with productivity growth; (2) public sector innovation can solve organizational problems; (3) policymakers can establish a benchmark to evaluate innovation and performance (so we can compare which agencies are doing better); (4) because technology and organizations are changing (innovating), public organizations should also innovate; and (5) innovation in the public sector will have a positive spillover effect to the private sector (due to partnerships). Because governments can provide incentives, rules, and regulations for private organizations (Potts & Kastelle, 2010), innovation in the public sector can also bestow large benefits on the private and nonprofit sector (Demircioglu & Audretsch, 2019; Edquist & Zabala-Iturriagagoitia, 2012; Kattel et al., 2013; Leyden & Link, 1992; Link & Siegel, 2007). In addition, innovation positively impacts environmental and social revitalization while public, private, nonprofit, and other actors learn from each other and share information (Bekkers et al., 2011b).

Similarly, Alsos et al. (2016, p. 82) explain the importance of public sector innovation as follows:

The public sector is tremendously important for the economy, social security and people's well-being, and innovation in the public sector can have dire implications for citizens' quality of life. One way its importance can be measured is by looking at public-sector expenditures as a share of gross domestic product (GDP). Among the OECD countries, the share of public expenditures in GDP varies from 30% (South Korea) to 58% (Iceland), and countries such as the USA, Germany and France all have a share of 40% or higher. Almost all countries on the top 10 on the Economist's 'quality of life' index have a well-developed public sector and a high share of public-sector expenditure, in addition to being among the countries in the world with the highest GDP per capita. However, the economic crisis has put the public sector under pressure in most developed countries. Arguably, the symptoms have been there for some time: An aging population, high health care costs, and a burgeoning administration have put the public sector under strain. It is increasingly claimed that the public sector has to change the way things are done, new services and products need to be introduced, established services need to be produced more efficiently, and new ways of organising the public sector need to be implemented to sustain the vital role that the public sector plays in the economic and social well-being of countries.

In a similar vein, Stewart-Weeks and Kastelle (2015, p. 71) explain why public sector innovation is vital:

Innovation drives economic development and growth. The public sector makes up more than a third of the economy in most places, which means that it must play a role in supporting and delivering innovation as well. It is not good enough to have this sector viewed as simply a drag on productive economic activity. Innovative regions need innovative public sectors. In fact, if you look at all of the important innovations driven by the public sector over the past century, it is clear that we all need innovative public sectors.

In addition to the size of the public sector and the share of public expenditures of the public sector, general government revenues as a percentage of GDP are also very high, particularly in the Nordic countries, where government revenues and expenditures are more than 50 percent of GDP (Alsos et al., 2016; Arundel et al., 2015; Arundel et al., 2019; Potts & Kastelle, 2010). Thus, a small innovation in the public sector may yield enormous social benefits. Table 6.1 reports government revenues[1] as a percentage of GDP and Table 6.2 reports government expenses[2] as a percentage of GDP in the OECD and other major economies in recent years. In addition, as a percentage of total employment,[3] public organizations employ a large share of the employees, particularly in the Nordic countries. Similarly, Figure 6.1 shows that the public sector is large and vital since the OECD average

---

[1] Government revenues "finance the goods and services provided by government and allow the state to carry out its redistributive role, as the two main sources of revenues are taxes and social contributions" (OECD, 2017b, p. 68).

[2] Government expenditures refers "to implementing the broad array of government objectives and delegated mandates, from the uniquely publicly-provided services, such as justice or voting logistics, to paying for wages of civil servants and transportation infrastructure, among many other government activities" (OECD, 2017b, p. 74).

[3] General government employment refers to employment in federal/central, state, local, and social security funds, and includes ministries/departments and agencies (OECD, 2017b, p. 90).

Table 6.1 *General government revenue as a percentage of GDP*

	Code	OECD country/region	Government revenue (%)
1	AUS	Australia	35.46
2	AUT	Austria	50.28
3	BEL	Belgium	49.93
4	CAN	Canada	42.29
5	CZE	Czech Republic	41.42
6	DNK	Denmark	53.45
7	FIN	Finland	52.96
8	FRA	France	52.61
9	DEU	Germany	47.53
10	GRC	Greece	50.56
11	HUN	Hungary	41.20
12	ISL	Iceland	41.37
13	IRL	Ireland	23.20
14	ITA	Italy	48.30
15	JPN	Japan	38.12
16	KOR	Korea	37.24
17	LUX	Luxemburg	43.64
18	MEX	Mexico	23.05
19	NLD	Netherlands	44.34
20	NOR	Norway	58.90
21	POL	Poland	42.26
22	PRT	Portugal	44.85
23	SVK	Slovak Republic	40.14
24	ESP	Spain	43.74
25	SWE	Sweden	49.23
26	CHE	Switzerland	35.93
27	TUR	Turkey	31.21
28	GBR	United Kingdom	40.62
29	USA	United States	32.87
30	EST	Estonia	39.05
31	ISR	Israel	37.17
32	SVN	Slovenia	44.91
33	EA	Euro Area	47.31
34	EU	European Union	46.89
35	NZL	New Zealand	40.53
36	LVA	Latvia	37.07
37	COL	Colombia	40.53

Table 6.1 (*cont.*)

	Code	OECD country/region	Government revenue (%)
38	CRI	Costa Rica	41.94
39	LTU	Lithuania	36.36
40	CHL	Chile	26.80

Note: The 2020 data are used for Turkey due to availability. For the rest of the countries, the 2021 data are reported.
Source: OECD (2023), general government revenue (indicator), https://doi .org/10.1787/cc9669ed-en (accessed July 12, 2023).
Used with permission of OECD.

Table 6.2 *General government spending as a percentage of GDP*

	Code	OECD country	Government spending (%)
1	AUS	Australia	41.48
2	AUT	Austria	55.96
3	BEL	Belgium	55.47
4	CAN	Canada	NA
5	CZE	Czech Republic	46.51
6	DNK	Denmark	49.88
7	FIN	Finland	55.77
8	FRA	France	59.05
9	DEU	Germany	51.25
10	GRC	Greece	57.45
11	HUN	Hungary	48.30
12	ISL	Iceland	49.33
13	IRL	Ireland	24.82
14	ITA	Italy	55.16
15	JPN	Japan	44.46
16	KOR	Korea	38.13
17	LUX	Luxemburg	42.89
18	MEX	Mexico	NA
19	NLD	Netherlands	46.65
20	NOR	Norway	48.29
21	POL	Poland	44.09
22	PRT	Portugal	47.75
23	SVK	Slovak Republic	45.51
24	ESP	Spain	50.62

Table 6.2 (*cont.*)

	Code	OECD country	Government spending (%)
25	SWE	Sweden .	49.20
26	CHE	Switzerland	36.47
27	TUR	Turkey	NA
28	GBR	United Kingdom	48.41
29	USA	United States	44.93
30	EST	Estonia	41.47
31	ISR	Israel	40.85
32	SVN	Slovenia	49.29
33	NZL	New Zealand	NA
34	LVA	Latvia	44.11
35	COL	Colombia	33.94
36	CRI	Costa Rica	39.93
37	LTU	Lithuania	37.52
38	CHL	Chile	34.14

Note: Because of the data availability, the 2020 data are used for Korea and Costa Rica. There are no data for Canada, Mexico, Turkey, and New Zealand. For the rest of the countries, the 2021 data are reported.
Source: OECD (2023), general government spending (indicator), https://doi.org/10.1787/cc9669ed-en (accessed July 12, 2023).
Used with permission of OECD.

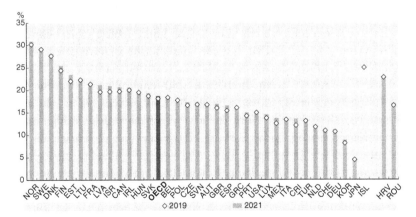

Figure 6.1 Employment in general government as a percentage of total employment, 2019 and 2021.
Reproduced from: OECD (2023). Used with permission of OECD; permission conveyed through Copyright Clearance Center, Inc.

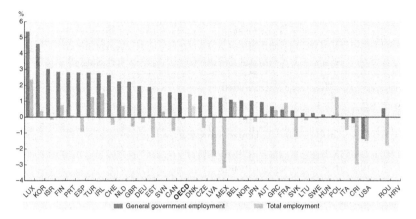

Figure 6.2 Annual average growth rate of general government employment and total employment, 2019–2021.
Reproduced from: OECD (2023). Used with permission of OECD; permission conveyed through Copyright Clearance Center, Inc.

is close to 20 percent, suggesting that almost one-fifth of employees are employed by the general government. Furthermore, Figure 6.2 demonstrates that general government employment increases in each country although total employment decreases in many countries. Hence, as general government employment is significant and even increasing, public sector innovation becomes even more important.

Results from innovation research make it clear that innovation is vital for economic growth (Leyden & Link, 1992), can enhance public value (Meijer, 2018), and can increase the welfare of citizens (Windrum, 2008). Moreover, public sector innovations can also increase prosperity, competitiveness, and employment (Cantwell, 2006; Fagerberg et al., 2006; Leyden & Link, 1992; Pianta, 2006; Verspagen, 2006). Innovation can also positively affect public sector entrepreneurship (Hayter et al., 2018; Leyden & Link, 2015) and sustainability (Lundvall, 2010). Public sector innovation is also a solution to the grand challenges or wicked problems of contemporary governments, such as aging populations, climate change, natural disasters, immigration, and the increasing costs of health care (Albury, 2005, 2011; Alsos et al., 2016; Chicot & Matt, 2018; Demircioglu & Vivona, 2021; Geels & Schot, 2007; Kuhlmann & Rip, 2014; Mazzucato, 2018; Nowacki & Monk, 2020; Osborne & Brown, 2011;

Sarros et al., 2008). As Nowacki and Monk (2020, p. 2) articulate, "generating new ideas may be the most important activity for governments to face Grand Challenges."

Research suggests that public sector innovation is considered a solution to economic crises (Hansen & Pihl-Thingvad, 2019) and positively influences the private sector's ability and motivation to innovate (Bloch, 2011). For example, a recent study of Sweden and Finland demonstrates that the public sector is crucial in stimulating private sector innovations in these countries. Researchers find that around 50 percent of the innovations between 1970 and 2013 have been sparked by funding from the government, and between 25 and 65 percent of innovations emerged from collaborating with public research in Finland (Torregrosa-Hetland et al., 2019). These findings are consistent with Mazzucato's (2015, p. 15) observations:

While innovation is not the State's main role, illustrating its potential innovative and dynamic character – its historical ability, in some countries, to play an entrepreneurial role in society – is perhaps the most effective way to defend its existence, and size, in a proactive way. Changing the way we talk about the State is not just about changing rhetoric – it is about changing the way we reason about the State, its role and structure.

As discussed in Chapters 3 and 4, although risk is involved in public sector innovation, it is also risky if governments do not innovate, as public organizations cannot lag behind private organizations. Citizens' confidence and trust diminish if public organizations do not innovate (Bartos, 2003). In this regard, "it is not only important that innovative practices are generated but, perhaps even more so, that these are then spread to and implemented in other settings" (de Vries et al., 2018, p. 160). Likewise, Bysted and Hansen (2015, p. 699) argue that "the positive effect of innovation has resulted in a desire for more innovation in public organizations."

It is not surprising that innovative countries are also more developed and wealthier. There is also a strong correlation between innovation and development at the national level: "The most innovative countries are those with the greatest investments in R&D. Little innovative output is associated with less developed countries, which are characterized by a paucity of production of new economic knowledge" (Acs & Audretsch, 2003, p. 61). Table 6.3 shows countries from the Innovation Index (Dutta et al., 2022). Countries that top the list tend

Table 6.3 *2022 Global Innovation Index*

Rank	Economy	Score
1	Switzerland	64.6
2	United States of America	61.8
3	Sweden	61.6
4	United Kingdom	59.7
5	Netherlands	58
6	Republic of Korea	57.8
7	Singapore	57.3
8	Germany	57.2
9	Finland	56.9
10	Denmark	55.9
11	China	55.3
12	France	55
13	Japan	53.6
14	Hong Kong	51.8
15	Canada	50.8
16	Israel	50.2
17	Austria	50.2
18	Estonia	50.2
19	Luxembourg	49.8
20	Iceland	49.5
21	Malta	49.1
22	Norway	48.8
23	Ireland	48.5
24	New Zealand	47.2
25	Australia	47.1
26	Belgium	46.9
27	Cyprus	46.2
28	Italy	46.1
29	Spain	44.6
30	Czech Republic	42.8
31	United Arab Emirates	42.1
32	Portugal	42.1
33	Slovenia	40.6
34	Hungary	39.8
35	Bulgaria	39.5
36	Malaysia	38.7
37	Turkey	38.1
38	Poland	37.5

Table 6.3 (*cont.*)

Rank	Economy	Score
39	Lithuania	37.4
40	India	36.6
41	Latvia	36.5
42	Croatia	35.6
43	Thailand	34.9
44	Greece	34.5
45	Mauritius	34.4
46	Slovakia	34.3
47	Russian Federation	34.3
48	Viet Nam	34.3
49	Romania	34.1
50	Chile	34
51	Saudi Arabia	33.4
52	Qatar	32.9
53	Iran (Islamic Republic of)	32.9
54	Brazil	32.5
55	Serbia	32.3
56	Republic of Moldova	31.1
57	Ukraine	31
58	Mexico	31
59	Philippines	30.7
60	Montenegro	30.3
61	South Africa	29.8
62	Kuwait	29.2
63	Colombia	29.2
64	Uruguay	29.2
65	Peru	29.1
66	North Macedonia	28.8
67	Morocco	28.8
68	Costa Rica	28.7
69	Argentina	28.6
70	Bosnia and Herzegovina	28.5
71	Mongolia	28
72	Bahrain	27.9
73	Tunisia	27.9
74	Georgia	27.9
75	Indonesia	27.9
76	Jamaica	27.7
77	Belarus	27.5

Table 6.3 (*cont.*)

Rank	Economy	Score
78	Jordan	27.4
79	Oman	26.8
80	Armenia	26.6
81	Panama	25.7
82	Uzbekistan	25.3
83	Kazakhstan	24.7
84	Albania	24.4
85	Sri Lanka	24.2
86	Botswana	23.9
87	Pakistan	23
88	Kenya	22.8
89	Egypt	22.7
90	Dominican Republic	22.7
91	Paraguay	22.6
92	Brunei Darussalam	22.1
93	Azerbaijan	21.4
94	Kyrgyzstan	21.1
95	Ghana	20.8
96	Namibia	20.6
97	Cambodia	20.5
98	Ecuador	20.3
99	Senegal	19.9
100	El Salvador	19.9
101	Trinidad and Tobago	19.8
102	Bangladesh	19.7
103	United Republic of Tanzania	19.4
104	Tajikistan	18.8
105	Rwanda	18.7
106	Madagascar	18.6
107	Zimbabwe	18.1
108	Nicaragua	18.1
109	Côte d'Ivoire	17.8
110	Guatemala	17.8
111	Nepal	17.6
112	Lao People's Democratic Republic	17.4
113	Honduras	17.3
114	Nigeria	16.9
115	Algeria	16.7

Table 6.3 (*cont.*)

Rank	Economy	Score
116	Myanmar	16.4
117	Ethiopia	16.3
118	Zambia	15.8
119	Uganda	15.7
120	Burkina Faso	15.3
121	Cameroon	15.1
122	Togo	15.1
123	Mozambique	15
124	Benin	14.6
125	Niger	14.6
126	Mali	14.2
127	Angola	13.9
128	Yemen	13.8
129	Mauritania	12.4
130	Burundi	12.3
131	Iraq	11.9
132	Guinea	11.6

Source: Dutta et al. (2022).

to be wealthier whereas countries at the bottom tend to be developing countries.

At the organizational level, public sector innovations can increase effectiveness, legitimacy, and even citizen involvement (Bysted & Hansen, 2015; de Vries et al., 2016; Hansen & Pihl-Thingvad, 2019; C. Jung & G. Lee, 2016; Lœgreid et al., 2011; Tõnurist et al., 2017; Torfing & Triantafillou, 2016). As Kattel et al. (2013, p. 2) argue, "[p]ublic sector innovation promises to deliver more with less," suggesting that innovation can increase efficiency in the public sector. Leman (2002) gives examples from the United States, including the national parks system, government construction projects, the US Census, IT usage in government organizations (particularly in the military), NASA, and the US Geological Survey, all of which have implemented many innovations over the years that have had major positive impacts on society and citizens.

Innovation is also crucial at the individual level, such as for employees. As Afsar and Masood (2018, p. 410) argue:

The rapid changes in technology, high level of competition to innovate regularly and frequently, shortened product life cycles, and greater pressure on organizations to respond quickly and creatively to frequent technical problems have made the structured procedures and systems ineffective. Employees, therefore, need to be able to perform tasks that go beyond the established routines for a team, group, or organization.

When employees are innovative, they can increase the performance, efficiency, and effectiveness of organizations and employees (Bysted & Hansen, 2015; van de Ven et al., 1999; Walker, 2008). Demircioglu and Berman (2019) state that an innovative workplace can increase employee job satisfaction and reduce employees' intention to leave organizations in the public sector. Therefore, it is not surprising that recent graduates and highly talented people want to work at Google, Netflix, Amazon, and Facebook because these companies are innovative and offer employees a challenging and creative workplace in addition to an attractive salary. Thus, it is crucial that public organizations are innovative in order to attract more individuals (particularly young, bright, and competent professionals) to the public sector.

If public organizations do not innovate, then citizens, legislators, and some interest groups will challenge those public organizations. For example, after the September 11 terrorist attacks and a series of national disasters in the 2000s, many people challenged the intelligence sources and government organizations of the United States. A significant criticism of governments is that they are not innovative enough to deal with new internal and external threats. Similarly, the 3/11 disaster when a tsunami and earthquake hit Japan's Fukushima nuclear power also led to the government being challenged by Japanese citizens, as this disaster would have been predictable and preventable if the government had been more innovative (see Kapucu & Boin, 2017; Kapucu & van Wart, 2006; Kettl, 2008; van der Wal, 2017; Wise, 2006). In this regard, innovation matters for citizens in addition to nations, organizations, and employees.

Conclusion

This chapter has looked at the rationale for public sector innovation. More specifically, it has examined why policymakers, practitioners, and citizens should care about innovation in public organizations and public services. An important reason why public organizations prioritize innovation is legitimacy concerns – via pressure from other organizations and citizens – that focus on the efficiency, effectiveness, and performance of public organizations, providing public services, and solving and preventing problems before they occur (Lœgreid et al., 2011; Verhoest et al., 2007).

An older view was convinced that innovation was better left in the hands of the private sector. After all, it has been innovative activity in the private sector that has transformed economies and their entire societies, enabling them to harness the opportunities afforded by change rather than succumbing as a victim. While robust studies have linked innovation in the private sector to economic development and societal prosperity, research has not yet identified such a causal link between innovation in the public sector and economic performance, broadly considered. Still, both anecdotal evidence and compelling case studies point to the rich potential of public sector innovation. A generation ago, a partisan audience snickered as President Ronald Regan wrote off even the possibility of public sector innovation with his now famous punchline, "I'm from the government and I'm here to help." In our contemporary world besieged by pandemics, war, and environmental and social crisis, no one is laughing now. The promise of societal and economic progress is inextricably linked to innovation in the public sector.

7 | Drivers and Conditions for Innovation

Introduction

How can public organizations and public sector employees innovate? As already mentioned, there are differences between public and private organizations that lead to different conditions for innovation. For instance, growth expectations, market share, profit, number of sales, and salaries are essential motivators for private sector managers and employees to improve their performance and adopt innovations (Christensen et al., 2004). However, public sector employees tend be motivated to improve their personal and organizational performance. For instance, when public organizations and public managers motivate employees to perform well, inspire them to do a good job, and encourage creativity, and when public organizations and employees are serving citizens more efficiently and effectively when they create public value, then public sector employees will have the motivation to improve individual and organizational performance and thus to be more innovative (Perry & Wise, 1990; Rainey, 2009). Likewise, the conditions of innovations may be different for an organization with a large budget and many personnel than for a small organization.

Furthermore, there may be specific conditions for public organizations to innovate based on presidential and parliamentary democracies and autocratic regimes. Thus, each context may require different conditions. Thus, this chapter explains specific conditions and factors that can affect innovation at the individual, group, organizational, and national levels. Accordingly, we can consider drivers and conditions as inputs, as they can affect outputs such as innovations. Other inputs in the form of sources or actors also influence innovation. Without sources, innovations cannot occur. We devote an entire chapter to sources of knowledge and innovation (Chapter 8). There are also specific impediments or factors increasing barriers to innovation, which

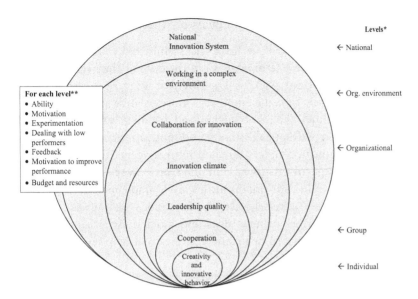

Figure 7.1 Conditions for innovations.
Source: Adapted from Demircioglu and Audretsch (2020). Used with permission from Springer Nature. Frameworks based on Christensen et al. (2004); Demircioglu and Audretsch (2017); Sahni et al. (2013).

we explain in Chapter 9. In other words, this chapter and Chapters 8 and 9 are highly related.

The primary framework we use in this chapter is Demircioglu and Audretsch's (2020) work on how different levels affect innovation in the public sector. The second framework is based on findings that ability and motivation are necessary for innovation (Christensen et al., 2004; Sahni et al., 2013). The third framework is based on Sahni et al.'s (2013) work as well as the work of Demircioglu and Audretsch (2017), who offered some further changes. This framework states that in order to implement innovations in public organizations, the following conditions need to be present: experimentation, dealing with low performers, feedback, and motivation to improve performance (Figure 7.1). There are mixed findings regarding budget changes, which we explain later. First, we use Demircioglu and Audretsch's (2020) framework of the unit/level of analysis. In doing so, we link this analysis with Christensen et al.'s (2004) ability and motivation framework and adapt it to different levels (individual, group, organizational, and national).

Public Sector Innovation and Levels of Analysis

We start from the employee level. As Demircioglu and Audretsch (2020, p. 824) argue, "[e]mployees are the core of the organization, and its most important asset," suggesting that we must start from the employees and how to make employees more creative and innovative. Employees' abilities (i.e., knowledge and training) and motivation drive innovation. Without the ability and motivation, employees cannot pursue innovation unless directed by managers. Thus, the more employees engage in creativity and innovative work behavior, the more likely they and their organizations are to implement innovations (Demircioglu & Audretsch, 2020; Fernandez & Wise, 2010). Additionally, exposure to new ideas and moving away from stable, specialized, and insulated tasks and routines will help employees be more creative (van de Ven, 1986).

Individual factors such as awareness, personal values (e.g., individual's pro-innovativeness), and social norms affect innovation. Analyzing environmental innovations in Canada, Yuriev et al. interviewed some key informants. One specialist stated: "We want to talk about sustainability, but it's a sensitive subject nowadays. Before, you weren't allowed to talk about politics and religion. Now, you also have to be careful encouraging pro-environmental measures!" (Yuriev et al., 2021, p. 11). Likewise, to demonstrate social norms, they provided another quote from a director in a ministry (department): "When I tell employees that I bike to work, I feel like I'm the only one" (Yuriev et al., 2021, p. 11). Thus, norms and institutional factors also affect innovations in the public sector.

Organizational leaders should support employees by encouraging them to be creative. For instance, providing autonomy to employees (Demircioglu, 2021), empowering them (Fernandez & Moldogaziev, 2013), and increasing their networking capabilities (C. Jung & G. Lee, 2016; H. Jung & J. Lee, 2016) can increase employees' innovative work behavior, creativity, and thus innovation in the public sector.

However, extrinsic and carrot–stick approaches to innovation do not lead to sustained or high-quality innovations. In particular, studies find that intrinsic motivation is more important than extrinsic motivation for innovation (Angle, 2000). An important reason why intrinsic motivation is more important than extrinsic motivation is that employees' commitment, focus, and concentration could be higher when they are internally motivated, as demonstrated by self-determination theory (Demircioglu & Chen, 2019; Ryan & Deci, 2000, 2017). Nevertheless, when employees are motivated externally, such as through carrot and stick approaches, if these motives become less important (e.g., an organization may eliminate a bonus system) employees' motivation to innovate may decline significantly.

Cooperation and collegiality among groups and teams are crucial for innovations at the work group level. Cooperation among employees' work groups can increase employees' abilities (e.g., employees can share ideas with colleagues and (co)learn from them) and motivation (employees feel supported). For instance, Yuriev et al.'s (2021, p. 13) research with Canadian bureaucrats demonstrates the following points. One specialist they interviewed states that: "Initiatives tend to fail when employees' colleagues are negative." Another interviewee, who is a director in a large ministry, stated: "I recently met the head of another department to discuss an idea and he said, 'This isn't our mission, why would you even come to me with this project?'" Thus, a lack of collaboration, cooperation, and support from employees' work groups reduces innovative activities.

Without support from colleagues, employees and managers may feel discouraged and thus not be willing to take action for innovation. One study found that employee cooperation, collegiality, and effective communication led to innovation in the Veteran's Benefits Administration of the United States (Fernandez & Pitts, 2011). Effective communication is vital for innovations (McLean, 2005), and research finds that both information flows and effective communication positively affect innovation, particularly communication among dissimilar and diverse employees, as innovative ideas from different and diverse views can generate innovation (Angle, 2000; McLean, 2005). Thus, work groups and organizations with no communication problems could be more innovative. In fact, McLean's (2005, pp. 235–237) synthesis of the literature shows that what matters most for creativity and innovation is organizational support, which includes "organizational encouragement," "supervisory encouragement," "work group encouragement," "freedom and autonomy," and "resources." McLean's synthesis of the literature is also relevant at the organizational level.

At the organizational and external environment level, what matters most is the leadership quality, climate of innovation, and culture. Innovative culture and climate (or supportive innovation culture or climate) refer to organizational leaders' support, motivation, and empowerment of employees while encouraging them to experiment and providing incentives (Hijal-Moghrabi et al., 2020). Borins (2002, p. 475) argues that: "Creating a supportive climate would entail consulting staff, instituting formal awards and informal recognition for innovators, promoting innovators, protecting innovators from control-oriented central agencies, and publicly championing bottom-up innovations that have proven successful and have popular appeal."

If the organization and leaders encourage innovations and empower and support employees, then the organization and employees working in that organization would be more innovative (Demircioglu & van der Wal, 2022; Engelen et al., 2015; van der Wal, 2017). Additionally, the innovation climate of an organization – which can be defined as organizational practices and routines facilitating knowledge, sharing ideas, aiming to increase creativity, providing policies and practices, enhancing new ideas, and formalizing the process for innovation (Demircioglu, 2021; Demircioglu & Berman, 2019; Popa et al., 2017) – can increase innovation for the following reasons. For innovations, leadership support and an innovation climate are needed (Albury, 2011; Borins, 2002). Additionally, the right nurturing environment and a supportive organization can increase motivation and performance (White, 1959).

Recognition and affirmation can affect public sector innovations:

Innovation needs to be recognised and supported by the people with power. That means ministers within each department with a remit to protect and nurture innovation, and, where relevant, board members responsible for providing the money and backing. It means paying attention to how the future is unfolding (for example, situating health innovations within the broader shift to greater self-management of long-term conditions and the steady move away from a health service centred around hospitals and acute illness). (Mulgan, 2014, p. 17)

As Demircioglu and Audretsch (2020, p. 826) observe, "[i]f an organization or a leader does not support employee efforts to be innovative by providing resources, then there will be no motivation and incentive for public sector employees to champion complex innovations," suggesting that both the quality of leadership and an innovation climate can enhance innovations. Likewise, a report published by the Australian government states that leaders of the APS "play a dominant role in shaping the culture and behaviour of their organisations ... A culture of innovation and collaboration will only flourish across the APS if it is supported and demonstrated by leaders at all levels" (Australian Government, 2010, p. 45). Furthermore, analyzing the effects of leadership on creativity and innovation, Yoshida et al. (2014) explored how psychological connections and collegiality increase employees' creativity and innovations at the work group level. They recommend that leaders focus on mentoring skills and increasing innovation and team climate:

A team climate which prioritizes innovation provides the conditions that are conducive to employee creativity, and hence becomes the most potent means to enhance creative outcomes ... [Leaders should] generate followers' trust, identification, and perceptions that the leaders represent the team's beliefs, norms and attitudes becomes more critical when creativity and innovation are a priority organizational goal. (Yoshida et al., 2014, p. 1402)

In this regard, employees can innovate when leaders encourage innovation and creativity and when agencies motivate and inspire them to achieve the organization's objectives.

The government may encourage smooth competition among government agencies at the organizational environment level. However, a significant challenge for competition among public organizations is that there are no clear benchmarks, and it is hard to compare different types of organizations. For instance, the mission, operations, interaction with different stakeholders, and organizational and demographic context of the US Treasury, Department of Foreign Affairs, and Department of Human Services are very different (Wilson, 2000). Thus, competition may be difficult because it is hard to compare different agencies. Still, governments can compare agencies based on similar missions or duties, past and present. In addition, it is also challenging to measure outputs in the public sector because it is hard to measure innovative activities. Therefore, the government may look at and compare innovative activities in the public sector, such as employee creativity.

Collaborating and networking with other actors and stakeholders can enhance innovation by exposing organizational members to new ideas and feedback; collaboration can increase knowledge, access to knowledge, and resources, and encourage people to engage in boundary-spanning roles (Demircioglu et al., 2023). Even though employees initiate many innovations, the same employees interact with service users and businesses (Altshuler & Zegans, 1997). Many innovations in the United States are developed by collaboration with different firms and organizations (H. Jung & J. Lee, 2016). Demircioglu and Audretsch (2020, p. 828) argue that "if an organization does not require employees to deal with a complex working environment, then employees have only a limited opportunity to communicate and interact with the external environment."

Additionally, identified demands from external environments such as new laws or regulations, political mandates, new policy priorities, use of external knowledge, and external trends such as the adoption of certain policies by other organizations and governments also push public organizations to be more innovative (Clausen et al., 2020). Likewise, norms, regulations, and technology are external drivers of innovation (Wirtz et al., 2021).

At the national level, Chapter 10 provides more comprehensive information, so we do not focus on government failures in this chapter. Why some countries are more innovative than others is an important question. For example, at the national level, while the United States is considered an innovative country, its neighbor, Mexico, is not innovative (Acemoglu & Robinson, 2013; Dutta et al., 2022). Likewise, why is Singapore innovative but its neighbors Malaysia and Indonesia are not as innovative (Dutta et al., 2022)? Indeed, research has found that institutions and what has been characterized as constituting the National Innovation System of each country matter for innovative activities (Acs et al., 2017; Donges et al., 2022; Gregory, 1993; Intarakumnerd et al., 2002; Nelson, 1993) and shape both the nature and amount of innovative activity, and this accounts for cross-country variations in innovation. Those countries with the requisite institutions conducive to innovation tend to exhibit a greater degree of innovative activity. By contrast, those countries with weaker institutions that are important to innovation tend to be less innovative. For example, institutions such as the apprentice system have been found to contribute to the innovative activity of manufacturing firms in Germany. Similarly, the great research institutions of Stanford University and the University of California at Berkeley have fueled the dominance of innovation in the tech industry in Silicon Valley, just as Harvard University and the Massachusetts Institute of Technology have contributed to the enviable innovative performance in the Boston area.

Similar to the other levels, ability, motivation, experimentation, and budgets affect innovation at the national level. Additionally, perception becomes more important than reality because perceived necessity drives innovation in many countries (Demircioglu, 2019). For instance, although Norway is an oil-rich country, innovations in Norway are driven by perceived necessity.

A former top civil servant of Singapore, Peter Ho, argues that experimentation is not only leading innovation in Singapore but has also made Singapore's government more effective and the country more prosperous (Ho, 2015). For example, he quotes several speeches of Lee Kuan Yew: "The crucial thing [for policy and implementation of new ideas] is: do not be afraid to innovate" (Ho, 2015, p. 91). He provides several examples: "willingness to try things out spawned a generation of state entrepreneurs who created, almost out of nothing, national icons such as Singapore Airlines, DBS, ST Engineering, Changi Airport, SingTel, and so on. The national computerisation programme, started in the Ministry of Defence, is another example of a [successful] policy that transformed Singapore" (Ho, 2015, p. 92).

Long-term thinking and investments, focusing on good governance, and creating strong institutions can increase innovations in nations:

Smaller nations that had started to make significant investments in science, innovation and education already in the 1990s (like Finland or Switzerland, the latter still not a member of the EU), attract more and more international investment. The same holds true for some of those regions which – while being part of a nation state – enjoy a high degree of political autonomy; they used to afford and maintain for many years strong innovation infrastructures and would now be keeping abreast with the mentioned smaller nations. They may even establish inter-regional transborder coalitions for concerted innovation policies, mutually matching local strengths and weaknesses of innovation-related institutions. They may also launch EUREKA-like "bottom-up" inter-regional industrially oriented innovation support initiatives – imagine e.g. an "innovation belt" of regions and nations surrounding the Alps, reaching from Bavaria, through Baden-Württemberg (two federal states of Germany), Switzerland (independent), Rhône-Alpes (French region), northern Italian regions like Lombardy to Slovenia (independent). (Kuhlmann, 2001, p. 969)

For countries, globalization and networks can increase innovation by nations, organizations, and individuals. For example, "networks have proven to facilitate innovation by sharing resources such as unique knowledge" among countries (Efrat, 2014, p. 17). In his famous book *Diffusion of Innovations*, Rogers (2003) spends an entire chapter (chapter 8, pp. 300–364) on "Diffusion Networks" to emphasize how powerful networks are in implementing innovations. Among many others, he gives examples from medicine and reports that "doctors with more network links were more innovative in adopting ... [a novel medicine], while doctors who were isolates [*sic*] ... were later in adopting the new drug ... The degree of network interconnectedness of a physician was a better predictor of innovativeness than any of the other independent variables [e.g., income, communication channels, and individual traits]" (Rogers, 2003, p. 327).

Ability and Motivation

Christensen et al. (2004) find that ability and motivation are the two main factors for innovation and that when both are present, innovation will happen. While education and training can increase employee abilities (Sanger & Levin, 1992), engaging with employees and focusing on their well-being and development increases their motivation (Demircioglu & Chen, 2019). Furthermore, as innovations require ability and motivation, the existence of an innovation climate such as leadership support, providing resources to try out new ideas, autonomy, policies encouraging creativity, and some level of risk-taking can increase both ability (e.g., employees learn from each other and work hard to develop innovations) and motivation (e.g., employees feel that they are supported and encouraged to be innovative).

According to Christensen and colleagues: "Actions that increase ability or motivation tend to increase innovation; actions that put up barriers to ability or motivation tend to decrease innovation" (Christensen et al., 2004, p. 92). Likewise, Sahni et al. (2013, p. 31) state: "Though there is no silver bullet for our problems, ensuring that the ability and motivation to innovate effectively exists throughout the public sector is a vital piece of any solution we develop." Similarly, McLean (2005) has underlined that innovation occurs when enabling conditions such as ability and motivating conditions are present. Furthermore, analyzing twenty-five successful public sector innovations, Sanger and Levin (1992, pp. 112–113) find that "a willingness and an ability to look outside the narrow confines of one's intellectual and organizational environment are most likely to generate innovative ideas … Producing future innovators will clearly require a conscious effort to abandon the constraints these artificial boundaries impose on innovation."

Organizations' abilities and capabilities are quite similar. Regulation (e.g., whether process and procedures enhance or inhibit innovation), budgeting (e.g., whether there are funds and flexibility to mobilize resources), human resources (e.g., whether leadership and the organization support and develop skills for innovation), managing risk, and space for experimentation are part of organizations' abilities and capabilities (OECD, 2017). While capacity is crucial for government responses and effective governance (O'Flynn, 2021), resources, capabilities, and leadership styles are internal drivers of innovation (Wirtz et al., 2021). Capabilities and incentives increase innovation (Jia et al., 2019). Yuriev et al. (2021) finds that the main factors affecting the implementation of innovations were the creativity and problem-solving skills of government employees. The same factors can also affect employee motivation to innovate. For instance, in terms of human resources, the rewards for and recognition of innovation efforts can motivate employees (OECD, 2017).

Two Innovation Models

The Demircioglu and Audretsch model and its comparable framework developed by Sahni, Wessel, and Christensen both state that experimentation, dealing with low performance, feedback at the organizational level, and motivation to improve performance can enhance innovation within organizations at an aggregated level (Demircioglu & Audretsch, 2017; Sahni et al., 2013). Additionally, resources and budgets have different effects on innovation. As Albury (2011, p. 233) states: "Thinking about innovation, allowing space for innovation and adaptation, openness and deregulation are all absolutely key to whether innovation happens and whether it spreads. Unless we are attentive to those wider conditions and determinants of innovation we won't really foster high levels of public sector innovation and its diffusion." This suggests that public organizations can be highly innovative under the right conditions, particularly with experimentation.

In fact, innovative public organizations are the result of "encouraged experimentation … Encouraging staff to innovate and supporting their attempts is a crucial element of leadership and organizational culture" (Albury, 2011, pp. 229–230). To provide more information about the importance of experimentation, Chesbrough (2007, p. 17) observes that:

[A]n organization must give a senior manager the resources and authority to define and launch business model experiments. This will require cooperation from many other parts of the organization. Once the data from these experiments are received, the senior executive can decide which experiments to continue, which new ones to initiate, and whether and when enough information exists to justify the wider adoption of a new business model.

Thus, experimentation is helpful not only for leading innovations but also for increasing individual and organizational learning and the advancement of the innovation process.

Stewart-Weeks and Kastelle (2015, p. 71) also attest to the importance of experimentation for organizations:

If there is one critical innovation skill that public sector organizations should build, it is experimentation. The idea behind experiments is to trial new ideas at the smallest possible scale. A good example of this is the Innovation Growth Lab13 (IGL) developed through NESTA [National Endowment for Science, Technology and the Arts] in the United Kingdom. This international program trials multiple ways to support the growth of small, innovative firms, testing the outcomes of different methods in an effort to develop knowledge about what works and what does not. This is a relatively large-scale experiment, but many problems can be attacked with this approach. Doing this regularly has several benefits. First, when a small-scale experiment does not work as expected, it is not front-page news. Experiments keep the cost of ideas that do not work low. When we are spending the public money, we obviously want to do so wisely. On the other hand, if we only do things that we know will work in advance, we are missing important opportunities. Trying ideas at a small scale is a good way to resolve this tension. The second advantage is that experiments drive learning. That is the point behind IGL – the question of how best to support the growth of innovative firms is not a solved problem. Consequently, running experiments that gather data is one of the most valuable things to do right now. If done properly, this will lead to improved policy. Finally, experiments make the idea-selection process easier. This is a common area of weakness. However, if new ideas are tested through prototyping, small-scale experiments, pilots, or incubator programs, then the most promising can be chosen to scale up based on data, not best guesses.

The OECD's 2017 *Government at a Glance* report argues:

A common feature of innovative organisations is their acceptance of experimentation and learning through trial and error. The challenge, for public sector organisations in particular, is to find ways to enable experimentation while mitigating the risks that will be borne by society as a whole. An associated challenge is finding ways to reward public servants who undertake well-structured experimentation, even when it does not succeed. Motivating professional public servants to be innovative requires careful consideration of the range of incentives and disincentives that operate simultaneously within an organisation. These can include extrinsic factors such as the way that pay is structured and the way promotions are granted. It can also include the quality of relationships among staff and management, the way teamwork is used and effort is recognised. Intrinsic motivation can be affected by making staff aware of the impact of their work – how close they are to the beneficiaries of the policies that they develop, how they see value created as a result of their ideas and their labour. To be innovative, professional public services must also have the right skills to apply to the problems they are being asked to solve. Employees who feel less capable to complete tasks will be less motivated to undertake them, while those with new skills will be keen to put them to use. Some of these skills are likely related to specific technical abilities, such as the ability to understand and manipulate big data sets or the ability to manage prototyping or experimental approaches to service design. Other skills include the ability to make connections between ideas that are not apparent, to ask the right questions and network with the right people. acquiring and reinforcing these skills in the public sector workforce likely entails thinking about employee and workforce development in new and creative ways. (OECD, 2017, p. 42)

Similar to experimentation, employees of innovative public organizations enable an organization to "make mistakes and to quickly correct upon those mistakes. The key issue is to recognise that innovation requires risk taking and that entrepreneurship will invariably lead to some failures. In recent years, there has been a significant growth in the type and number of organisations and structures dedicated to supporting innovation in the public sector" (OECD, 2017, p. 43). However, the context also matters for experimentation. For example, "[e]mployees' willingness to experiment and take risks also may depend on the tightness of the resource and time constraints that they face at work" (Afsar & Masood, 2018, p. 58). Additionally, the contexts we discussed in Chapter 2 are also relevant here because employees face different resources and time constraints. While encouraging experimentation, policymakers and public managers should consider the purpose (e.g., experimentation in general or for a specific policy), feasibility (e.g., whether the experimentation is measurable and testable), reliability (e.g., whether the same experimentation has led to similar results in other places or times), and value (e.g., whether the experimentation increases performance) of the experiment (Hartley & Knell, 2022).

Dealing with low performers is another condition for innovation. As low performers negatively affect other employees and the work itself, it is imperative to respond to them. Demircioglu and Audretsch (2017, p. 1683) have suggested that "if employees have low ability and experience, the organization can help them through training. If, however, employees have low conscientiousness, the organization can deal with those employees via motivating low-experienced employees and via rejecting (e.g., firing) high-experienced employees" (see also LePine & Dyne, 2001). Designing effective training and mentoring employees can make employees more skillful in terms of innovation (ANZSOG, 2019). In this regard, organizations and organizational leaders should respond to low performers differently depending on employees' ability, motivation, and other factors.

Another condition for innovation is the existence of feedback loops. Studies find that constructive feedback motivates employees (Ryan & Deci, 2000) and increases their socialization, job satisfaction (Anseel et al., 2015), capability, competence, and performance (Demircioglu & Audretsch, 2017). Without feedback loops, employees keep making the same mistakes without learning and improving. Employees could also be frustrated and eventually want to leave their job without an effective feedback loop (Bentley & Bentley, 2022). In other words, feedback loops help individuals and organizations improve through innovation. Meanwhile, innovations – specifically the development of products, services, and processes – increase organizational learning in public organizations (Osborne & Brown, 2013). Thus, while experimentation and feedback increase organizational learning and thus innovation, implementing innovations and evaluating these innovations also increases individual and organizational learning.

Motivation to improve performance and innovate is another condition for innovation. According to Ryan and Deci (2000, p. 54): "To be motivated means to be moved to do something … someone who is energized or activated toward an end is considered motivated." When employees and organizations are motivated to improve their performance, they can focus on achieving this objective and become more creative and innovative (Demircioglu & Audretsch, 2017; Sahni et al., 2013). Klein and Sorra (1996, p. 1060) find that innovation can be fostered by "(a) ensuring employee skill in innovation use, (b) providing incentives for innovation use and disincentives for innovation avoidance, and (c) removing obstacles to innovation use."

Albury's findings show that innovative public organizations are the results of employees' and leaders' motivation to innovate. Without motivation, organizations cannot innovate. For example, most schools operate in almost the same way they did a century ago. On the one hand, this may be because education is highly centralized and regulated, and schools do not have the ability, capacity, and motivation to innovate. On the other hand, schools primarily focus on metrics such as inspection reports, student–teacher ratios, and so on. Thus, "[s]chools are not motivated to provide space to innovate, to collaborate with niche players, to acquire new ideas to experiment" (Albury, 2011, p. 233). Albury further observes that innovative public organizations have "encouraged experimentation … tolerated failure … [and learned] from mistakes … Encouraging staff to innovate and supporting their attempts is a crucial element of leadership and organisational culture" (Albury, 2011, pp. 229–230).

White's (1959) seminal research on the competence of organisms found that not all environments and niches provide motivation for them to make exploratory activities and improvements. The right environment will increase motivation and thus increase capability and mastery: "Such activities … must therefore be conceived to be motivated in their own right. It is proposed to designate this motivation by the term effectance, and to characterize the experience produced as a feeling of efficacy" (White, 1959, p. 329). Along with the efficacy, increasing motivation for innovation can also increase employee creativity and innovation. For example, Berman and Kim (2010) provide evidence that in the Seoul Metropolitan Government in South Korea, providing monetary incentives and top prize awards for the best and most creative ideas drastically increased creative ideas from employees. Thus, a monetary incentive can be an effective motivator for many employees.

Finally, changes in budget and resources may affect innovations differently. According to Thompson, to make innovative organizations, the priority needs to go toward resources, such as money, skills, and time. Additionally, diversity of inputs such as training and experience is crucial (Thompson, 1965). Finally, rather than extrinsic factors (e.g., power, status, or money), "satisfactions [that] come from the search process, professional growth, and the esteem of knowledgeable peers" are the most important conditions for innovation (Thompson, 1965, p. 12). In fact, for Thompson (1965), there are both general and structural requirements for innovation in organizations. The former involves resources (physical, financial, human, and psychological), diversity, conflict, autonomy, professional growth, and dispersed power. The latter involves job descriptions, structural looseness, group process, and a freer communication style.

Analyzing successful public sector innovations in India, Mitra (2022, p. 7) finds that "[l]essons from India include that organizational slack was often used to make room for innovations. Innovations that provided well-defined new products to a specific clientele both survived and expanded. Most local and state innovations were driven by middle managers. Legitimacy enhancement was a powerful driver of initiatives and innovations." Likewise, analyzing environmental innovations in Canada, Yuriev et al. (2021) find that time (which could be considered another resource) is an additional critical factor affecting innovations in the public sector. For example, in their interviews, many specialists and directors state that because employees already have so many tasks, they cannot find sufficient or even any time to innovate.

However, a reduced budget and fewer resources can indeed increase innovation because doing so requires public organizations, managers, and employees to be more creative, such as prioritizing some policies over others and incentivizing public organizations to innovate (Sahni et al., 2013). The Australian Public Service Commission (APSC, 2013) found that "a reduction in resources is seen as both an enabler and barrier to innovation." They give the example of public managers in Washington, DC who are aware that the mayor and that the city management support them to achieve the city's innovation goals, so that they are motivated to improve their performance and thus innovate (Sahni et al., 2013). Similarly, analyzing findings from 330 employees in 95 teams at the Taiwan Customs Bureau, Hirst et al. (2011, p. 630) have found that "challenging demands and limited resources made it essential for employees to display creativity in developing innovative solutions to problems."

NPM's "do more with less," such as decreasing resources, aims to increase innovation in public organizations around the world (Dudau et al., 2018; Knox & Marin-Cadavid, 2022). Overall, budget constraints can increase prioritizing some policies over others, so employees and organizations must become more creative and innovative in order to deliver the same public service. This trend is consistent with NPM reforms and the reinventing movement in the United States, suggesting that to do more with less can increase not only efficiency but also innovation (Bartos, 2003; Glor, 2001; Kettl, 2005; Osborne & Gaebler, 1992). However, other studies find that higher budgets mean that there will be more resources to for experimentation, so organizations with more funding and slack resources tend to be more innovative (Damanpour, 1991; Wynen et al., 2014). For example, mission innovations such as the moon mission and several NASA projects require significant resources.

Meanwhile, some studies do not find any relationship between changes in budgets and other resources on the one hand, and innovation on the other (Demircioglu & Audretsch, 2017; Lægreid et al., 2011). Therefore, we believe that context is attributable to conflicting studies about the effects of budgets and resources on innovation because as contexts differ, so will the outcomes (as discussed in Chapter 4). More specifically, administrative, political, temporal, and organizational contexts for innovations are different. Even if their budget is sufficient for innovation, organizations cannot innovate without political support. Additionally, different types of innovations also require different types of budgets. For example, while technological and mission innovations require resources and budgets, process innovations may require changing mindsets, routines, and practices, and thus diminishing budgets may increase these types of innovations.

In fact, not all organizations are the same. In their classic study, Burns and Stalker (1961) found that organic organizations are more innovative than mechanistic organizations because the former tend to interact more with the external environment (such as with other organizations). Similarly, Lawrence and Lorsch (1967) found that a complex and uncertain organizational environment forces organizations to be more adaptive and innovative. Thus, operating in a fast-changing environment and interacting with other organizations are considered conditions for innovation. Furthermore, Thompson (1965) observed that there was a belief among behavioral scientists that bureaucratic organizations were considered efficient but not innovative, so bureaucratic organizations (both in the public and the private sectors) needed to be more innovative. One way of making organizations more innovative is through technological changes, as changes force organizations to innovate.

Because too much conflict drives internal politics, dealing with unnecessary tasks, and employee turnover, organizations dealing with too much conflict typically perform worse than other organizations (Pfeffer, 1992). However, Thompson (1965) argues that because some amount of conflict results in "pluralism" and this type of healthy conflict requires organizations and employees to deal with and seek solutions, a minor to moderate amount of conflict positively influences the creativity and innovativeness of employees and organizations (Thompson, 1965). Thus, less bureaucratic and more dynamic organizations that include some healthy conflict along with minor uncertainty may be more creative and innovative (Thompson, 1965).

Still, financial and extrinsic incentives matter. Albury argues that: "It is not sufficient merely to have reputational rewards in place, they need to be complemented with financial incentives, additional innovation funding, and performance bonuses" (Albury, 2005, p. 231). For innovations, public organizations can initiate more innovation-friendly policies such as awarding innovative ideas. For instance, the Seoul Metropolitan Government provides financial incentives for innovative ideas (Berman & Kim, 2010).

Creating Innovation Units or Labs

An important approach is creating innovation units, centers, or labs to foster innovation. Innovation labs – or creating organizational forms to encourage innovation – can help organizations experiment, support innovative activities, change organizational culture by encouraging more innovation, entrepreneurship, and risk-taking activities, and support solving certain problems (ANZSOG, 2019; Lee & Ma, 2020; Tõnurist et al., 2017). Thus, innovation labs can enhance innovative activity both directly (creating labs for implementing innovations) and indirectly (e.g., changing culture to encourage employees to experiment). For example, national institutions such as NESTA in the UK and the National Fund for Research and Development (SITRA) in Finland advance innovation and solve public and policy problems (ANZSOG, 2019).

To demonstrate the benefits of innovation labs and specialized innovation teams, Mulgan (2014, p. 14) observed the following and offered some recommendations:

There is a value to having separate specialised innovation teams, as they bring in new methods and new people and also act as catalyst for change. But it is also vital that these teams work with existing agencies and departments – for instance, by using their budgets and some of their staff – otherwise new ideas are seen as being created by outsiders and are too easily rejected. Connectivity is the key. A high proportion of teams and networks of this kind then need to be deployed across organisational boundaries, reporting directly to central departments like the Cabinet Office, Treasury or Chief Executives' departments in local authorities. These teams may focus on problems (for example the rise of Alzheimer's disease or gun crime) on groups of people (such as migrants with poor English language skills) or places (for instance depressed seaside towns).

Likewise, an OECD (2017) document recommends that if innovation units and teams are not well implemented, they will not positively affect innovation. Therefore, innovation units must be well designed and innovation teams must work together well. Additionally, policymakers should pay attention to experimentation and the evaluation of innovations. Innovation units and teams should be flexible and adjust what they do based on the experimentation and evaluation of innovations, such as changing the location of the innovation unit. Even if there is no dedicated innovation unit, the organization should have an innovation climate and culture in which new ideas, experimentation, support, opportunities, and evaluation of innovations are encouraged (OECD, 2017).

External Shocks as Conditions

One major condition for innovation is the response to external shocks or crises such COVID-19. Early studies of public sector innovation in the United States suggest that innovations are typically a response to crises (Sadler, 2000; Wilson, 1966), so crises can be the most important condition for innovation. The crisis provides the opportunity for new solutions to address the challenges. Thus, the response to the COVID-19 crisis was a host of innovations, ranging from vaccinations and testing to the introduction of online services. Other examples of innovative responses to the COVID-19 abound. The "home office" emerged as a management innovation that became a staple of the organizational response to the COVID-19 crisis in the USA. The virtual workplace accomplished the need for physical distance and isolation during the pandemic, but it would not have been possible without the plethora of technological innovations enabling online platforms to be accessible and reliable. The pandemic crisis also provided a shift in attitudes to prioritize new and urgent values, encouraging resources to flow to activities addressing those challenges.

The COVID-19 pandemic provides another compelling example, where the public was much more understanding of the need to ramp up public sector programs to combat and overcome the pandemic. Thus, such crises can trigger innovations. Sanger and Levin (1992, p. 105) argue that "[c]risis presents problems, but also great opportunities for the freedom to innovate. Rather like the impetus provided by natural selection when old biological solutions and structures cease to meet the needs of a changing environment, crises in public organizations provide the fuel for change. Crisis often quells natural opposition and provides the political and organizational support for innovation." One example is the September 11 attacks; the attacks were "so profound and important that they led to substantive policy change and innovation" (Birkland, 2004, p. 180). Birkland provides several examples regarding this, including how regulations about cockpit doors, the duties of pilots, screeners, and other technological innovations were introduced for security reasons following the September 11 terrorist attacks.

The crises may also be related to international relations, economics, disasters, and other human or natural crises. Hurricanes in the United States, such as Hurricane Katrina, led to innovation in Federal Emergency Management Agency. The creation of the Department of Homeland Security is another example of how crises lead to innovations (Wise, 2006). Noordegraaff et al. (2019, p. 291) explain at length how crises are conditions for innovations:

A crisis might help. In 2015 and 2016 Europe experienced a "refugee crisis." The national governments had great difficulty finding adequate answers to handling the mass influx of migrants and therefore allowed experimental ideas and initiatives to be carried out at the local level. One example came about in the city of Utrecht, one of the mayor cities in the Netherlands. During Fall 2016 the local government received EU funding to start an experiment with innovative reception facilities; the Utrecht Refugee Launch

Pad (U-RLP). This is a co-housing and co-learning experiment. All facilities are open to locals as well as asylum seekers. For example, entrepreneurship courses (in English) are provided in mixed classes for asylum seekers and for people who have been living in the neighborhood for longer. The aim being that this will allow all of them to acquire "future proof" skills which they will benefit from, no matter whether they will continue to live in Dutch society, or if they will have to leave the Netherlands in case their asylum application would be rejected. Housing is facilitated for asylum seekers as well as for local youngsters. Local government, civil society organizations, knowledge institutes, and social entrepreneurs developed this local experiment together with asylum seekers as well as with grassroots initiatives by (young) citizens.

Innovation can often only be accomplished through collaboration (see Chapter 8). Under normal conditions, barriers to collaboration inhibit the ability of the public sector to attain its innovative potential. However, when confronted by a crisis, those barriers to collaboration crumble, resulting in waves of transformative innovations from the public sector. As the truism suggests, "necessity is the mother of invention."

Other examples of how crises, external forces, or necessity affect innovation come from Singapore. This small island country does not have any natural resources such as oil and water. It suffers from water scarcity although the country is surrounded by seas and oceans. The government announced the "Four National Taps" plan to overcome water scarcity in Singapore in 2002. As stated in the plan:

Singapore has built a robust, diversified and sustainable water supply from four water sources known as the Four National Taps – Water from Local Catchment, Imported Water, high-grade reclaimed water known as NEWater and Desalinated Water. In integrating the water system and maximising the efficiency of each of the four national taps, Singapore has overcome its lack of natural water resources to meet the needs of a growing nation. (Public Utilities Board, n.d., para. 1)

The Singapore government has invested many resources in water, such as funding the Institute of Water Studies, which has resulted in innovative solutions, and implementing innovations such as converting rivers into a reservoir and focusing on recycling water (NEWater). These necessities have forced the government to be more innovative regarding water safety and sufficiency. Focusing on fresh water is consistent with the Singapore government's other approaches, such as the motto of the "Garden City" and "City in a Garden" (Irvine et al., 2014; van der Wal, 2017). Irvine et al. (2014, p. 8) summarized the eight factors that made Singapore's water system innovative and effective: need, leadership and vision, political will, economic capacity, single lead agency (Public Utilities Board), openness to new ideas, education, and public–private partnership. Likewise, energy and technology are critical sectors for Singapore, and CleanTech Park is an eco-business park in Singapore. CleanTech Park allows and encourages R&D and the implementation of green technology and solutions.

In a *Straits Times* essay, Richard Magnus – who is the chairman of Temasek Foundation Cares (a nonprofit organization supporting social and citizen innovations in Singapore), a former senior judge, and the first representative to the ASEAN Intergovernmental Commission on Human Rights – states that COVID-19 has brought opportunities. He suggests that it increased our empathy, resilience, and unity against the common enemy: a global disease. He argues: "Empathy can lead to innovations for economic recovery, and give us relevance on the international stage … Empathy can lead to innovation. According to Microsoft chief executive Satya Nadella, the source of innovation is 'all about being able to meet the unmet and unarticulated needs of customers.' To do this successfully, you need to have empathy."

In this regard, crises can also help governments to become closer to the public, increase empathy among citizens and decision-makers, and motivate governments and public organizations to meet citizens' needs, mobilize resources, and innovate.

Beyond the Frameworks

There are different conditions for innovation based on different perspectives of scholars as well as the heterogeneous nature of innovations. According to Bartos (2003, p. 14), "a coherent idea," "political impetus," "willingness to implement change," "committed advocates for the innovation," and "a reason for change" need to be present to achieve successful public sector innovations. In another study, two practitioners, Loewe and Dominiquini (2006, pp. 26–27), find that the following factors lead to innovations in organizations regardless of the sector: allowing "divergence and exploration at the front end. This helps ensure that the new ideas generated aren't simply a re-hash of what has been done before"; synthesizing "individual ideas into bigger platforms before selecting individual ideas to develop further. This enables the company to avoid 'betting the farm' on one idea without first learning about the larger opportunities at hand"; using "experiments to test critical assumptions and refine the business model before locking it in. This helps minimize the risk associated with market entry and incorporate key learning into the business model before it is too late"; and "adjusting "evaluation criteria throughout the process to reflect the stage of development of the innovation. This helps ensure that promising ideas are not killed prematurely."

Regarding NASA, Romzek and Dubnick state that organizational structure and expertise were crucial for its success and innovativeness:

NASA's earliest programs had three important characteristics: they involved clearly defined outcome objectives, highly technical methodologies for achieving those goals, and almost unqualified political (and therefore budgetary) support ... Those early conditions had a significant impact on the development and management of NASA. The agency's structure and recruiting practices reflected an institutional willingness to respect the technical nature of NASA's programmatic tasks. NASA's form of organization emphasized deference to expertise and minimized the number of political appointments at the top of the administrative structure ... NASA's initial staff consisted almost entirely of individuals with the relevant substantive knowledge, primarily aeronautical engineers. These circumstances afforded NASA the opportunity to become among the most innovative organizations (public or private) in recent American history and a classic example of an agency operating under a professional accountability system. (Romzek & Dubnick, 1987, p. 231)

Chenok et al. argue that innovation is one of the most vital forces driving change in governments. They suggest that public organizations and public managers need to provide key incentives in order to increase the innovation climate and innovation itself: "government leaders need to go beyond simply fostering a culture of innovation to actively encouraging it" (Chenok et al. 2013, p. 21). They emphasize that government leaders can involve internal and external stakeholders in innovation; establish platforms to share innovative ideas; bring private sector employees into the public sector (e.g., through the Presidential Innovation Fellows program in the United States); offer incentives for trying new ideas and being an entrepreneur (e.g., going beyond the job description); acknowledge experimentation; consider innovation as a part of employees' annual review; allow people to make mistakes and learn from failures; and create programs for innovation, which results in the institutionalization of successful innovations (Chenok et al., 2013).

Although institutionalizing innovations is not easy, Mulgan (2014) claims that the following steps can help public organizations to institutionalize innovations and make public organizations more innovative: create an innovation ecosystem, recruit innovators, design and test novel and promising ideas, focus on improving outcomes, and create spaces to develop and implement breakthrough ideas. As the world becomes more connected, public organizations are also more connected to other organizations, citizens, and civil society (Chen et al., 2021), and thus they operate within an ecosystem.

Trust can also affect innovation positively because with trust, "uncertainty about opportunistic behavior is reduced, and the feeling that other actors will exercise their goodwill in the search for innovative solutions is increased" (Bekkers et al., 2011b, p. 26). Studies find that trust is vital to reducing transaction costs and increasing the learning, knowledge, innovation, and stability of organizations, particularly for collaborative innovations (Emerson et al., 2012). Seeking legitimacy is another innovation driver (Feller & Menzel, 1977), even in autocratic regimes. For example, Huang and Yu (2019) find that innovations are used by local governments to respond to increasing demands for public services by citizens of authoritarian governments such as China's.

Analyzing different conditions for innovation together is vital because all of the conditions impact each other. As de Vries et al. (2016, p. 162) observe, different conditions for innovation "are often addressed independently, ignoring possible connections between them." They recommend more work encompassing different factors at different levels to analyze how they affect innovation (de Vries et al., 2016, 2018). In fact, innovations are more effective and significant when both supervisors and senior executives support innovative ideas together (Demircioglu & van der Wal, 2022) and when collaboration exists among different organizations. Additionally, the involvement of different stakeholders can ease the difficulty of implementing innovations. For example, in the context of the United States, Sapat (2004, p. 148) observes that innovations become successful when all relevant stakeholders are involved during the innovation process and when sufficient resources are provided. Similarly, Ansell et al. (2021, pp. 949–950) state: "Turbulent problems call for cross-boundary collaboration, public innovation, and, perhaps most importantly, the development of robust governance strategies that facilitate and support adaptive and flexible adjustment and entrepreneurial exploration and the exploitation of emerging options and opportunities." Likewise, innovation "requires openness, delegated governance, leadership, and an environment that is supportive of experimentation and future-oriented initiatives" (Ek Österberg & Qvist, 2020, p. 293).

For all these levels, important drivers include leadership support and quality as well as employees themselves. As mentioned in Chapter 3, public organizations tend to be more risk averse and thus seem to be less innovative. However, the degree and types of innovations between public and private organizations are different as public sector innovations do not focus on commercial considerations, so even without incentives for innovation, public sector employees can still initiate innovative activities (Borins, 1998; Sadler, 2000). Therefore, our argument is not that all organizational levels should be supportive of and prepared to implement innovations, as this is not always possible. Our argument is that while each unit or level is not essential to all innovations, ultimately the more factors that are present, the more likely it is that organizations will innovate. Thus, practitioners may find the levels and steps of innovation illustrated in Figure 7.1 useful for their organizations and employees.

In addition to encouraging public sector employees to innovate, leadership also matters. However, not all leaders are the same, as different types of leadership behavior affect innovation differently. For example, Yoshida et al. (2014) find that servant leadership positively impacts employee creativity and team innovation while Demircioglu and Chowdhury (2021) find that relations-oriented leadership has a positive impact on public sector entrepreneurship. Effective and high-quality organizational leaders can provide intrinsic incentives to employees and allow them to experiment.

We should also remember that innovating and implementing innovations are not simple, straightforward processes. Innovations require commitment, dedication, hard work, and engaging with employees. As Stewart-Weeks and Katelle (2015, p. 63) argue: "To be effective, innovation has to engage an almost emotional, visceral level of commitment and energy. That is what makes it so compelling and, sometimes, so difficult." Similarly, analyzing six cases of public organizations in the United Kingdom and conducting thirty-six semi-structured interviews with senior leaders and managers, Knox and Marin-Cadavid (2022) find that "organizations that were able to engage employees demonstrated greater learning and innovation outcomes, while those that were unable to engage employees demonstrated lower learning and innovation outcomes" (Knox & Marin-Cadavid, 2022, p. 18). According to Cohen and Levinthal (1990, p. 131), a diversity of knowledge and information "facilitates the innovative process by enabling the individual to make novel associations and linkages." Thus, even if all the conditions are present, without commitment, dedication, and hard work, innovations cannot be implemented. The important question then becomes: Who will influence innovation or who is more committed to implementing innovations? We answer the "who" question in Chapter 8.

Under the right conditions, organizational structure, and leadership, and with capable employees, organizations and employees can focus on both exploration and exploitation. Both exploration and exploitation are needed for effective innovations. While "exploration" refers to discovery, creativity, and experimentation, "exploitation" refers to implementation (Bekkers et al., 2011b; March, 1991). Combining these two practices will lead to successful outcomes for innovations.

Greenhalgh et al. (2004, p. 593) argue that "innovativeness is seen as dependent on good leadership, sound decision making, and effective human resource management." Likewise, Marcum (1999, p. 46) suggests that: "Whereas the 'motivating' boss of the traditional organization thinks in terms of being in control, running a tight ship, and giving directions, the engaging leader is a coach and facilitator scrambling to keep up with the pack." Thus, the best ways for leaders to motivate employees to engage in innovation occur via experimentation, offering incentives, creating a workplace that encourages innovation, and providing feedback and direction without reducing employee autonomy. Additionally, employee empowerment and job engagement may be essential conditions for innovation (Fernandez & Moldogaziev, 2013).

Conclusion

This chapter has discussed how individuals, work groups, organizations, and countries implement innovations. We are particularly interested in whether any specific factors are associated with innovation.

Promoting innovation across different public organizations, experimentation, developing and testing new ideas, funding innovation, and developing capacities and capabilities for innovation can increase public sector innovation (OECD, 2017).

Although each context is different, we can generalize about the determinants and conditions for innovation in the public sector. We need to consider innovation as an ecosystem, since multiple units of analysis need to be considered, including the individual, group, organizational, national, and external levels. Each unit needs to have both the ability and the motivation to innovate. For instance, at the employee level, employees need to have ability (e.g., be able to understand the work process) and motivation (e.g., individual motivation and encouragement from leaders) in order to innovate. At the organizational level, ability reflects more the availability of key resources, motivation, and desire for innovation by organizational leaders. At the national level, ability is reflected more by state capacity and budgets, and motivation is more relevant in terms of political leadership, such as policymakers' willingness to create innovation spaces. However, we also believe that not all conditions have the same effect. We believe that experimentation is perhaps the most important condition for innovation, followed by motivation. We explore more about the government's roles in innovation in Chapter 10.

Certain organizational and leadership characteristics tend to facilitate innovative activity while other characteristics tend to inhibit innovation. For example, Demircioglu and Audretsch (2017) have found that the ability to experiment, dealing with low performers, feedback loops, and motivation to make innovations are associated with innovations in the public sector. In some cases, there will be pressure from government leaders or citizens to innovate in the public sector. However, COVID-19 clearly shows us that perhaps the most important driver for innovation is an external shock (e.g., the pandemic); in extraordinary times, the major drivers or conditions of innovation are often not internal but external. In addition, organizational resources, job involvement, empowerment, and other contextual variables may affect innovative activities in the public sector. As the Australia and New Zealand School of Government (ANZSOG) advises: "With imagination and courage, immense opportunities are available to reinvent government for the 21st century by building on the skills and dedication of the public servants" (ANZSOG, 2019, p. 55).

8 | Sources of Knowledge and Collaborative Innovation

Historical Developments and the Framework

What is the source of an innovation? Whereas antecedents of innovation refer to conditions or driving factors affecting innovation – and these include centralization, communication, formalization, tenure, specialization, and complexity, among many other factors (e.g., Damanpour, 1991; Greenhalgh et al., 2004) – sources refer to actors (such as the government) that provide innovation ideas or implement innovations (Bason, 2010; Demircioglu & Audretsch, 2019). Innovations in public organizations are affected by different factors and sources. To put it simply, actors are sources of knowledge for innovations. Understanding the sources (or actors) is also crucial because actors/sources bring resources (e.g., financial, expertise, knowledge) to a situation (Ostrom, 2005), which is no less true for innovative activity. Furthermore, an early study of public sector innovation argues that a significant issue for public sector innovation research is that the source of innovation is often neglected in the literature (Perry & Kraemer, 1978).

The impact and role of each innovation source in the public sector may differ depending on the context (see Chapters 3 and 4). In some contexts (i.e., country, state, organization, or work group), innovations may be top down, so the government and organizational leaders are crucial sources of innovation. In other contexts, innovations may emanate more from a bottom-up process, suggesting that employees and members of the public provide more ideas spurring innovative activity. Some agencies (e.g., departments/ministries of science and technology or of trade) collaborate with industry and business stakeholders, so collaborative innovation may be more important for these agencies and work groups. Innovation units, labs, or science parks could be responsible for innovations in some cases. Although there may be a tendency to move to more collaborative innovation, top-down innovations will still be expected due to contextual differences between countries and sectors.

Most previous studies on innovation in both the public and business management fields have focused on the antecedents or outcomes of innovation rather than on the sources of innovation and the nature of their involvement in innovation (Demircioglu et al., 2019). Regarding innovation indicators and the measurement of innovation, sources of innovative ideas is a new innovation indicator (Smith, 2005). In addition, many previous studies about innovation consider innovation at the national or organizational level and from the perspective of particular national agendas (Acs et al., 2017; Suzuki & Demircioglu, 2019). Fewer papers in public management scholarship consider innovation at the individual level other than analyzing innovative work behavior and creativity (Demircioglu et al., 2023). Finally, studies and published papers on public sector innovation are predominantly case studies rather than empirical work (Arundel & Huber, 2013). Thus, a gap in research and practice exists as to sources of innovation as we still have limited knowledge and information about innovation sources, particularly in the context of public organizations.

As Demircioglu et al. (2019, p. 1366) have pointed out, "[t]he famous conclusion attributed to Solow that innovation 'falls like manna from heaven' … ignore[s] that innovation activity emanates from earthlier source," suggesting that if there is an innovation, then there are the sources for the innovation. In other words, innovation cannot happen without sources. Innovation depends on knowledge sources, and sources are even more important than all other innovation factors (Feldman, 1994). Likewise, Leckel et al. (2020) state that studies must link innovation with sources.

Contrary to Solow's argument that knowledge comes from random and stochastic sources, such as heaven (Demircioglu et al., 2019), Romer (1990) and Feldman (1994) argue that innovative activities spill over from external sources, and that the location of innovation matters. Acs et al. (2009, 2013) call this phenomenon "the knowledge spillover theory" of entrepreneurship. The concept of knowledge spillover has been mainly studied in the private sector, research has found strong evidence that the positive spillover effect between businesses and universities occurs frequently, and the knowledge spillover effect has been found to be a crucial source for innovation, particularly in urban areas (Aryal et al., 2018; Audretsch & Feldman, 1996, 2004).

While the traditional view of innovation started with the organization and then analyzed strategies to spur innovative activity, by contrast, the knowledge spillover theory of entrepreneurship does not assume the organization to exist but rather the idea or knowledge that is embedded in an individual or individuals. In an effort to actualize and transform that idea into reality through innovation, a new organization is created since none of the existing incumbent organizations deem the idea sufficiently worthy. Thus, the organization is created endogenously, as a response by individuals to equilibrate the value of their endowment of knowledge and ideas. While the traditional view in economics and strategy takes the organization as given and then analyzes what strategy it should deploy, the knowledge spillover theory of entrepreneurship instead focuses on the strategy of the individual who is endowed with knowledge and ideas.

In other words, ideas and new knowledge are created in the context of a legacy organization or firm. However, many of the new ideas are rejected as not being valuable and are not pursued. This means that the legacy firm will not commercialize that knowledge or innovation, even though it undertook the research, development, and work by employees to generate those new ideas. If, however, an employee, or group of employees deems the new idea to be valuable, they can attempt to commercialize that knowledge by starting a new company or organization. Thus, the new organization is created only in response to knowledge and ideas that are left uncommercialized by the legacy companies. The new organization is the endogenous response to knowledge created by legacy firms.

The first innovation theory we are aware of that identified articulating sources of innovation is Alfred Marshall's 1890 theory on knowledge and innovation externalities (Carlino, 2001; Demircioglu et al., 2019). Marshall observed how smaller organizations interact with larger organizations and learn from them, suggesting that innovative ideas could emanate from larger organizations to smaller organizations (Hart, 1996). Hart has also reflected on Marshall's views: "The availability of external economies to small firms is seen to increase with the scale of industry output, a factor which also induces the average size of firms to increase, and therefore the accessibility of internal economies" (Hart, 1996, p. 356).

Industries and large organizations are important sources of innovation. At the same time, research also demonstrates that employees and workers are vital sources for innovative ideas in the private sector (Demircioglu et al., 2019; Nakamura, 2000). Thus, innovation could come from external sources such as other organizations or internal sources such as employees within the organization. Because innovations do not typically follow a linear process (e.g., from idea to creation to diffusion), different actors are involved in different stages of the innovation (Qiu & Chreim, 2021). Normally, however, one source is dominant during the innovation process.

We can classify or approach sources of knowledge and innovation using two methods: from the origin and by the level of analysis. The first approach (the origin) is whether innovations are top down or bottom up and whether innovations are external or internal. Top-down innovations mean that the sources of innovations are organizational leaders inside the organization or a higher authority such as the president, ministers, or politicians. Thus, top-down innovations could be internal (e.g., employees' supervisors and senior executive service employees) or external (e.g., ministers). Bottom-up innovations mean that employees or their work groups are the sources of knowledge and innovation (for private organizations, see Daft, 1978; van de Ven et al., 1999; for public organizations, see Arundel et al., 2019; Borins, 2001; Demircioglu, 2021). Thus, bottom-up innovations are internal by nature.

Another source of innovation is external innovations, meaning sources that operate outside of an organization without government authority. Other public organizations, private organizations, science parks, nonprofits, universities, citizen groups, and citizens are external sources of innovations. Table 8.1 shows this typology. For the rest of the chapter, we explore and explain how these sources are vital for innovation.

The second approach is to analyze sources of innovation using different levels of analysis. For example, at the individual level, the sources would be leaders, employees, and members of the public. At the organizational level, the sources would be other organizations, governments, industry stakeholders, and universities. At the national level, the sources would be other governments and international organizations (e.g., OECD, UN, NATO, and EU). In this chapter, we cover the important sources of innovation, which are outlined in Table 8.1.

Table 8.1 *Sources of innovation*

	External without authority or control	External with authority or control	Internal
Top down	Outside of the organization, such as firms, nonprofit organizations, and other public organizations	Higher authority, such as the federal or central government, prime minister's office, courts	Organizational leaders
Bottom up	Citizens	NA	Employees and their work group

Internal Innovations: Top Down versus Bottom Up

Different studies consistently demonstrate that the most crucial source of innovation in public organizations is the organization itself, which include both top-down-internal (e.g., managers) and bottom-up-internal sources (e.g., employees themselves and their work groups) (Borins, 2001, 2014; Demircioglu, 2021). Several studies distinguish between top-down and bottom-up innovations (Fromhold-Eisebith & Eisebith, 2005; Gaynor, 2013; Saari et al., 2015). This distinction is relevant because "innovation can either be generated from the bottom up by civil servants in the frontline or be initiated by executive leadership" (OECD, 2017, p. 16). Likewise, Fernandez and Pitts (2011, p. 204) point out that "it is important to consider where in the organisation innovations are likely to emerge. Are innovations mostly generated or adopted by those toward the top of the organisational hierarchy or by front line employees?"

The main difference between top-down and bottom-up innovations is the following: Top-down innovations stress the leading role of government and organizational leaders in the adoption of innovations whereas bottom-up innovations stress the importance of frontline employees and members of the public (Fernandez & Pitts, 2011). Additionally, this difference between top-down and bottom-up innovation reflects whether employees are involved in the innovation process and are empowered. Hence, it shows whether organizations manifest democratic features. Additionally, while top-down innovations are typically responses to crises or a new agenda by a new administration or new managers, bottom-up innovations typically result from internal problems or innovative employees' proactive behaviors (Borins, 2010, 2014; Lœgreid et al., 2011), thus suggesting that motivations and rationales for sources of innovation also differ. Moreover, bottom-up innovations are typically focused on the development of new products and services, indicating that the outputs and outcomes of sources of innovation also differ (Lœgreid et al., 2011).

There are also different strategies to differentiate between top-down and bottom-up innovations:

Strategies to identify and promote innovative behaviour are top-down and bottom-up. From the top down, one could implement management tools and programmes to build the innovative capacity of public organisations and the innovative capabilities of employees and managers. From the bottom up, one could identify ways to encourage employees to experiment with new approaches, to explore new avenues and to celebrate this kind of behaviour to inspire others to act in similar ways. (OECD, 2015, p. 23)

Thus, strategies and tactics between top-down and bottom-up innovations differ.

Furthermore, these approaches reveal differences in terms of the cultures of organizations and nations:

"[T]op down" governance structure could be a common innovation method for agencies, particularly in risk-averse environments or where there is staff resistance to change. Bottom-up methods should be relatively common in Northern Europe where work is more likely to be organized around discretionary learning than in Southern Europe and reflect a pro-innovation culture. Newer approaches to innovation such as lateral and networked innovation could also exist. In respect to beneficial outcomes from innovation, it is impossible to predict the types of innovation methods that lead to better outcomes because there has been very little research on this topic. (Arundel et al., 2015, p. 1273)

Likewise, many organizational cultures do not encourage or even accept bottom-up innovations because (as innovations require both resources and support) employees must be supported by managers and provided with resources in order to innovate (Gaynor, 2013).

Although several studies have addressed the issue of where innovation comes from and the sources/actors that contribute to innovation (e.g., Dawson & Denford, 2015; Hüsig & Mann, 2010; Osborne & Brown, 2011), how these different sources affect employee attitudes – such as job satisfaction – is not well known. An advantage of bottom-up innovations may be that employees feel more creative and encouraged to innovate (Fernandez & Moldogaziev, 2013). For example, analyzing the Korean interorganizational network with a focus on the Seoul Tourist Police, Seulki Lee (2021) finds that frontline employees become agents of collaboration and foster innovation while resolving accountability tensions and demands in their organizations. Likewise, organizations emphasizing empowerment and bottom-up approaches to innovation tend to have fewer barriers to innovation (Demircioglu, 2018).

Top-down innovations may not always be beneficial. For example, one reason employees may be dissatisfied with innovations coming from the top down is that, on average, top-down innovations require more time to implement than bottom-up innovations (Arundel & Huber, 2013). Analyzing innovation in the Australian Federal Government, Arundel and Huber have further found that over 40 percent of the innovations emanating from ministers and agency leaders took at least a year to complete. In contrast, nearly 60 percent of the innovations from frontline employees took fewer than six months to complete. Hence, employees may be overwhelmed by innovations that take so much time, which are typically top-down innovations, compared to innovations that take less time, which are bottom-up innovations. Additionally, because employees interact with service users and citizens more often than senior managers and the government (Fernandez & Pitts, 2011), this interaction and feedback can increase problem solving and the quality of services.

Research suggests that both top-down and bottom-up innovations are common and beneficial in the public sector although bottom-up innovations are rarely discussed in the literature (Yuriev et al., 2021). Most studies focus on how organizations adopt innovations, overlooking the people who made the innovation happen. Zhang and Zhu (2020) find that career bureaucrats and their cohorts in China are the ones who not only implement innovations but also that their innovations are similar. Examples of top-down innovation include innovations from Indianapolis Mayor Goldsmith, along with the governors of Florida, Georgia, Mississippi, and Massachusetts, who have implemented many innovations such as introducing TQM, pay-for-performance compensation, and privatizing social service delivery systems (Fernandez & Pitts, 2011). Regarding bottom-up innovations, most of these innovations come from middle managers and front-line employees (Borins, 2001; Kamensky, 1996). Employees are the source of many innovations, including environmental innovations, in Canada (Yuriev et al., 2021). However, studies find that regardless of the nature of the innovation (top down vs. bottom up), both types of innovation are common in the public sector (Arundel et al., 2015; Demircioglu, 2021) and that management plays a vital role in encouraging and supporting bottom-up innovations.

Both top-down and bottom-up innovations are necessary for successful innovations. Top-down-external sources of innovation are consistent with "overhead democracy and the traditional approach to policy implementation, where elected officials enshrine innovations in legislation and executive orders," and managers and employees follow orders and implement those innovations (Fernandez & Pitts, 2011, p. 203). Top-down-internal sources of innovation are common in the United States (Kamensky, 1996). However, Windrum (2008, p. 14) argues that "[f]ar less attention is paid to bottom-up innovation." Bottom-up-internal sources of innovation focus on "changing the incentives employees face in doing their work, rather than investing the administration's political capital in restructuring the missions and organization of the government" (Kamensky, 1996, p. 248). Studies suggest that most government innovations in the USA after the 1990s focused on receiving ideas from the employees themselves (Fernandez & Pitts, 2011; Kamensky, 1996). Likewise, analyzing innovation in the public sector in Europe, Herrmann and Peine (2011) found that most innovative ideas and innovations are generated by employees. Furthermore, citizens and service users are crucial sources for innovative activities (OECD/Eurostat, 2005). Arundel and Huber (2013) summarize research on public sector innovation by focusing on sources of innovation (in countries such as the UK, Australia, the USA, Canada, Denmark, and many other European countries) and report that both top-down, bottom-up, internal, and external sources of innovations are important for and common in these countries. Finally, bottom-up innovations are consistent with democracy and empowerment (e.g., via participation).

Bekkers and Noordegraaf (2016) argue that the two of the most important sources of innovation come from public managers that are intentional, top down, and initiated by strategic agendas as well as from staff and professionals that are bottom up, flexible, and based on service and citizens' interests. They call the former "enforced innovation" and the latter "free innovation." While top-down innovations are the most reported type of innovations (Windrum, 2008), other research shows that bottom-up innovations are widespread in public sector organizations (Borins, 1998, 2001, 2014; Sadler, 2000). For example, Borins (1998, 2001, 2014) consistently finds that most innovations in the public sector originated not from politicians and senior executives but from employees themselves, mainly by the middle-level managers and frontline employees.

There are also unique advantages of bottom-up innovations:

Frontline staff are one of the most important sources of ideas ... Not only does it save money, it is also an effective risk management approach. That is the experience of MindLab's BenchKode team, which sought to innovate government's online business registry. What MindLab's team found was that there was a lot of intelligence in the front line where public servants interacted with citizens. Those insights can help create better service and also help innovation teams build legitimacy. This legitimacy can help toward earning a mandate, which will help thwart risks and uncertainties by having the self-interest of the organisation work with, rather than against, the innovation. (OECD, 2017, p. 185)

In addition, employees' involvement of innovations increases democracy within organizations and increases democratic culture (Vivona, 2023). However, research also suggests that public sector innovations have broader and more positive impacts if both top-down and bottom-up innovations are applied simultaneously, such as when managers encourage communication and are capable of using both sources' strengths (Saari et al., 2015).

Although public organizations operate differently than private organizations (as mentioned in Chapter 3), public organizations can also learn some best practices from private organizations. More specifically, in the private sector, bottom-up innovations are more common and encouraged. For example, in the company Amazon, several projects are employee-driven innovations. Kantor and Streitfeld (2015, p. 4) provide several examples:

[S]ome employees said, Amazon can feel like the Bezos vision come to life, a place willing to embrace risk and strengthen ideas by stress test. Employees often say their co-workers are the sharpest, most committed colleagues they have ever met, taking to heart instructions in the leadership principles like "never settle" and "no task is beneath them." Even relatively junior employees can make major contributions. The new delivery-by-drone project announced in 2013, for example, was coinvented by a low-level engineer named Daniel Buchmueller. Last August, Stephenie Landry, an operations executive, joined in discussions about how to shorten delivery times and developed an idea for rushing goods to urban customers in an hour or less. One hundred eleven days later, she was in Brooklyn directing the start of the new service, Prime Now. "A customer was able to get an Elsa doll that they could not find in all of New York City, and they had it delivered to their house in 23 minutes," said Ms. Landry, who was authorized by the company to speak, still sounding exhilarated months later about providing "Frozen" dolls in record time. That becomes possible, she and others said, when everyone follows the dictates of the leadership principles. "We're trying to create those moments for customers where we're solving a really practical need," Ms. Landry said, "in this way that feels really futuristic and magical."

O'Leary, who has made significant contributions to analyzing and understanding the role of guerrilla employees, defines this concept as the following:

[T]he actions of career public servants who work against the wishes – either implicitly or explicitly communicated – of their superiors. Guerrilla government is a form of dissent that is usually carried out by those who are dissatisfied with the actions of public organizations, programs, or people, but typically, for strategic reasons, choose not to go public with their concerns in whole or in part. A few guerrillas end up outing themselves as whistleblowers, but most do not. (O'Leary, 2010, p. 8)

According to her, "guerrillas" can be innovative employees, as she found that:

[M]ore than 200 of the 216 managers who responded to my survey emphasized that dissent, when managed well, can foster innovation and creativity. In particular, dissent can help generate multiple options that might not normally be considered by the organization. Managers should think of dissent as an opportunity to discuss alternative notions of how to achieve a goal. Cultivating the creative aspects behind dissent can lead to greater participation, higher job satisfaction, and, ultimately, better work product, the managers told me. (O'Leary, 2010, p. 16)

Thus, she recommends that policymakers "create an organization culture that accepts, welcomes, and encourages candid dialogue and debate. Cultivate a questioning attitude by encouraging staff to challenge the assumptions and actions" (O'Leary, 2010, p. 16). Thus, having guerilla employees or rebels is not only an innovation source; they can also increase innovations in their organizations.

Finally, although they are top down, the features and nature of middle managers (e.g., supervisors) and agency heads (e.g., senior executives) are different. For instance, Demircioglu and van der Wal (2022, p. 1291) state that "while supervisors tend to have more detailed knowledge about their work unit and the execution of organizational tasks, senior executives are expected to employ a broader perspective on how the external environment affects the organization and formulate a strategic vision for institutional adaptation." They also observe that middle managers are primarily concerned about organizational processes and thus focus on internal innovations. At the same time, senior executives are most concerned about developing partnerships with other organizations and responding to politicians (Demircioglu & van der Wal, 2022). Borins (2001) also found that middle managers are initiators of more innovations than senior managers in the contexts of the United States, advanced Commonwealth countries (e.g., Australia, Canada, and the UK), and developing Commonwealth countries (e.g., India, Malaysia, and South Africa). In this regard, not all top-down innovations have the same features and effects.

Collaboration and Open Innovation as Sources

Sources of innovation include collaborative innovation (e.g., multiple actors' involvement). In the past, innovation was not considered a collaborative action. However, most innovations involve the collaboration of different actors. As mentioned earlier, if there is an innovation, there must be sources: champions, promoters, supporters, or collaborators. Thus, collaborative innovation refers to innovations with multiple sources. Collaborative innovation could be defined as more than one public organization engaging with other public organizations or any other organization, such as private organizations and nonprofit organizations, in a collective decision-making process to implement innovations (Agranoff & McGuire, 2004; Ansell & Gash, 2008; Hartley et al., 2013). In collaboration, there should be "two-way flows of communication or multilateral deliberation" (Ansell & Gash, 2008, p. 546).

Similar to collaborative innovation, another aspect of innovation is open innovation. A recent focus has emerged on what has been characterized as the open innovation phenomenon. In open innovation, different sources work together and participate in innovations using the concept of open innovation projects (Guenduez & Mettler, 2022; Leckel et al., 2020). Innovations, particularly public sector innovation, have become an open process, such that both internal and external sources influence them (Boon et al., 2021). In particular, with the idea of open innovations, citizens have become involved in innovation processes around the world (Hameduddin et al., 2020; Leckel et al., 2020; Mergel & Desouza, 2013). As we mentioned in Chapter 5, citizens are involved in many innovations worldwide from the open innovation perspective. In particular, "crowdsourcing," "challenges and contests," and "civic hackathons" are well-known tools of open innovation (De Coninck et al., 2021; Yuan & Gascó-Hernandez, 2021). With these tools, citizens participate and provide innovative ideas, primarily using digital platforms.

Hage (1999) observes that collaborative innovation, or interorganizational networks for innovation, is a new area for research for both public and private organizations. Although Weberian bureaucracy and NPM reforms emphasize public service delivery from one source (i.e., in Weberian terms, from the government, and in NPM, from the market), after the 2000s there was a shift toward collaborative innovation. The main reasons for these shifts include the influence of New Public Governance reforms, whereby public organizations began embracing the VUCA (volatility, uncertainty, complexity, and ambiguity) world (van der Wal, 2017), and a belief that more actors are needed to solve problems (Lodge & Gill, 2011). Sources of innovation and particularly collaborative innovation are crucial to solving grand challenges or wicked problems (Bekkers et al., 2011a). To deal with grand challenges and implement transformative changes, different actors – such as public and private organizations, civil society, and service users – need to work together. While doing so, different actors need to experiment with which innovation can solve policy problems and grand challenges (Nair, 2022), and experimentation allows actors to appreciate uncertainty and accept failure (Schot & Steinmueller, 2018). More specifically, Noordegraaff et al. (2019, p. 292) argue that:

[I]nvolving new actors seems crucial in being able to develop this local innovation aimed at tackling this wicked problem. Aiming to get away from the deadlock at the national level implied having to develop innovative practices at another level (local) and together with other actors (entrepreneurs, knowledge institutes). Being away from the spotlights removed some of the public and political attention and allowed professionals to become more open to exploring each other's perspectives, to experiment and to learn from mistakes.

In addition, as Smits and Kuhlmann (2004, p. 7) point out, "[o]rganisations are not innovating in isolation but in the context of a system," suggesting that collaborative innovation is the norm or what is expected. Furthermore, there is a belief and even a bias that collaborative innovation is better (Liu, 2017; Prpić et al., 2015; Vivona et al., 2022), so there is more discussion of collaborative innovation.

Borins's well-known studies of innovation awards demonstrate that collaboration between public organizations and other sources (e.g., businesses, citizens) increased dramatically between his first study (the early 1990s) and later studies (2010), suggesting that the propensity for the public sector to collaborate with partners to generate more innovations has increased over time (Borins, 2001, 2014). His results suggest that collaboration as a source of innovative knowledge has become more prevalent. Other research also support these claims that many innovations exist in a collaborative setting: "More and more innovation has become a network activity ... [and] this trend is the growing need for public–private partnerships (PPPs) in the area of research, technology and development" (Smits & Kuhlmann, 2004, p. 7).

However, studies also find that while collaboration with different organizations enhances innovative activities and innovation performance, too much collaboration has a negative effect on innovative activities and innovation performance in both the private (Terjesen & Patel, 2017; Xie et al., 2022) and public sectors (Demircioglu et al., 2023; Torugsa & Arundel, 2016a). This is primarily because networking and collaborative activities are costly in terms of time, resources, and coordination (Demircioglu et al., 2023; Vivona et al., 2022). The opportunity cost of such collaboration can crowd out other productive uses of those scarce resources. Thus, collaboration should not be taken for granted but employed strategically.

External Innovations from Government

In addition to internal innovations, which can be top down or bottom up, considerable knowledge and innovation sources are developed or implemented from external sources. Many innovations, particularly more radical ones, require political support. At the same time, politicians are the ones who direct public organizations and public sector leaders and employees to implement certain innovations. They provide resources and other support. Thus, it is common that governments and politicians serve as sources of innovation. One benefit of relying on external government innovation is that the innovation and the innovation process can be seen as more legitimate when external actors are involved in the process. To borrow Feller and Menzel's words: "The greater the 'legitimacy' within an agency of the external sources (government/professional associations/manufacturers), the greater the likelihood of adoption of innovations" (Feller & Menzel, 1977, p. 65).

A report published by the Australian government discusses not only the government's role in innovation but also how government and politicians are vital sources for innovation: "The AU [Australian] government is an important player in the innovation system. It helps to create the conditions for innovation by managing the economy responsibly, regulating effectively, and making specific investments in education, research and infrastructure ... maintains pro-business operating environment, with the emphasis on open communication and the free flow or products, people, and ideas" (Carr, 2009, p. 18). In sum, in many cases innovations are developed externally by the government.

External Innovations from Outside of Government

In addition to these government sources, both internal (top down and bottom up) and external, there are other sources for innovation such as universities, government research agencies, private organizations (e.g., firms), service users, and citizens. In many cases, including crises and disasters in democratic countries, nonstate stakeholders (particularly citizens), volunteer networks, and nonprofit organizations are the designers and initiators of innovations (Park, 2018; Park & Johnston, 2017). Thus, as Park (2018) suggests, scholars should focus on innovations driven by nonstate stakeholders. Furthermore, relying on external actors such as other government organizations and other nations' public services can help public organizations to increase organizational learning, seek inspiration, and support insights from other organizations (Albury, 2005).

Arundel and colleagues summarize many studies' findings that external sources affect innovations in public organizations around the globe. For example, other than government organizations, other organizations developed approximately two-thirds of public sector innovations in the UK and significant innovations in Scandinavian countries. External sources for innovation provide benefits (e.g., reducing cost and increasing quality of services) to public organizations in the APS (Arundel et al., 2015).

Business and Industry

Governments support private organizations and industry by subsidizing R&D, sharing resources, maintaining intellectual property rights, and using other tools to encourage innovation from private organizations (Leyden & Link, 1992; Svensson & Hartmann, 2018). In return, private organizations influence public organizations to adopt technological, product, and process innovations. Likewise, venture capitalists play a key role for startups and small businesses while providing funding and support for innovative ideas related to medical devices and semiconductors (Hochberg et al., 2015).

For instance, research finds that:

[W]ith the increasing opportunities to work with external partners, firms have begun to explore the resources of external sources and individuals in other areas as new ways to find innovative ideas and solutions ... Many large corporations such as IBM, 3M, DuPont and Boeing have leveraged the benefits of external innovation opportunities, moving major new initiatives from internal resources to those that focus on external networks and communities. (Lee et al., 2012, p. 148)

An important insight is that legacy companies invest in R&D and human capital to access knowledge that was created by other organizations and is external to the boundaries of the firm. It takes complementary knowledge to understand and access such external knowledge and to absorb it by bringing it into the legacy company. Just as no man is an island, so too the more innovative companies are apparently not isolated either. Rather, they engage in strategic investments to be able to access and absorb external knowledge as well as a host of networking and linkage activities, in order to create conduits and absorb external knowledge spillovers from other firms and organizations.

Citizens

Citizens also provide an important source of innovation (e.g., by participating in innovation). One compelling example of citizens as sources of innovative knowledge is crowdsourcing activities or open innovations (Hameduddin et al., 2020). Citizens are crucial sources of innovation, particularly in determining innovation outcomes. For example, public organizations may generate innovations, but these innovations may be meaningless to citizens and service users. Or, public organizations may generate innovations due to institutional pressures such as coercive or mimetic isomorphism. In both cases, the innovations do not benefit citizens or service users (Salge & Vera, 2012). Thus, we suggest that innovations – and particularly service innovations – should suit citizens' and service users' needs.

Furthermore, comparing public, private, and hybrid sector managers, Wittmer (1991) finds that while higher pay was the most important reward in the business sector, performing work to help others was the most important reward in the public sector. Public sector employees' interactions with members of the public not only help the former to receive innovative ideas, but these interactions are also intrinsic rewards that can increase employee motivation and job satisfaction. Because employees with higher motivation and job satisfaction tend to work harder, employees can bring about positive organizational benefits.

Because employees care about job conditions such as involvement and satisfaction, Hackman and Oldman (1980) propose that motivation, job satisfaction, and performance can be increased depending on the skill variety, identity, responsibility, feedback, and significance of the job. Engaging with employees and members of the public can increase employees' skills, identity, feedback, responsibility, and the significance of the job. For instance, technological innovation can be developed by industry, and public employees may learn about this innovation via interacting with citizens. Similarly, a service innovation may be developed by receiving feedback from citizens. These factors affect employees' self-determination by increasing employee autonomy (e.g., the significance of job and skill variety) and bring about positive effects from a significant innovation.

Lee, Hwang, and Choi (2012, p. 148) provide an example of how citizens are sources of innovations: organizations "take advantage of a growing number of citizen networks and new types of online intermediaries (e.g., ChallengePost.com) to enhance public value. For example, the Obama administration has signaled a commitment to the Open Government Initiative, allowing members of the public to contribute ideas and expertise to government policy making." Similarly, based on a systematic literature review on crowdsourcing, Liu (2017) provides many examples of citizens directly involved in an innovation, including 311 services in the United States that allow citizens to access and provide feedback regarding local government services: including, for example, the United States government's challenge.gov initiative in which government agencies launched challenges to address problems; the Citizen Archivist where citizens can contribute archival records to the National Archives Records Administration; and eRulemaking where citizens can participate in the US government's rulemaking process.

Service Users

Not all citizens are service users, and not all service users are citizens. Particularly in this globalized world, many individuals other than citizens can also involve innovative activities directly or indirectly. Analyzing how service users impact innovation is less studied, although empirical evidence shows that service users affect innovations significantly in the private (Baldwin & Von Hippel, 2011; Svensson & Hartmann, 2018; Von Hippel, 1988) and public sector (Callens, 2023). Service users, particularly "lead users," can significantly affect innovations, such as the many technological and manufacturing products that are developed or advanced by users who are not working for these firms (Von Hippel, 1986, 2005, 2017). As Svensson and Hartmann (2018, p. 279) observe, "the most commercially attractive user innovations are developed by lead users (per definition a minority of users with strong incentives to innovate). Lead users also have the strongest needs for those innovative solutions and therefore innovate more often than users with less extreme needs."

Thus, not only are there differences between different service users (e.g., passive user vs. lead user), but lead users can also significantly impact innovations. For example, drug developments for particular illnesses or cancer are lobbied by lead users, and health innovations are pushed not only by governments but also by users. More specifically, the developments of drugs and medical treatments for AIDS were pushed by lead users and opinion leaders in the United States (Rogers, 2003). In addition, a significant number of health innovations in Europe are created and developed by users in public–private collaborations (Callens, 2023).

Smits and Kuhlmann (2004, p. 6) provide a rationale for why users represent vital innovation sources: "users will play an increasingly important role in innovation processes, the reason for this being that users want more grip on innovation processes. The producers of innovations on the other hand are interested in broad societal acceptance of innovations." Through ICT and social media, service users (e.g., citizens, residents, and tourists) can interact with government organizations more frequently, so service users can influence policies while also becoming involved in innovative activities.

Universities, Research Centers, and Federal Labs

Historically, universities invested in the creation of scientific knowledge that provided the basis for a broad range of technologies and innovations (Demircioglu & Audretsch, 2019; Nelson & Winter, 1977). There are two key outputs emanating from university research and educational investments: knowledge through research and human capital through education. As Cheah (2016) points out, universities therefore have the potential to impact innovative activity in the public sector just as it does for private firms.

With the emergence of innovation as a driving force for competitiveness in global markets, the role of the university has become more important. This is because the twin outputs accruing from universities – knowledge and human capital – are vital to innovation. During the second industrial era, which was characterized by the mass production of manufactured goods, scale and size bestowed competitive advantage; the university outputs of knowledge and human capital were not particularly relevant to enhancing scale and size in most industries, resulting in a marginalized role of universities.

However, with the advent of the third industrial area and the primacy of innovation as the driving force of global competitiveness, the university emerged as a key institution providing the coveted resources of knowledge and human capital.

Studies find that universities provide innovative ideas not just to firms in the private sector, or to rural firms (Aryal et al., 2018) and larger firms (Walsh et al., 2016), but also in the context of the public sector. In the public sector context, universities develop medical and public health innovations (Windrum, 2008). In particular, universities are vital sources for public sector innovations in Nordic countries, as close to half of their innovations come from universities (Bugge et al., 2011). Additionally, in the APS, Demircioglu and Audretsch (2019, p. 607) find that when universities are sources of innovation, it provides many benefits to public organizations: "ideas and information emanating from universities [to public organizations] are associated with larger organizational benefits, in particular increasing the quality of government products and services, employee job satisfaction, and collaboration in the public sector."

Link (2017) finds that information sources are crucial for developing new technology and innovation. He finds that in the context of the US research joint ventures (RJV), the most important innovations come from in-house R&D (53.7 percent), followed by research reported at scientific conferences (16.4 percent), a member of the RJV (10.8 percent), competitors (7.1 percent), and scientific publications (6.5 percent).

In addition to universities, many innovations are developed by innovation labs and federal labs. For example, studies find that private organizations in the United States benefit from US federal labs. There is a social gain from these technology transfers, such as customers and service users receiving high-quality products at low prices as firms produce products and services innovatively and more cheaply when US federal labs provide technologies to other organizations (Leyden & Link, 1992; Link & Scott, 2019). Moreover, the research labs of universities represent another vital innovation source. As Acs and Audretsch (2003, p. 65) observe: "The research laboratories of universities provide a source of innovation-generating knowledge that is available to private enterprises for commercial exploitation ... the knowledge created in university laboratories 'spills over' to contribute to the generation of commercial innovations by private enterprises."

More specifically, federal and national labs owned by the United States are engines for many technological and scientific innovations. Interestingly, there are more PhD holders in science at federal and national labs than at research universities in the United States. Specifically, California has nearly fifty federal labs, including the Lawrence Berkeley National Lab, the Stanford Linear Accelerator Center, the Ames Research Center, and the Jet Propulsion Laboratory. These labs not only help government organizations to become more innovative (e.g., adopting technological innovations), they also provide technology transfer and positive spillover effects to private organizations. For instance, the Department of Energy in the United States' Lab Corps Program provides entrepreneurial training for faculty, postdocs, and graduate students.

In addition to federal and national labs, there are also science, technology, and research parks. In recent years, investment and support for these parks have increased. Universities such as the National University of Singapore have established science parks and incubators while creating startups based on university-owned (or licensed) technologies. Public universities (and some private universities) also view these institutions as fostering regional economic development. Even when institutions are private, they also receive public investment; many incubators and accelerators are purely public sector institutions.

Siegel and Wright (2015) have reviewed the academic literature and find that the bulk of research focusing on technology transfer and the entrepreneurial activities of scientists have analyzed the institutional context of universities. It is important to emphasize that there are other key public institutions generating research, such as federal and national laboratories. Bozeman and Crow (1991), Crow and Bozeman (1998), and Rahm, Bozeman, and Crow (1988) have provided pioneering studies of technology transfer from national laboratories. Still, there is much to be garnered from the technology transfer efforts in particular, and knowledge spillovers more broadly, emanating from federal laboratories. Like their counterparts at universities, federal laboratories have a technology transfer mission and technology transfer offices.

The magnitude of spending on R&D at the federal laboratories should not be underestimated. For example, the forty-eight federal laboratories in California, which includes six major national labs: the Lawrence Berkeley National Lab, the Lawrence Livermore National Lab, Sandia National Labs, the Stanford Linear Accelerator Center, the Ames Research Center, and the Jet Propulsion Laboratory, expends more on R&D than do the ten regional campuses comprising the University of California system. The preponderance of spending on R&D accounted for by the public research laboratories reflects that for the entire country. For example, the US federal government provided $42 billion for research to the federal and national laboratories in 2016 but only $38 billion to US universities (Audretsch, Siegel, & Terjesen, 2020).

Investing in research is not the same as generating innovations. Rather, the gap between inputs and outputs, or between research and innovation, frustrates public policy on the one hand, while on the other its elimination holds the promise for igniting sustainable economic growth. Public policy recognizes the priority of enhancing the commercialization of research and federal laboratories. For example, in 2019 the National Institute of Standards and Technology emphasized the need to prioritize the commercialization of research emanating from federally funded research. Similarly, the former US commerce secretary, Wilbur Ross, warned that the commercialization processes and procedures prevalent at the federal laboratories are antiquated and outdated, hampering the ability of entrepreneurs and legacy companies to innovate. Similarly, the largest federal laboratories are managed by the Department of Energy. In its concern to accelerate the commercialization of research, it authorized an encompassing review of its technology transfer procedures.

We note the extent of interest from governments to enhance the commercialization of research undertaken at the national laboratories, and more generally, funded by the governments. In searching for solutions, a number of key issues are apparent. First, are the incentives at public institutions for scientists to commercialize sufficient, and if not, how can they be improved? Second, how can a culture conducive to the commercialization of research be injected into public research institutions? Third, how can the workplace be redesigned through issues, such as organizational justice, identity, role conflict, work–life balance, and championing/leadership (Balven et al., 2018) in a government lab context? These issues, which are at the heart of refocusing public management and policy to enhance the innovative activity emanating from public R&D, should fuel a new revolution in public management and policy research.

Conclusion

This chapter has identified the main sources of innovation, including the government, organizational leaders, employee work groups, industry, business stakeholders, universities, members of the public, other government organizations, nonprofits, and other stakeholders (APSC, 2011; Arundel et al., 2019; Demircioglu, 2017; Demircioglu & Audretsch, 2019; Gault, 2018). A report by the OECD (2015) argues that wicked problems or grand challenges require more collaboration with public, private, nonprofit, and academic sources. Thus, we have also explained collaborative and open sources of innovation. We have also noted two significant sources for innovation: federal/national labs and incubators/research parks. As we discuss in Chapter 10, these represent vital parts of the National Innovation System.

Sources of and actors' involvement in innovation differs depending on the context. In some contexts (a country, organization, or work group), innovations may be top down, so the government and organizational leaders are crucial sources of innovations. In other contexts, innovations may involve a more bottom-up process, so employees and members of the public provide more innovative ideas. Some agencies tend to collaborate with industry and business stakeholders, such as the Department of Science and Technology or the Department of Trade, so collaborative innovation may be more critical for these types of agencies and work groups. Although there may be a tendency to move toward collaborative innovation, top-down innovations will remain common due to differences between countries and sectors. As a policy recommendation, public sector employees, public organizations, and governments should learn from other employees, other public or private organizations, and other countries in pursuing innovation.

Perhaps one of the most salient insights garnered from real-world experiences both from the private sector and the public sector across a broad spectrum of national contexts and institutions is that many, if not most, ideas for important and even disruptive new ideas emerge in those employees and workers closest to the actual knowledge. This means that important new ideas are more likely to be generated at the lower levels of a decision-making hierarchy. For those ideas to see the light of day, managers need to relax their fears about failure and less than desirable outcomes. They also need to listen to workers and employees lower than them in the hierarchy.

Another key source of knowledge is from external organizations. The propensity to devalue and downgrade new ideas not emanating from the organization, or the "not invented here syndrome," poses a deadly impediment to innovation. To access and absorb external ideas and knowledge requires a very different culture, one that prioritizes relationships, networks, contact, and interfaces outside of the organization. It is important for employees to attend networking events, conferences, and other opportunities to learn about new ideas and thinking beyond the organization.

While open innovation is celebrated as a new paradigm, in fact, this novelty is in the realm of large and legacy organizations. Accessing and absorbing knowledge has always been the primary source of innovation for new and small organizations. The current interest in open innovation reflects the increased priority for innovation for all organizations. As the founder of Intel, Andrew Grove, called his best-selling book: *Only the Paranoid Survive*. Perhaps it might also have been aptly titled: "Only the Innovative Survive." Since knowledge that could serve as the source for potential innovations external to the firm dwarfs internal knowledge, even for the largest organizations, it is no surprise to observe an increased priority for collaboration, partnerships, and other instruments to access the wealth of external knowledge.

Although the state of research and knowledge about the sources of knowledge driving public sector innovation is in its incipiency, one finding jumps out. It may take a village to raise a child, but it takes committed partnerships and collaboration to fuel innovative activity. As public sector organizations increasingly emerge from their historical isolation, research shows that they have a unique opportunity to pay attention to both the success and failure of analogous organizations around the world.

9 | *Barriers to Public Sector Innovation*

Public versus Private?

Barriers to innovation can be defined as "obstacles or difficulties in implementing innovations that may cause organizations not to adopt or delay effective innovations" (Demircioglu, 2018, p. 1303). Barriers to innovation are not specific to public organizations. Studies report that private organizations have struggled with barriers to innovation for a long time. As early as 1965, Thompson observed that bureaucratic organizations are considered efficient but not innovative. Not only public organizations but also private organizations can be bureaucratic. He recommends that bureaucratic organizations need to be innovative to perform better. One way to make organizations more innovative is through technological changes, since technology and technological changes induce public and private organizations to be more innovative (Thompson, 1965). Similarly, private organizations also suffer from bureaucratic cultures, hierarchy, lack of management, organizational support, and encouragement, and lack of communication, as they are major barriers to innovation in private organizations (Kanter, 1983).

Additionally, according to McLean (2005, p. 238), a major organizational barrier in any organization is control, which prevents organizations from innovating and performing better:

[C]ontrol in decision making, control of information flow, or even perceived control in the form of reward systems that put too much emphasis on increasing extrinsic motivation. A culture that supports and encourages control will result in diminished creativity and innovation … [although] in stable and predictable environments, some degree of formalization and centralization of decision making might actually increase an organization's ability to implement innovations.

Furthermore, legal restrictions and government policies are not only barriers to public sector innovation but also major barriers to private

133

sector innovation. For example, Acs and Audretsch (2003, p. 67) summarize studies about German small to medium-sized enterprises that are impeded by "legal restrictions and restrictive government policies, too long of duration required to obtain government approval for a new product, and shortage of finance capital, a lack of competent employees, and too high of a risk," which are all major barriers for the private sector. Thus, factors affecting barriers to innovation in both the public and private sector resemble each other.

Two business practitioners, Loewe and Dominiquini, from an innovation firm, collected data from 550 large companies regarding innovation. They found that six barriers to innovation across all companies include: "short-term focus," "lack of time, resources or staff," "leadership expects payoff sooner than is realistic," "management incentives are not structured to reward innovation," "lack of a systematic innovation process," and "belief that innovation is inherently risky" (Loewe & Dominiquini, 2006, p. 25). Although their observation is relevant to private organizations, we believe the same barriers exist for public organizations. Sectoral differences explain how organizational structure affects barriers, yet the sector does not matter much regarding management practices. For instance, short-term focus and lack of time, resources, or staff are barriers regardless of the sector – public or private.

Several studies compare public and private organizations in terms of innovative activities. One study shows that even innovative employees in innovative public organizations reported a high level of risk-aversion, which was different in private organizations (e.g., innovative employees in innovative private organizations were risk-takers) (Sadler, 2000). According to Sadler (2000), the main reasons why even innovative public sector employees are risk aversive are that they are using public money, they are accountable to citizens and politicians who are expected to be reelected, and public organizations attract of a huge amount of media attention. Likewise, another study corroborates these findings, arguing that risk-taking is perhaps the biggest barrier in the public sector and the major difference between public and private organizations. For example, while taking risks allows private organizations to survive and prosper, there is little gain from taking risks, but they may have drastic losses if something fails after taking a risk. Additionally, public organizations have less to lose if they are not risk-takers. Thus, even innovative public sector employees are, or need to be, risk averse to some extent in order to be innovative.

To sum up, barriers to innovation exist in any organization, regardless of whether the organization is public or private. As public organizations have a high level of formalization, public scrutiny, and more control than private organizations, the former tend to have more barriers to innovation (Qiu & Chreim, 2021). However, barriers to innovation are overrated for the public sector (Hartley, Sørensen, & Torfing, 2013). There are certain characteristics (e.g., organizational structure and design) of public organizations that affect employees' and organizations' barriers to innovation, so many barriers exist due to the organizational structure and design of public organizations. The following section explores overall barriers in public organizations.

Overall Barriers in the Public Sector

As the bureaucratic structure of public organizations aims to reduce making mistakes and unethical behavior such as corruption and bribery, and they are concerned about accountability and transparency, many constraints and thus barriers exist in public organizations (Borins, 2001, 2002; Demircioglu, 2018; Rainey, 2009; Torugsa & Arundel, 2016a). Public organizations' structure and design create a risk-averse culture and thus limit experimentation and innovative leadership (Albury, 2005, 2011; Bommert, 2010; Mulgan, 2014). In addition, as the public sector does not have a clear bottom line (e.g., financial success) that measures public sector innovation and its value, public organizations do not have financial incentives to innovate. Thus, barriers to innovation in public organizations are typically unintentional yet present (Demircioglu, 2018).

Hartley, Sørensen, and Torfing (2013, p. 823) summarize this clearly:

Public organizations have no clear financial bottom line to use in measuring the value of innovation, and the public value of innovations is hard to assess. Public organizations and partnerships often lack financial incentives to innovate and are rarely allowed to keep the cost savings from innovations. Public organizations develop innovations in the presumption of openness and transparency and often with contested goals and outcomes, magnified by media interest, which has enhanced the view that public organizations are risk averse ... Finally, public organizations are governed by politicians who have to take account of multiple stakeholders in innovation while knowing that innovation failure may be exploited by the political opposition.

Likewise, Vigoda-Gadot et al. (2005) explain why and how innovation in public organizations is challenging and thus why barriers to innovation exist:

The challenge of creating successful innovation in any organization, despite and regardless of many barriers, is immense. Public organizations, where wider social considerations are also involved, face even more complex tasks. Many obstacles must be removed before a creative idea realizes its full potential ... Individuals and organizations tend to oppose rapid changes that contradict their cultural orientations. In a public sector sphere, where the tradition of past knowledge, experience, and conservative institutional solutions strongly influence managers' decisions, such a resistance to creativity and change is widespread. Beyond such cultural barriers, bureaucracies are much less amenable to transformation and to innovation due to their complicated and inflexible organizational design and increasing red tape. (Vigoda-Gadot et al., 2005, p. 61)

Cinar et al.'s (2019) systematic review shows that the most common barriers to innovation include organizational barriers (40 percent), followed by interaction-specific barriers (30 percent), perceived attributes as barriers (18 percent), and contextual barriers (12 percent). Barriers to innovation in public organizations are mainly organizational barriers or come from the bureaucracy of the organization itself, which we can call organizational barriers.

Additionally, common organizational barriers include ineffective administration, resistance or lack of support by employees, lack of available resources, and rigid organizational structure. In particular, lack of resources is a critical barrier to implementing innovations in the public sector. To support the importance of resources, Yuriev et al. (2021) shared some quotes from Canadian public sector employees. As a lucid example, a director in a large organization stated: "We don't have an excess of money in the organization, so we are extremely selective about new projects." Another employee who is a specialist argues: "Some ideas are promising, but they require solid investments. Not everyone supports sustainability efforts. How would we explain these expenses to citizens?" Another employee who is also a specialist observes: "Over the years, I've noticed that the main reason why I wasn't able to launch some projects was a lack of financial resources" (Yuriev et al., 2021, p. 14).

Second, regarding interaction-specific barriers, lack of shared understanding, collaboration, and cooperation across public, private, and nonprofit organizations along with political entities and citizens are reported as barriers. For example, lack of shared understanding, communication, networks, funding, and turf fights are major barriers across different organizations. Third, incompatibility, complexity, software problems, and inflexibility are major barriers regarding perceived attributes. Finally, regarding contextual barriers, laws and regulations are the most common barriers to innovation (Cinar et al., 2019).

Studies have explored barriers to innovation in different countries. Analyzing public sector innovations in Canada, Yuriev et al. (2021, p. 16) reaches similar conclusions that public sector–specific barriers to innovation include hierarchy, political context, legal obligations, and accountability. Regarding the hierarchy, one employee states: "Every time I suggest something, I can't get authorization to go further." Regarding political context, another employee argues: "Even now, it's difficult to implement our initiatives. What will happen if the ruling party changes?" Regarding legal obligations, another employee states: "Getting other departments to engage in new projects is challenging because the SDA [Sustainable Development Act, which was adopted in Quebec in 2006 and is still active] has many counter-intuitive requirements. So, instead of being a useful tool, it's basically a compliance checklist." Finally, regarding accountability, another employee states: "For us, the accounting and reporting is quite burdensome. We put multiple specific actions in our sustainability plan, and there's so many of them now that it's difficult to report on them." All these quotes suggest that barriers to innovation in the public sector are common.

In the context of the Netherlands, Meijer (2015) has classified barriers into two categories. The first dimension (domain) comprises government versus citizen barriers while the second dimension (types) involves structural versus cultural barriers. Regarding government barriers, these explanations – or barriers emanating from the bureaucratic structures and specific characteristics of public organizations (e.g., personnel capacity, financial, and legal structure) – are common barriers. Citizen barriers occur when citizens aim to use public services; in this regard, the digital divide and citizens' views of government can be cited as examples. Regarding citizen barriers, in many cases technological innovations are not integrated into people's lives, or public organizations fail to adopt innovations to respond to citizens' demands.

Structural barriers are related to the structures of public organizations, such as legal constraints and funding. In contrast, cultural barriers are related to organizational cultures, such as autonomy, privacy, and the values of employees and citizens. More specifically, government–structural barriers are a lack of resources, employees, skills, and political and managerial support, and legal constraints. Government–citizen barriers are a lack of technology, infrastructure, knowledge, competence, and time. Government–cultural barriers are resistance to change and the feeling that innovation reduces the quality of government. Finally, citizens–cultural barriers are citizens' lack of interest and belief in government and lack of interest in technology use (Meijer, 2015).

Analyzing barriers in Australian public organizations, Moussa (2021a) finds that the main barriers for public organizations are organizational barriers (rules and regulations as well as funds and budget), leadership characteristics, and organizational climates discouraging innovation. However, the "most noticeable barriers that hinder a culture of innovation in Australian public sector organisations involved rules and regulations and funds and budget. For example, it is found that the Australian government's capacity to enhance innovation through direct funds for encouraging innovation projects is inadequate" (Moussa, 2021a, p. 190).

Light (2014, p. 11) has analyzed forty-one government failures in the United States government, which include the 9/11 terrorist attacks, the 2008 financial collapse, Hurricane Katrina, and food safety. He finds that there are five major causes for these government failures. These are policy (e.g., the policy may be too difficult to solve or outsourced to an unreliable organization), resources (e.g., public organization may not be provided with sufficient resources, budget, staff, or technology), structure (e.g., too much hierarchy or duplication of tasks and responsibilities), leadership (e.g., unqualified top managers and poor decisions and delays for appointments due to the presidential appointment process), and culture (e.g., confusing missions and problems of performance measurement).

There are also other barriers to innovation not explored in these studies. One barrier to innovation in the public sector is the competing interests of different individuals and stakeholders, as public organizations are confronted with numerous constituents (Qiu & Chreim, 2021). Public sector innovations also challenge existing policies, practices, and strategies, as well as the interests of employees (Meijer & De Jong, 2020; Qiu & Chreim, 2021), so these can also contribute to imposing barriers to innovation in the public sector.

In addition, using insights from Boukamel and Emery (2017) and March (1991), Nowacki and Monk (2020, p. 2) argue that "[a] key obstacle to government innovation ... [is] that the bureaucracy is primarily organized for activities of 'exploitation' of existing resources and capabilities, which are often incompatible with activities of 'exploration' leading to innovative products and practices." According to them, exploration and exploitation should exist together because organizations solely focused on exploiting existing services and processes become stagnant and unable to be creative and innovative. On the other hand, organizations primarily focused on exploration and developing new services and processes often fail to benefit from their discoveries due to insufficient implementation (Nowacki & Monk, 2020). Thus, an important recommendation is to balance exploration and exploitation activities in the public sector.

Furthermore, the innovation process in public organizations is dominated by organizational leadership inside the organization, limiting the integration and collaboration of other sources, such as citizens and private organizations (Bommert, 2010). Thus, the quality and quantity of innovative ideas are limited for public sector innovations. Additionally, this closed nature of the bureaucracy of public organizations reduces transparency, communication channels, and feedback loops, thus inhibiting the implementation of innovations and the quality of innovations in public organizations (Bommert, 2010).

In sum, many barriers to innovation confront public organizations. Some of these barriers are conflicts among employees, work groups, units, or organizations; opposition from employees, middle managers, or top managers; lack of resources (e.g., budget restrictions) and funding; lack of sufficient employees or skillful employees; lack of coordination, cooperation, and collaboration across individuals, teams, and organizations; lack of technology; and lack of effective leadership (Borins, 2001; Cinar et al., 2019; Torugsa & Arundel, 2016a). We can classify these barriers as bureaucratic (i.e., bureaucratic attitudes, turf fights, and staff and management resistance), internal (i.e., logistics and coordination problems, technology, and union opposition), political (i.e., lack of resources, too many regulations, and political opposition), and external (i.e., public opposition and private sector competition) (Borins, 2001). The following section classifies some of these critical barriers according to the level of analysis.

Barriers to Innovation and Levels of Analysis

We can analyze barriers to innovation from two angles. The first is whether barriers are related to inputs (or independent variables) or outputs (or dependent variables). The second is from the level of analysis. If we consider barriers as inputs, or independent variables, then we are interested in the outcomes of barriers. For example, how barriers to innovation impact innovation, performance, employee job satisfaction, motivation, and turnover intention have emerged as key priorities in scholarly literature. However, if we consider barriers to innovation as endogenously determined (e.g., as outputs or outcomes, or simply a dependent variable), then we are interested in why there are more or lower barriers to innovation in specific organizations. For example, researchers and practitioners may be interested in why employees in a certain agency (organizational level) or working with certain organizational leaders (individual level) report more barriers than others. Perhaps the reason would be based on individual, group, and organizational factors. Thus, our second angle – the levels of analysis – will help us to explore barriers to innovation in the public sector in a more systematic way. As we demonstrated in Chapter 7, some specific conditions for innovation can be analyzed based on different levels of analysis (see Figure 7.1).

As seen in Figure 7.1, the opposite or lack of conditions conducive to innovation could be interpreted as reflecting high barriers to innovation. For example, while ability, motivation, experimentation, dealing with low performers, feedback loops, and motivation to improve performance can increase innovations in public and private organizations, lack of the same factors or conditions may lead to barriers to innovation and thus impair the implementation of innovations. Similarly, while employees' creativity and innovative behavior, group cooperation, leadership quality of the teams and organizations, an innovation climate, collaboration, and working in a complex environment increase innovation, a lack of the same factors (e.g., lack of employees' creativity) could lead to barriers to innovation. However,

Vigoda-Gadot et al. (2005) observe that many employees in many public organizations produce creative ideas, but most of these ideas are never implemented, so a major problem in the public sector is not creativity but implementation (Vigoda-Gadot et al., 2005).

Many public sector employees are still not creative, which could stifle innovations. Thus, we can analyze barriers to innovation based on different levels of analysis. In particular, national, organizational, and individual levels are more relevant and common. For example, Chapter 10 explains barriers at the national level. Barriers at the national level may exist due to too much regulation, lack of national resources and infrastructures, the quality of institutions, lack of existing rule of law, lack of high-quality research centers and universities, and so on. For example, regulations become barriers to innovation because they "protect boundaries and turf and keep out competition ... [and] can provide a false sense of control in the sense that every possible scenario or option has been anticipated even if implementation is unworkable or the regulation too complex to follow as a result" (OECD, 2017, p. 42).

Barriers at the organizational level may exist due to budget limitations and leadership. Barriers at the group level may exist due to a lack of cooperation among group members. Finally, barriers at the individual level may exist due to a lack of employee creativity or employees' inability to innovate (e.g., they did not receive sufficient training to generate and evaluate innovative ideas). Table 9.1 demonstrates how barriers can be matched with the level of analysis, reasons, and potential remedies.

The most studied barriers to innovation are those at the organizational level. In fact, different surveys have been designed and conducted to measure barriers to innovation in organizations although individuals (employees and managers) fill out these surveys. For example, the APSC (2011, p. 114) has identified the following organizational barriers to implementing innovations in workplaces:

- unwillingness of managers to take risks;
- resistance to change by managers;
- employees believe that their ideas are not seriously considered by managers;
- budget restrictions;
- political uncertainty, such as frequent changes of ministers or government;

Table 9.1 *Barriers to innovation and levels of analysis*

Unit of analysis	Reasons	Potential remedies
National	Lack of state capacity	Increasing human capital, economy, investment, foreign direct investment (FDI), state capacity
Organizational	Financial	Providing resources, financing projects, encouraging interagency collaboration, selecting entrepreneurial leaders and training them
Individual	Lack of creativity	Increasing creativity, providing training for employees, encouraging collaboration

- lack of incentives;
- technological barriers.

Similarly, the European Commission (2011) has identified the following barriers to innovation in public organizations:

- lack of management support;
- lack of incentives for employees;
- staff resistance;
- uncertain acceptance by the users of public services;
- regulatory requirements;
- lack of sufficient human or financial resources;
- risk-averse culture in organizations.

These barriers to innovation are common in the context of public organizations. They can also affect other levels. For example, a lack of management support and regulatory requirements may reduce employees' creativity and innovative behavior (individual level). Some existing barriers to innovation can also be related to other existing barriers. For example, technological barriers may exist due to budget restrictions and a lack of management support. Likewise, regulatory requirements affect the lack of incentives. Likewise, lack of sufficient human or financial resources also affects staff resistance. Therefore, studies may analyze interlinkages among different barriers as well as how barriers exist at different levels of analysis.

Deterring versus Revealed Barriers

A significant development in the study of barriers to innovation is D'Este et al.'s (2008, 2012) pioneering study (deterring versus revealed barriers) and its adaptation to public sector settings. As has been argued, "public innovation research has tended to focus on the negative side of barriers; only recently has some attention been given to the positive effects of barriers" (Qiu & Chreim, 2021, p. 15). In fact, a systematic literature review finds that barriers to innovation are not necessarily negatively associated with innovation (Cinar et al., 2019; Demircioglu & Audretsch, 2017; Torugsa & Arundel, 2016a). These studies argue and find evidence that barriers are not only different, but that some barriers (i.e., revealed barriers) may even have positive effects on innovation, as we explain later. According to these studies, two distinct types of barriers are deterring and revealed barriers (D'este et al., 2008, 2012).

"Deterring barriers" are barriers that block or prevent organizations from undergoing innovation. "Revealed barriers," however, are barriers that increase awareness of the factors constraining innovative activities. As D'Este et al. (2012, p. 482) observed, while the former are seen by organizations "as being unsurmountable," the latter can be considered an organization's "awareness of the difficulties involved as a result of engagement in innovation activities." In other words, while the former seem negative because these barriers can block innovations, the latter seem positive because they increase awareness of innovation and innovative employees are the ones who can identify these barriers. Thus, innovative organizations discover revealed barriers and analyze how to reduce them, as argued by public sector innovation scholarship (Demircioglu & Audretsch, 2017; Torugsa & Arundel, 2016a).

For example, one study claims that "financial constraints have often been cited as an important barrier for public innovation … While constraints are often perceived as limiting factors, they can also enable creativity (e.g., financial constraints act as incentives for people to innovate)" (Qiu & Chreim, 2021, p. 17). This suggests that the same idea, resource, or constraint could either enable or disable innovation. A qualitative study finds that budgets are typically not barriers to innovation in Australian public organizations (Moussa, 2021b).

We believe that these findings about the effects of budget and resources on innovation are not surprising, as studies have conflicting findings (as discussed in Chapter 7). Perhaps one reason why the same factor (e.g., resources) can increase or decrease innovation would be the importance of context, leadership, and employee ability and motivation. Regarding context, the legal system, state structure (e.g., federal vs. unitary government), and administrative culture impact innovations and barriers to innovation (OECD, 2017; Pollitt & Bouckaert, 2011). For instance, common law countries (e.g., the UK and Australia) tend to be more innovative than civil law systems (e.g., France and Germany) because while the former focus on what is prohibited and allow creativity for nonprohibited aspects, the latter focus on rules. Since public sector employees are already expected to follow rules and what is expected from them has already been written into law, this may reduce employee motivation to be innovative.

As a policy recommendation, D'Este et al. (2012, p. 487) suggest that policymakers focus on minimizing the effects of revealed barriers. Working with these barriers encourages positive learning and changing the culture to embrace an innovative culture, as not all innovations are successful. Innovators – both organizations and individuals – aim to find solutions and creative ideas in response to these barriers and learn to innovate more effectively, so these barriers can bring opportunities to organizations and employees, especially to particularly innovative employees (Borins, 2014; Cinar et al., 2021). In other words, innovative employees are the ones who can identify the barriers, so they can understand the process of both innovation and its barriers. In other words, it is not surprising that research finds a strong and positive correlation between barriers to innovation and the implementation of innovation. For example, empirical findings by Torugsa and Arundel (2016a, p. 410) demonstrate that barriers to innovation do not reduce the benefits of innovations, suggesting that "employees are able to control, manage and overcome these barriers … [E]mployees reporting several types of barriers are highly motivated and creative. These characteristics could enable them to find means of overcoming barriers to complex innovations and to ensure that these innovations produce large benefits." These findings are consistent with a qualitative study analyzing innovative activities and barriers to innovation in Japan, Italy, and Turkey by Cinar et al. (2021) that finds that barriers provide opportunities for organizational learning and develop innovations further while also increasing individuals' and leaders' determination to succeed and better manage the innovation process.

In sum, in many cases, barriers to innovation can be positive as they can bring about opportunities to develop innovations (Qiu & Chreim, 2021) and lead to greater awareness of innovations. We believe that more studies are needed to unlock the effects of barriers as well as under what circumstances the same barriers could deter innovations (i.e., block) and reveal innovations (i.e., awareness). For example, as mentioned in Chapter 7, there are certain conditions for innovations. One condition with mixed results was budget constraints (Demircioglu & Audretsch, 2017). Budget and resource limitations can block innovation because some innovations require budgets and resources, as seen with technological innovations such as the creation of the picture phone in the United States in the 1960s (Gertner, 2012) and mission innovations such as the moon mission (Kattel & Mazzucato, 2018). However, the same concept, budget, resources, and constraints can help organizations and leaders to be more creative and innovative in different situations. Thus, studies may look at other conditions. Understanding the barriers to innovation is critical. At the same time, organizational managers and policymakers should aim to reduce barriers to innovation if they are deterrents. Although barriers to innovation may be helpful as they can increase awareness of the innovation process, most of them are harmful. Thus, policymakers should aim to minimize barriers to innovation because doing so can enhance innovative activity.

Reducing Barriers to Innovation

We understand that different types of barriers exist in public organizations, that barriers exist at different levels, and that not all barriers are negative. Still, a vital and practical question is how to reduce barriers to innovation. Studies suggest that fixing and framing are two strategies for reducing barriers (Cinar et al., 2021; Meijer, 2015). In order to fix structural barriers, organizations can create prizes for innovative ideas (see also Berman & Kim, 2010), modify innovations, find resources to develop innovations, and receive support from other actors such as collaborators. In order to frame cultural barriers (e.g., overcome resistance through persuasion and motivation), organizations should create incentives for experimentation (see Demircioglu & Audretsch, 2017), consulting and providing training to employees, and building political and stakeholder support (Cinar et al., 2021; Meijer, 2015).

In this regard, Demircioglu (2018, p. 1304) argues that "although innovations are intentional actions, barriers to innovation are typically not intentional but present. However, organizational leaders and managers in public organizations have power and incentives to reduce barriers to innovation." A vital question, then, is how to reduce those barriers, especially when they are deterring barriers. Different governments have different abilities, capabilities, capacities, and motivations. At the national level, governments can make sure to allocate sufficient resources to agencies and encourage public organizations to hire more talented and highly motivated employees. While doing so, governments can change some regulatory practices and policies if they are not up to date. Governments can also encourage entrepreneurship in public organizations and public sector employees, particularly managers, while encouraging proactiveness, creativity, innovativeness, and risk-taking.

To reduce barriers, identifying problems and generating ideas to solve these problems are crucial (OECD, 2017). Public organizations can also use social media and other technologies to engage with citizens (Gintova, 2019). Governments can allocate sufficient resources for technologies or develop innovations, address cultural and organizational factors, and measure results through tools such as satisfaction surveys of service users or citizens (Gintova, 2019). Governments must also find innovative ways to respond to citizens' changing expectations and needs.

In addition, modifying innovations to fit into a particular context and providing training can reduce barriers to innovation (Cinar et al., 2021). The importance of leadership is vital to reducing barriers and increasing innovation in the public sector. As Loewe and Dominiquini (2006, p. 26) observe: "Without this leadership, innovation efforts are doomed to fail." Encouraging risk-taking and changing the organizational culture can also reduce barriers (Stewart-Weeks & Kastelle, 2015). Additionally, challenging existing rules can reduce barriers: "The permission to question rules and, if they are considered a true obstacle, to challenge them, is a rule that itself nurtures an innovation culture and mindset" (OECD, 2017, p. 42).

Furthermore, the media and opposition parties commonly highlight unsuccessful innovations or failures (Bloch & Bugge, 2013). Thus, because public sector leaders and employees may wish to avoid media scrutiny, governments aim not to fail, which means that public organizations may hesitate to implement innovations. Thus, politicians and policymakers can engage media and opposition groups, build trust, and admit that there is always a possibility that some innovations may not be successful. Still, if governments stop innovating and taking risks, it will only lead to more negative outcomes. Demircioglu and Vivona (2021, p. 10) suggested the following strategy: "the media's role is not only crucial but also that policymakers should communicate with the media. Nevertheless … the media was not considered as a potential partner with whom enhanced communication would be desirable … public sector innovators respond more directly to these negative perceptions and actively involve the media in councils and forums." Thus, while communicating with the media regularly, public organizations can also build an effective marketing team and respond to concerns from the media or opposition groups.

In sum, leadership and management matter most to reduce barriers to innovation. Resistance to innovation by some employees is a natural part of innovations, so managers should aim to win the hearts and minds of employees, build alliances, get political support, consult with affected parties, and be open and clear about the benefits of programs (Borins, 2001; Cinar et al., 2019; Osborne & Gaebler, 1992; Osborne & Plastrik, 1997). Additionally, managers and organizational leaders should recognize and overcome problems sooner rather than later.

Conclusion

Barriers to innovation are both complex and dynamic, suggesting that there are variations across innovative processes, interrelationships across different actors, and contexts and time pressures that affect the process of barriers to innovation (Cinar et al., 2021). For instance, as demonstrated by Cinar et al. (2021), a particular barrier in one stage may cause further barriers in future stages, as they are interrelated. Thus, reducing the barriers to innovation is not an easy task. However, contrary to some early conceptualizations that public organizations suffer from too many barriers, this chapter has found evidence that despite certain barriers, public organizations are still innovative. As Hartley, Sorenson, and Torfing (2013, p. 823) find: "The barriers to public sector innovation have been overplayed." We agree with this statement.

What matters most in studies of organizational behavior is to understand and manage the workforce (Denhardt et al., 2015; Word &

Sowa, 2017). For example, organizational leaders should not aim to entirely eliminate conflict among work groups or team members but to make the workforce more collaborative and cooperative. The same logic applies here. Organizational leaders should focus on understanding the causes of barriers to innovation instead of focusing on eliminating barriers immediately: "If government innovation is indeed held back by unnecessary constraints, it is important to better understand how, why and to what extent that happens, and to find out what can be done about it" (OECD, 2017, p. 28). As mentioned earlier, employees and managers who identify barriers are the ones who are innovative. Thus, organizational leaders and managers should discuss barriers with employees as well as how to overcome them.

Although studies of barriers to innovation focus primarily on structural barriers, less attention is paid to employee engagement (Knox & Marin-Cadavid, 2022) and other behavioral factors such as employees' lack of commitment to organizations. As some frontline employees, middle managers, and top executives drive innovations (Borins, 2001, 2014; Demircioglu & van der Wal, 2022; Hartley, 2005), low levels of employee engagement can undermine innovative activities (Knox & Marin-Cadavid, 2022). It is vital to analyze how employees, regardless of their rank, impact both innovations and barriers to innovation.

10 | *National Systems of Innovation and Market and Government Failure*

Market Failure

Market failure exists when markets fail to implement efficient, just, and effective policies and solutions to problems, or to deliver products or services (Howlett & Ramesh, 2014). According to welfare economists, although the market is the more efficient process, it does not always work well (Howlett et al., 2009). For instance, without government control and intervention, private organizations consider their own interests rather than society's interests, leading to market failures (Leyden & Link, 1992). Examples of market failures are monopolies, externalities such as pollution, information asymmetries, destructive competition, the tragedy of the commons, and credible commitments (Howlett & Ramesh, 2014; Howlett et al., 2009; Leyden & Link, 1992).

Market imperfections or imperfect information in the market is a natural shortage rooted in market mechanisms. There are several reasons for market imperfections, such as "loss of economic efficiency due to classic market failures," "lack of mechanisms to pursue goals other than efficiency," "market power," "transaction costs," "public distrust toward profit motive in essential services," and "bounded rationality" (Wu & Ramesh, 2014, pp. 307–308). For markets to work efficiently and effectively, actors must have close to perfect information. For instance, buyers need to understand and evaluate quickly the products and services they are purchasing. However, definitions of innovation include taking risks and being proactive. Thus, any daily transaction activities among public and private actors and citizens include risks and thus innovations (Peters, 2015). In other words, naturally, there may be market failures involved in daily activities, let alone innovations. An example of market failure includes environmental regulations, which force private organizations such as factories to reduce and internalize costs (i.e., pollution) (Lim & Prakash, 2014).

In the absence of such government policies, pollution would reflect a failure of the market to internalize negative production externalities.

The literature of market failures demonstrates that the pursuit of private interests causes inefficient outcomes (e.g., natural monopoly, externalities, and information asymmetry), particularly in delivering public goods (Weimer & Vining, 2005; Wu & Ramesh, 2014). In pursuing innovation, markets underinvest in knowledge production and R&D (Leyden & Link, 1992). As Leyden and Link (1992, p. 2) conclude, "[t]he cost of inadequate investments in innovation is particularly high in today's globally-competitive environment where continued technological advancements are critical to sustaining, if not advancing, the economic prosperity of [nations, including the US]."

Government Failure

Government failure occurs when governments do not adopt efficient and effective solutions to problems (Howlett & Ramesh, 2014). When government failure exists, the government cannot improve the market. Examples of government failures include information gaps, lack of incentives, principal–agent problems, rising costs, and political interference (Howlett & Ramesh, 2014; Howlett et al., 2009). Compared to market failures, government failures are less well analyzed and tested (Wu & Ramesh, 2014).

When market failures exist (such as economic imperfections in capital markets), governments aim to correct the market – for example, by providing finance to some firms affected by the imperfections (Hyytinen & Toivanen, 2005). In other words, market failure is a primary motivation for the government to enter the market, particularly regarding innovation (Noble et al., 2019). For instance, one study in Finland demonstrates that government funding reduces market imperfections, suggesting that financing private organizations and R&D are vital instruments for innovation policies (Hyytinen & Toivanen, 2005). As these private organizations do not have much incentive to correct market failures, governments regulate the market – for example, by regulating the pollution level. However, not all regulations are the same. Suppose the regulation is solely based on command and control. In that case, the policy leads to inefficiencies and less innovation because it is expected that the firms simply comply with the regulations dictated by the government. Additionally, private organizations that have invested in certain technologies have little incentive to innovate due to technology-forcing aspects (Lim & Prakash, 2014), providing another rationale for government intervention.

Government imperfections or imperfect information is a natural shortage rooted in government operations. There are several reasons for government imperfections, such as "limited capability in accessing necessary information," "principal agent problems," "power of organized interests," "administrative costs," "strategic responses," "lack of competition," and "financial sustainability (e.g., many forms of government intervention – such as subsidies, grants, or public provisions – require budget outlay from the government, but their financial sustainability cannot be taken for granted)" (Wu & Ramesh, 2014, pp. 307–308). Thus, government imperfections exist on many levels that affect innovation: an innovation project (e.g., innovation lab) may be discontinued when it does not receive financial support (financial sustainability), the ruling political party or its preference has changed (power of organized interest), or it becomes too costly (administrative costs). For instance, "to address equity and efficiency in the provision of social goods, it may be necessary to undertake social regulation design that would impose certain choices on consumers, especially where governments believe that the consumption is sub-optimal" (Chindarkar et al., 2017, p. 8).

In sum, market failure is the primary rationale for government intervention to choose a policy tool to solve the market failure (Kleiman & Teles, 2008). However, government intervention in the market may lead to government failures. Thus, market and government failure are highly related to and affect one another.

Market Failure, Government Failure, and Innovation

In their pioneering research on artificial intelligence (AI), Acemoglu and Restrepo (2020) offer reasons for market failures in innovation. First, innovation creates externalities and spillover effects, but markets are inefficient in dealing with externalities. Second, markets prefer one paradigm (e.g., a popular one) over others even though other paradigms could be more efficient and effective. Third, historically, governments (particularly the US government) have used PPPs and collaboration across sectors for better outcomes leading to innovations in technology, pharmaceuticals, and medicine. However, in recent years, the US government has started cutting budgets for R&D while the private sector has become more dominant in the economy, particularly in high-technology fields. This reduction of budget discourages innovation related to social and environmental issues such as employment opportunities and sustainability initiatives. Fourth, there is a strong bias in industry, the private sector, and even some universities and research centers that focus on one narrow definition of innovation, which is the Silicon Valley model. This model rewards the development of high-tech products and automation but less so other innovations, including frontier and basic technologies. This is unfortunate because innovation should not focus solely on economic benefits. Fifth, the social value of innovation is typically overlooked. Sixth, as tax policies in Western countries tax employment, technological innovations such as AI make organizations more profitable. Likewise, as labor is costly, private organizations aim to implement technologies such as AI beyond the optimal level, leading to further market failures (Acemoglu & Restrepo, 2020).

Governments use several measures such as tools (e.g., R&D support and tax incentives or increases) to reduce the uncertainty linked to innovation, and governments encourage (e.g., via lowering risks) the private sector to develop innovations (e.g., process and service) (Noble et al., 2019). However, well-intended policies that are not well thought out and well designed create more problems than benefits. This is particularly relevant in welfare states such as western European nations and the Nordic countries where governments are bigger and government funding is the norm (Hyytinen & Toivanen, 2005). However, as suggested, we should "not overlook the risk that government funding may end up crowding out potentially profitable businesses of private financiers, distorting the private sector's investment incentives and even sustaining socially wasteful business activity" (Hyytinen & Toivanen, 2005, p. 1402).

Additionally, the application of innovative HR practices such as meritocracy matter for market and government failures. For example, high-quality governments prioritize the rule of law, professional bureaucracy, political neutrality, and principles based on meritocracy (Evans & Rauch, 1999; Jia et al., 2019; Rauch & Evans, 2000; Suzuki & Demircioglu, 2019). In these contexts, we observe less government failure because governments tend to operate more efficiently and effectively as they are run by capable employees. For low-quality governments, Jia et al. (2019, p. 225) observe that "government officials are generally held less accountable for advancing the state's interests." Hence, public sector employees "shirk their responsibilities" and do not care much about their work, the value of their organizations, or serving citizens. Thus, in low-quality governments, such as countries with less meritocracy, government failures could be the norm rather than the exception.

Overall, there is a positive and strong correlation between meritocratic recruitment and country growth (Evans & Rauch, 1999; Rauch & Evans, 2000), suggesting that meritocracy can reduce government failure because the government will operate more efficiently and effectively under a meritocratic system. However, too much focus on meritocracy may cause elitism and a lack of compassion while providing services and dealing with citizens (Suzuki & Demircioglu, 2021; Tan, 2008), suggesting that it may also lead to government failures.

To correct both market and government imperfections, Wu and Ramesh (2014) suggest using policy mixes (e.g., using multiple tools or instruments). Their rationale is the following:

Any single policy instrument aimed at addressing either market or government imperfections will inadvertently and inevitably induce the effects and the imperfections of the other. For example, the presence of natural monopoly (resulting from market imperfections) necessitates regulation, which is potentially subject to several government imperfections, such as information asymmetry and rent-seeking behavior on the part of producers. The inherent government imperfections, in turn, call for use of measures such as competitive bidding and yardstick competition to offset the government's shortcomings. Policy mixes consisting of regulation, competiveness bidding, and yardstick competition are thus necessary to correct the duality problem in monopoly sectors. In addition to addressing concerns over the duality between market and government imperfections, the design of policy mixes may also include consideration of how to take advantage of the strengths of both market and government. The strengths of the market may include the following: (1) efficiency gains from competition, (2) freedom of choices for consumers, (3) faster responses to changing circumstances, and (4) financial sustainability in service provision. Strengths of the government include the following: (1) economy of scale at the societal level, (2) pursuit of goals other than economic efficiency, (3) quick and sure change due to the use of coercive power, (4) the ability to alter incentive structures, and (5) accountability to a public majority in some cases. These strengths of market and government mechanisms provide another compelling reason for the use of multiple policy instruments, that is, policy mixes, as a policy response to the duality between market and government imperfections. Policy instruments based on the strengths of the market can be combined with those based on the strengths of the government to benefit from both while also minimizing their respective disadvantages. Because market mechanisms are employed to deal with government failures, and government intervention is used to reduce the impacts of the market failures, it is possible simultaneously to take advantage of both. (Wu & Ramesh, 2014, p. 309)

Additionally, to reduce market failure, governments (and particularly entrepreneurial states) should become more active in the economy by changing government policies, using government money for research, creating opportunities for employment, and commercializing products and services developed or supported by the government (Mazzucato, 2015, 2016). In other words, "the entrepreneurial state shifts the locus of that entrepreneurial decision to the state" (Audretsch & Fiedler, 2022, p. 2).

To further support her claim, Mazzucato (2016) states:

In the few countries that have achieved innovation-led smart growth – like the U.S., Israel, Denmark, and even China today – public actors have not just enabled the private sector. They have actively taken risks as an investor of first resort, not just a lender of last resort. In Silicon Valley, what was critical was the decentralized network of intelligent public organizations that facilitated feedback loops throughout the whole innovation chain. This includes basic research, applied research, and downstream patient and strategic long-term finance to companies. It also includes policies that directly and indirectly shaped demand for new goods and services. Contrary to the dominant view that policy is meant to simply "fix" market failures, public agencies like DARPA [Defense Advanced Research Projects Agency] and SBIR [Small Business Innovation Research] in the U.S., Yozma in Israel, and Sitra and Tekes in Finland have actively shaped and created markets. These kinds of direct investments are more successful at generating new private investment than the same money spent through indirect measures like tax credits. This approach means going beyond leveling the playing field, and instead actively tilting it in a particular direction. That doesn't mean betting on single technologies (all eggs in one basket), but rather backing a portfolio of different technologies (driven by problems to solve) that are encompassed under a mission (the big problem). The usual critique that governments cannot pick winners ignores the fact that the internet was picked through such mission-oriented investments, as were nearly all the technologies in the iPhone (including GPS [Global Positioning System], Siri, and touchscreen).

And in the energy sector, solar, nuclear, wind, and even shale gas, were primed by public finance. Elon Musk's three companies Solar City, Tesla, and Space X have received over $4.9 billion in public support. Sometimes these investments succeed (Tesla), sometimes they fail (Solyndra) – but any venture capitalist will tell you this is normal.

Likewise, as new startups lead to innovation, employment, and economic growth, many countries around the world support the creation of startups (Audretsch, Colombelli, et al., 2020). Government support for these innovative startups and new companies can also reduce market failure. There are also other strategies to reduce market failure. For instance, if used smartly, public procurement can reduce market failure, such as correcting information asymmetries (Edler & Georghiou, 2007) while providing other benefits, such as increasing innovations in public organizations (Demircioglu & Vivona, 2021). For instance, Edler and Georghiou (2007, p. 956) argue that public procurement (i.e., demand) can positively impact innovation because "the concrete state demand for innovations leads not only to technological capacities, but at the same time to increased production capacities for innovations."

Imperfect information means that not all of the organizations, firms, and individuals in society possess the complete set of information about all of the possible situations and scenarios that potentially could arise. Imperfect information characterizes the typical purchasing context by organizations, where they are not in possession of the complete set of facts and experiences about the entire set of products and services that they could potentially purchase. Market information about purchasing inputs in the production process led to the now famous industry-wide mantra guiding the purchasing decision of organizations for decades: "Nobody ever got fired for purchasing IBM." The power of this now famous mantra lies in the recognition that all purchasing agents and departments are confronted by a daunting degree of imperfect information, rendering it difficult and costly to identify which products and services should be purchased and which should be eschewed. The cost of identifying the pros and cons associated with each of the thousands of products and services purchased by even a small organization was sufficiently prohibitive that the solution for generations of purchasing departments and agents in countless organizations was simply to go with the tried and the true: IBM.

As if imperfect information in markets was not daunting enough, when it comes to the decision to pursue and invest resources in a particular innovation, an organization is always confronted by the hyper-uncertainty, high degree of asymmetry, and prohibitively expensive cost of transactions inherent in innovative activity. As Arrow (1962) pointed out, inherent in the concept of a significantly new product or service are the twin conditions of not being certain whether it can actually be produced and delivered and to what extent demand actually exists. Not only is the outcome associated with innovation inherently uncertain, in terms of both production and demand, but the valuation of the outcome varies dramatically across organizations and agents within each organization. What is deemed to be potentially valuable by one manager may be deemed as a waste of resources by her colleague or superior. The cost of transacting the knowledge underlying the valuation of a potential innovation can be prohibitive given the high degree of tacitness inherent in that knowledge. Such tacit knowledge typically draws on experience and intuition, which reflects the uniqueness not just of the experience set of each individual but ultimately of the individuals themselves.

Thus, while governments can do little to reduce the uncertainty inherent in knowledge, the opposite holds when it comes to information. In fact, an important role for government policy (and government's role for innovation) is to reduce information gaps by providing key and value guidance to consumers of products and services, thereby reducing the high cost of obtaining information. This is just as true for purchasing agents and departments within organizations as it is for consumers (Edler & Georghiou, 2007).

Another example of how governments can reduce market failure comes from Singapore. As Han (2019) explains, building green buildings is a low saliency issue (e.g., they are not easy to distinguish from traditional buildings, and the environmental harm caused by traditional buildings, such as air pollution [externality problem]). Since stakeholders such as owners or potential owners of buildings may not have access to knowledge, they may not be willing to access the relevant information and take action. Even if they are willing to take action, other firms may not want to take similar actions (the free rider problem). Thus, these factors result in market failures. In the Singapore case, for instance, the government led the green urbanization of environmentally friendly buildings while collaborating with other actors (Han, 2019). In other words, the government's involvement in this market has reduced market failure.

However, as governments attempt to reduce market failures, they may inadvertently cause government failures. For instance, analyzing public policies in Singapore, Audretsch and Fiedler (2022) find that economic and innovation policies that center on the government instead of private organizations crowd out individual entrepreneurship. For example, capital accumulation dramatically increases economic growth, but this growth is unevenly distributed such that smaller companies not linked with the government cannot compete with government-led corporations or government-supported firms. Thus, many private companies do not have any incentive to be innovative. Additionally, knowledge accumulation discourages risky behavior and thus discourages innovation by government-supported firms and government-led corporations.

Furthermore, human capital accumulation in public organizations (e.g., hiring talented, entrepreneurial, intelligent, hardworking individuals to government positions) crowd out opportunities for other entrepreneurs, so the country remains dependent on foreign employees. Thus, the authors conclude, "even the outstanding success of Singapore as part of the East Asian growth miracle has resulted in worrisome barriers impeding the transition to an entrepreneurial society" (Audretsch & Fiedler, 2022, p. 14). In other words, although the Singapore government's innovation policies and economic strategies have not induced dramatic government failures, they have at least led to a lack of efficiency.

Likewise, although providing incentives enhances innovation, it may create market failures for several reasons. Since innovation is complex, risky, and involves uncertainty, organizations or innovators may fail to execute innovations. Additionally, due to information asymmetry, organizations or innovators will not know all the necessary information in advance (Jia et al., 2019). Thus, the conditions for innovation that we discussed in Chapter 7 (such as providing incentives and encouraging experimentation) may not always work. In this regard, developing innovations and building innovation capacities are complicated and subject to many limitations, which may lead to both market and government failures. For example, private and public sector employees may be incapable or not diligent. When employees in private organizations hide information, they are less efficient, less capable, and more corrupt, leading to market failures (as we have seen with the company Enron). Still, the Enron example reflects moral failure. It is important to note that market failure by private companies reflects the inability of markets to provide the correct allocation of goods and services at the least expensive cost to the public. Market failure is the result of market power, externalities, and the public good nature of certain goods and services. All of these sources lead to lower market outcomes compared to those that would maximize the utility of consumers by aligning their demand with the true costs of production.

However, when public organizations or employees are less efficient, less capable, or more corrupt, we observe government failure, which may cause more extensive problems such as undermining trust and institutions. Government failure occurs when it fails to provide public goods and services that are valued by the public. That is, the public would be willing to incur the costs incurred through the provision of those goods and services, but imperfections impede the government from actually providing those goods and services.

Critics of Market and Government Failure: Research and Practice

We believe that there are certain limitations to the concepts of both market and government failures as they are related to innovation. First, in addition to market and government failures, other types of failures are not analyzed but are still important. One failure is a network failure, which could occur when "networks are weak and may be difficult to establish, be they corporatist or otherwise in nature" (Howlett & Ramesh, 2014, p. 320). Another failure is a social failure:

Failures in society that may necessitate the intervention of the public sector are not so readily classifiable as those in the economy, but they are nonetheless real. Issues such as crime, poverty, family breakdowns, school dropouts may have some economic element, but they also have a strong social and cultural component. And the absence of clear categories, such as those in economics, make these issues all the more difficult to address through public sector action. (Peters, 2015, p. 15)

How can policymakers reduce all these failures: market, government, network, and social? We believe that innovation and innovative activities such as innovative leadership in public organizations can solve not only market and government failures but also network and social failures. Additionally, the existence of an innovation climate, such as supportive leadership and criteria to evaluate new ideas in organizations (Demircioglu, 2019; Demircioglu & Berman, 2019), can reduce all types of failures.

The second limitation we observe in studies is that there is no clear norm or practice to determine the feature and extent of market and government failure. In other words, there are no objective criteria to calculate or measure market and government failures, suggesting that scholars and practitioners may disagree on which policy leads to market or government failures. This issue is particularly relevant and important because the effects of any policy (e.g., innovation policy) may differ based on short- and long-term perspectives. For instance, changing some rules and regulations may bring about short-term losses, but these same new policies could improve the quality of institutions and thus may positively impact society and the economy in the long term.

The third limitation is that, as mentioned in Chapter 4, the success of innovations, markets, and governments is also context dependent. For instance, the same innovation tool (e.g., R&D support) may induce market or government failure in one context but not in others. Likewise, the same innovation tool may cause market or government failure in one year but not in other years. For example, Keynesian economic policies focusing on bigger government worked well after the Second World War but not in the 1980s. Likewise, NPM reforms focusing on businesslike government worked relatively well in some contexts in the 1980s but not in the 2000s.

The fourth limitation is that market and government failure focus predominantly on efficiency criteria, overlooking other criteria such as effectiveness, equity, and justice (Wu & Ramesh, 2014). Thus, policymakers and academics must provide and analyze a more holistic understanding of market and government failure as some innovations have effects (such as increasing equity) other than increasing efficiency.

The fifth limitation is the notion that market and government failures are always negative. Although government regulations may cause government failure, they can still bring benefits to public and private organizations through innovations. For instance, according to Lim and Prakash (2014, p. 235), although regulations may increase government failures, they can also increase innovation with two mechanisms:

(1) economic and (2) organizational politics. Regarding the former: "Regulations such as recycling laws may involve more complex issues, forcing firms to innovate to reuse their materials or use less of disposable components. Regulations may also touch on truly complex issues, which require fundamentally reformulating products or reengineering production processes to remove, say, toxic components are two mechanisms induce innovations." Regarding the latter: "Regulatory pressure can encourage firms to examine their internal operations and seek ways to work more efficiently, just as external competition and consumer and stakeholder pressure do." Thus, government intervention to correct market failure does not always lead to major market or government failure; on the contrary, it could lead to further innovations. Additionally, in many cases, government intervention to correct market failure works well. For instance, one study finds that funding from the government to the market reduces market imperfections, and financing business R&D can be a vital policy tool for innovation (Hyytinen & Toivanen, 2005).

Related to the previous point, two additional points deserve discussion. Not all market and government failures are the same or have the same effect. In other words, some market or government failures may have more negative effects than others. Thus, studies should differentiate between the level and the intensity of market and government failures. Additionally, a minor level of market or government failure may help to avoid a larger or more significant level. For example, one output of government failure is rising costs, as seen in increasing government spending on healthcare, so it was suggested that minor market failure could be less costly than government failure (Howlett et al., 2009). To support this claim, Howlett et al. (2009, p. 25) provide the following observations:

Rising costs are another instance of government failure. Governments receive tax revenues and, unlike their private counterparts, are not under pressure to generate revenues by competing in the marketplace. Without the fear of going bankrupt, a real possibility for private producers, it is argued that governments do not have the same incentive to control expenses and instead may allow them to continually balloon in size. Again, it is argued that due to this limitation, a government must carefully weigh the costs and benefits of altering market relations, and in some cases allowing "minor" market failures to persist may be cheaper than engineering a government takeover of that activity ... [G]overnment replacement of market-based goods and service production should be carefully assessed, and that the "opportunity costs" associated with such actions should be factored into the government decision-making calculus. (Howlett et al., 2009, p. 25)

Textbooks are replete with the famous agency problem, in which individuals within an organization make decisions and undertake actions to maximize their own interests rather than those of the organization in which they are employed. An analogous concept is organizational displacement, which describes a public organization, or department within a public organization, which eschews the mandated public goals instead of the subservient goals for its own interests or those of certain managers and decision managers. Decisions that would lead to increased budgets and size may be more commensurate with private interests or those of the public organization rather than the overall public interest itself.

Governance of public organizations confronting both imperfect information and the uncertainty, asymmetries, and high transactions costs of knowledge inherent in all innovation requires a workplace organization that may not replicate that typically found in the private sector. To avoid short-term biases and a longer-term decision horizon, along with organizational displacement, job security and longer-term incentives may be more effective in human resource management than prioritizing flexibility and market-level financial compensations (Williamson, 1999). The organizational aspects of public sector governance are essential to avoiding or at least minimizing regulatory capture, as Bernstein pointed out in 1955.

In sum, although market and government failures are not desired, we should also remember that not all market and government failures negatively impact society. In addition, the relationship between market and government failure is complicated, and it has longer-term effects. Fortunately, governments can use multiple instruments or policies to reduce those failures. In this regard, the National Innovation System (NIS) and the government's role become vital for correcting failures and innovation. In the following section, we provide information about and insights into the NIS and the government's role in innovation.

The National Innovation System and the Government's Role in Innovation

The government's role in innovation is widely discussed in the literature, such as how governments provide financial support to the private sector's R&D to increase national growth and development (Hyytinen & Toivanen, 2005; Leyden & Link, 1992). A typical way to consider the government's role is within the NIS framework. As Autio et al. (2014, p. 1098) argue, NIS "is one of the most important and most cited concepts in innovation studies." What is NIS?

"NIS" can be defined as "the set of organizations, institutions, and linkages for the generation, diffusion, and application of scientific and technological knowledge operating in a specific country" (Galli & Teubal, 2005, p. 345) or "organizations and institutions directly related to searching and exploring technological innovations, such as R&D departments, universities, and public institutes" (Chung, 2002, p. 486). The concept of an NIS is "the array of public and private institutions and organizations within an economy that fund and perform R&D, translate the results of R&D into commercial innovations, and affect the diffusion of new technologies" (Mowery, 1992, p. 125). Instead of focusing only on company profitability, NIS offers a framework for innovation in which multiple actors and institutions contribute, including the public bureaucracy (Acs et al., 2017), private and nonprofit organizations, and universities (Leyden & Link, 1992). These interrelated actors or sources create, mediate, or implement innovations. Public organizations, public research institutions, industry, and academia are the main actors of NIS (Acs et al., 2017; Chung, 2002; Galli & Teubal, 2005; Nelson, 1993). NIS is different from entrepreneurship because the unit of analysis in NIS is the institutional context that embodies all levels. In contrast, the unit of analysis in entrepreneurship is the individual level or organizational level (Autio et al., 2014). In NIS, innovation sources, individuals, groups, organizations, and the institutional context all affect innovations, so NIS functions as an ecosystem (Acs et al., 2017).

In NIS, the innovation ecosystem interacts with many factors and actors, including the economic situation of countries and institutions. Additionally, innovations and government objectives and policies are affected by NIS (Noble et al., 2019). According to Kuhlmann (2001, p. 958), NIS includes all institutions "which are engaged in scientific research, ... educate and train the working population, develop technology, produce innovative products and processes, and distribute them; to this belong the relevant regulative bodies ... [and] the state investments in appropriate infrastructures." Thus, NIS includes all the institutions that are directly or indirectly parts of the ecosystem.

In particular, the university, industry, and government relationship is vital, which is called the Triple-Helix model (Kuhlmann, 2001; Vivona et al., 2022).

Likewise, Smith (2005, p. 90) observes that an "integrated set of public and private organizations, regulatory systems, and the policy system make up a 'national system of innovation': an overall context of economic and technical behavior that shapes the technological opportunities and capabilities of firms." In NIS, government authorities such as national, regional, and local governments play a vital but not dominant role as they act more as mediators (Smits & Kuhlmann, 2004) while also correcting market failures. Thus, successful public policies occur when a consensus among different actors is reached (Smits & Kuhlmann, 2004). NIS also includes infrastructures, regulation systems, political cultures, social values, and policy environments. Smith (2005, p. 89) observes:

The cohesion of any system thus appears to rest on two sets of infrastructure: physical infrastructures usually related to energy and communications, and science-technology or knowledge infrastructures such as universities, publicly supported technical institutes, regulatory agencies, libraries and databanks, or even government ministries. These infrastructures in turn operate inside an institutional framework which in one context emphasizes regulation: technical standards, risk management rules, health and safety regulations, and so on. The regulatory system includes not just formal rules, but also the general legal system relating to contracts, employment, and intellectual property rights (patent and copyright law) within which firms operate. Finally, there is the wider context of political culture and social values, which shape public policy objectives and particularly the macroeconomic policy environment.

In particular, the role of R&D, scientists, universities, and national labs impact NIS and successful innovations. For instance: "Government R&D expenditure is perhaps the most visible element of infrastructure support, typically involving about 1 per cent of national income in the OECD economies. There is wide international variation in policy institutions – research councils, ministries, state enterprises, etc. – through which these resources flow, both in terms of the balance between institutions and their respective missions and internal organization" (Smith, 2005, p. 96). However, our understanding of NIS is also evolving. Arundel et al. (2007, p. 1176) put it clearly (see also Meissner & Kergroach, 2021):

More recent work within the national innovation systems perspective highlighted the importance of other factors to successful innovation, particularly in low and medium technology sectors, where formal R&D frequently plays a secondary role. These other factors include interactions with suppliers and customers, other forms of "open innovation," and feedback mechanisms from the market. These interactions frequently form within localized networks, creating unique innovation systems at the regional or national level.

However, contextual differences across different countries can affect NIS, governments' roles in innovation, and outcomes. In this book, we have reiterated the importance of national and cultural context. For instance:

The socio-historical context of the systems of innovation literature is important. It arose in an attempt to explain the insurgence of East Asian economies, first Japan, then the four "tigers" (Taiwan, Korea, Singapore, and Hong Kong) and, most recently, China. The explanation is that these countries had become competitive thanks to their national systems of innovations, which made it possible to participate in a positive way in the globalisation of trade and finance. (Schot & Steinmueller, 2018, p. 1558)

Thus, context impacts NIS and its outcomes.

In addition, countries differ in their innovativeness and adoption of innovation due to cultural differences (Kaasa, 2013; Rinne et al., 2012; Shane, 1993; Waarts & van Everdingen, 2005). For instance, analyzing thirty-three countries, Shane (1993, p. 59) found that "rates of innovation are most closely associated with the cultural value of uncertainty acceptance, but lack of power distance and individualism also are related to high rates of innovation." Similarly, analyzing the effects of national culture on innovation outputs, Waarts and Van Everdingen (2005) found that while uncertainty avoidance, masculinity, and power distance are negatively associated with country-level innovation, higher levels of long-term orientation are positively associated with innovation. By analyzing the effects of power distance, individualism, and uncertainty avoidance using the Global Innovation Index, Rinne et al. (2012) found that while power distance and individualism are positively associated with innovation inputs and outputs, uncertainty avoidance does not have any statistical effect.

Thus, contextual factors affect NIS, and NIS positively affect nations' economies. We agree with the following statement by Efrat (2014,

p. 19), who suggests that organizations should "take national culture into account when determining the location of organizational units involved in creating any type of innovation. More specifically, they should consider national culture when establishing their expectations regarding the units' outputs and when planning the management of such units."

For instance, in the USA and Germany, public and private organizations have research labs, but in France, there is a separation of research and higher education, which reduces innovation in France (Hage, 1999). In other words, the NIS of the USA and Germany is different from the NIS of France, leading to different innovative activities and outputs. In Singapore, the government prioritizes innovation in the private sector, such as providing incentives for innovative companies to invest in Singapore and update their regulatory policies (Carney & Zheng, 2009). In addition, at least four government agencies in Singapore support innovative activities within and beyond the public sector: the Agency for Science, Technology, and Research (A*STAR); the Economic Development Board; Standards, Productivity and Innovation Board Singapore; and International Enterprise (Ho et al., 2016). These agencies can increase the economic growth and development of the nation through innovation (Ho et al., 2016). Likewise, in the context of Australia, one report shows that the Australian government is a vital player in NIS: "It [the Australian government] builds capacity and provides incentives to innovate. It builds capacity by educating and training the workforce (including researchers and managers), facilitating collaboration, brokering partnership, providing advice, and collecting data. It provides support in the form of grants and tax incentives to overcome market failures that discourage private investment in innovation... It also funds vital research" (Carr, 2009, p. 18).

These examples suggest the vital role played by governments in encouraging innovation. National and regional innovation policies and clusters are crucial tools to enhance national innovation (Giest, 2017).

It is true that not all innovation agencies or labs are successful, but these institutions could prove vital in the long term and increase the innovation culture and climate of a nation. Breznitz and Ornston (2018) have analyzed the five innovation agencies from the following five countries: Finland (SITRA); Israel (the Office of the Chief

Scientist); Singapore (A*STAR); Sweden (the Governmental Agency for Innovative Systems [VINNOVA]); and Ireland (the Policy Advisory Board for Enterprise and Science). They found that:

Just as policymakers can foster experimentation within mature, high-profile policy domains … innovation agencies can contribute constructively to national innovation systems. For example, while A*STAR was not a radical disruptor, it expanded support for research and upgraded FDI. VINNOVA did not fundamentally transform Swedish policymaking or production, but it used its position as a broker to modernize established industries. In a similar vein, a politicized SITRA has struggled to target fundamentally new industries and activities but has emerged as an important vehicle for social inclusion … DARPA's retreat from early-stage research and new technologies did not represent its "death" but, rather, a commitment to developing established industries and technological platforms. (Breznitz & Ornston, 2018, p. 738)

However, the limitations of NIS include not considering individual and micro-level innovative activities, focusing mainly on technological innovations and inventions but not process innovations, and that innovative leadership and entrepreneurship were ignored in the innovation system (Autio et al., 2014). Additionally, bureaucracy and public organizations need to be innovative in order to be part of the NIS, a factor that is not discussed in the literature. As Drechsler (2020, p. 1) argues: "Innovation bureaucracies are necessary because no policy implements itself, and innovation bureaucracy ecosystems need to be calibrated towards meeting the needs of the specific situation within the national innovation process, sometimes reacting in an agile manner, sometimes giving the stability the system needs."

In this regard, although we can benefit from the NIS framework, we need to go beyond different units of analysis, understand and evaluate governments' roles in innovation, and make government operations more innovative. Cinar (2020, pp. 82–83) summarizes how governments take on different roles in promoting innovation:

As a regulator, public sector decisions on innovation policy, education policy, infrastructure investment and regulations and laws have significant impact on innovation management. Second, several significant innovations such as GPS technology, two-way radio communication, and fingerprint tracing have been developed within government labs which illustrates the research role that is played by the public sector … Third, the governments can also be the buyer for many innovative products and services such as medical scanning products, enterprise resource planning systems and big data analytics software. In addition to these roles, governments can lead and introduce innovations to solve a complex set of problems and provide better services to their citizens.

More specifically, Guenduez and Mettler (2022) divide the government's role in innovation into four functions. First, governments are regulators (e.g., rule setters). Second, governments are enablers (e.g., reducing barriers to innovation, implementing innovative policies, and ensuring property rights). Third, governments are leaders (e.g., leading R&D and investing in technologies and innovative organizations). Finally, governments are users (e.g., using innovations and technologies for their operations). Thus, governments' major roles in innovation include regulation, enabling, leading, and acting as users for innovation. More specifically, governments use a combination of supply-side and demand-side innovation policies. While the former policies "represent the older tradition of aid through finance (grants, tax incentives and public venture capital) and aid through the provision of public services (brokerage services, incubators, science parks, etc) … [the latter policies] include relatively new tools … such as the use of regulation and standard-setting to incentivise innovation and promote 'lead markets'" (Flanagan et al., 2011, p. 703).

Governments' roles are particularly vital in less developed countries because governments in less developed nations have more leverage to make more considerable scale changes, including catch-up via subsidization, PPPs, and industrialization (Breznitz & Ornston, 2018). For example, before Singapore was economically advanced and developed, the country faced major problems, including housing. As Quah (2018, p. 18) observes, "when Singapore faces problems which other countries cannot solve, the PAP [People's Action Party, which has been the ruling party since 1959] leaders initiate innovative solutions to solve these problems," such as creating the HDB in 1960 to provide affordable houses to all citizens. The country built around 1,130 thousand flats by 2016, resulting in the ownership of housing rising from less than 10 percent to over 80 percent in 2016 (Quah, 2018). While building HDBs, the Singapore government implemented many innovations while collaborating with citizens and citizen groups.

Finally, the COVID-19 pandemic demonstrates the vital role of public organizations regarding how government capacities and policies impact the lives and well-being of citizens, economies, public, private, and nonprofit organizations, and universities, as well as promoting innovations (Sarkar, 2021). COVID-19 pushed all organizations to implement many innovations (particularly technological ones) while governments provided financial support for innovative vaccine developments (Raghavan et al., 2021a). In fact, Gold (2021, p. 10) argues that the assumption that science and inventions are developed solely in universities, industry labs, and research centers is wrong. For instance, the vaccine for Ebola "was created, developed and trialed solely by the public sector" and "the largest pre-clinical drug deal in Canadian history" was developed by the public sector with a partnership.

Conclusion

In Chapter 8, we discussed different sources of innovation such as industry labs, science parks, and universities. These sources also represent a part of NIS that we explore in this chapter. The role of government in the economy and society has evolved considerably over time. The second industrial era centered around mass production in manufacturing. During this era, the role of government typically revolved around three instruments: regulations, competition policies or antitrust, and public ownership (Audretsch, 1991). Various countries deployed these three instruments differently. In today's world, perhaps the most important instrument to use is innovative activities, including innovative policies, which may subject to market or government failures.

Why should we care about market and government failures, NIS, and the government's role in innovation? They are all interrelated. Market failures resulting in less efficiency lead to higher prices, lower-quality products and services, and diminishing citizen welfare. Additionally, when markets fail, the government collects fewer taxes. With market failure, the population withdraws its trust in the institutions of a market economy. The desires, needs, and demands of consumers are not met by the mechanisms inherent in a market economy: demand and supply. The result is often populism: a rejection of market-based capitalism with the demand for something better. Then, populist and utopic policies may be adopted by governments, which may lead to government failures. In other words, market failures provide governments with a compelling reason to adopt certain types of policy tools, but the outcome may not be always desirable.

One major consequence of government failure is that citizens' trust in government declines (Kettl, 2008; Merritt et al., 2021; Wilson, 2000). Then, the desires, needs, and demands involving the provision of public goods are not met by the public sector. This also often results in populism: a rejection of the social market-based capitalism, which depends on a vital public sector for the provision of goods and services falling into the public sphere and the call for something different and better. Societal, political, and economic stability are inextricably dependent on the ability of markets and the public sector to fulfill their roles effectively and efficiently. Thus, governments can play multiple roles in advancing innovation, which in turn impacts market and government failures and society.

11 | *Outcomes of Public Sector Innovation*

Defining and Understanding Outputs and Outcomes

Not all public sector innovation is created equal, just like its counterpart in the private sector context. As Salge and Vera (2012, p. 550) put it, "rigorous research is required to examine whether and – perhaps more important – under which conditions innovative activity contributes to tangible improvements in the quality of public services." One vital insight into an innovation involves the outputs or outcomes. To put it simply, when or if an innovation is implemented, can we observe any outputs, outcomes, or benefits? An innovation reflects a new idea, or a practice adopted by an organization, and it is expected to have a positive impact or output (Demircioglu & Audretsch, 2019; H. Jung & J. Lee, 2016). However, many innovations fail to or do not yield the expected benefits.

One of the crucial dimensions of measuring innovation in general and public sector innovation in particular is whether or how a particular innovation is linked with any outputs or outcomes. Innovations can be considered useless if they do not contribute any positive impact on society, citizens, organizations, the private sector, government, or public sector employees. Therefore, outputs and/or outcomes reflect the importance of innovation. Indeed, in any type of organization – public or private – leaders and employees typically aim for generating innovations that have positive outputs or outcomes. For instance, they want to solve problems, do more with less, and bring benefits to society or a segment of society (e.g., migrants). The important question is: What are the output and the outcome?

Hatry (2006, p. 16) defines "output" as "the amount of products and services delivered (completed)" and stresses that "outputs are things that the program's personnel have done, not changes to outside people or changes that outside organizations have made." "Outcomes," according to Hatry (2006, pp. 16–17), are "the events, occurrences, or changes in conditions, behavior, or attitudes that indicate progress toward a program's mission and objectives." He stresses that "outcomes are not what the program itself did but the consequences of what the program did" (Hatry, 2006, p. 17). He provides the following example from the Texas Governor's Office of Budget and Planning to distinguish between the two terms: "The number of patients treated or discharged from a state mental hospital (output indicator) is not the same as the percentage of discharged patients who are capable of living independently (outcome indicator)." If we apply this definition to innovation, output could be considered in terms of whether innovation reduces costs or even whether organizations implement innovation, and the outcome could be how this innovation impacts citizens.

Thus, "outcomes" typically refer to the long-term effects of the "outputs." In other words, when we analyze the effects of innovations, we should not only look at the immediate impacts but also at the long-term effects of policies. In this regard, the adoption of an innovation may not have an immediate effect, but that does not mean that the policy will generate effects in the long term. This distinction is important because, as Pollitt (2011, p. 42) observes, studies on public sector innovation focus on the short term, such as "on the moment of innovation itself." However, "what leads up to it, and what makes some innovations 'catch on' by attracting the right kind of 'early adopters' ... the later stages of development? ... [and] what proportion of administrative innovations is short-lived, and is there any pattern to those that become perennials rather than fade after the first bloom?" (Pollitt, 2011, p. 42). Thus, the impacts of innovations are typically understudied. Likewise, even if an innovation is beneficial today, it may not bring about positive effects in the future (Hartley & Knell, 2022). Therefore, we should not overly weigh the usefulness of innovation in the short run but rather evaluate its longer-term outcomes. Similarly, we should not take the usefulness of an innovation for granted, and we need to constantly evaluate the outcomes of innovation.

Because outputs and outcomes overlap and many studies use the terms interchangeably (e.g., Griffith et al., 2006; Rana et al., 2019; van Dooren et al., 2015), we do not strictly differentiate between the two terms throughout this chapter. For simplicity's sake, we refer to both terms ("outcomes" or "outputs") to characterize any effects from innovation.

Despite these definitions, there is no unified scholarly understanding of innovation outputs and outcomes. For example, some scholars consider innovation outputs as types of innovation, such as product and process innovations (Hashi & Stojčić, 2013). The degree of novelty, intensity of the innovation, number of innovations, and innovation complexity may also factor into innovation outputs and outcomes (Demircioglu & Audretsch, 2020; Kattel et al., 2013). Likewise, as the 2011 APSC data show, efficiency, effectiveness, improving process and procedures, increasing employee satisfaction and user satisfaction, and increasing interagency collaboration is a part of innovation outputs and outcomes.

Additionally, outcomes of innovation can also include changing organizational structures. For instance, Boyer et al. (2019) observe that innovating while responding to clients' needs induces more decentralized work environments because typical top-down and chain-of-command organizational structures could not solve citizens' problems. Thus, while organizational structure and design impact innovations, innovations can also impact organizational structure and design by making public organizations more collaborative.

Furthermore, during the COVID-19 pandemic, many agencies implemented technological and process innovations – such as working from home – that led to changes in organizational cultures. For instance, working from home and using Zoom have become a "new normal" or routine for many public organizations, motivating changes in organizational structures (Raghavan et al., 2021). In other words, regardless of whether innovations occur internally (e.g., leadership demand) or because of external causes (e.g., COVID-19 and other external shocks), innovations have different outcomes.

Some innovations, such as public procurement for innovation, can increase trust and longer-term outcomes, so particular innovations may have different outcomes, including spillover effects. For instance, Edler and Georghiou (2007, p. 957) observe that "the state – supported by its purchasing power – may help to create meaningful standards, with convergence on a standard allowing firms to internalise spillovers and hence to increase the incentive to invest in R&D. Those standards further contribute to trust building for innovative products."

However, despite numerous attempts from the research community, little is known about the long-term effects of innovations in the public sector. Pollitt (2011) makes an analogy with public sector reforms: The effects of public sector reforms diminish after they appear, so it may be true that the effects of most innovations also diminish over time. Thus, it will be important to analyze why some innovations survive and others do not (Mitra, 2022; van Acker & Bouckaert, 2018), as well as the longer-term and positive effects of innovations (Hood & Dixon, 2013, 2015). Meanwhile, policymakers and citizens expect that innovations should have longer-term outcomes (e.g., integrating migrants and solving climate change). Nevertheless, it is not always possible to estimate the long-term effects of innovations, as uncertainty is part of innovative activities.

Regarding uncertainty, Smits and Kuhlmann (2004) argue that uncertainty is part of innovation, so it is hard to grasp the effects and outcomes of innovations. As many sources from different stakeholders and viewpoints are involved in the innovation process, it becomes complex and challenging to understand innovative activities and outcomes. Although technologies provide opportunities for decision-makers and service users, they will not automatically provide solutions to public administration and policy problems. In this regard, any innovation is subject to failure and negative impacts, and it seems impossible to predict innovation's effects. However, before we discuss the potential negative impacts of innovation, we first analyze how sectoral differences impact the outputs and outcomes of innovation.

Sectoral Differences and the Outcomes of Innovation

Differences exist between public sector and private sector innovations in terms of inputs such as conditions, drivers, and outcomes. For the private sector, the traditional innovation measures and outputs are patents. Patents capture some aspects of innovation, primarily technical and product innovations (Griffith et al., 2006). As Wang and Hooi (2019, p. 866) state, in the industry and private sector, "[p]atents are a direct outcome of the creative process, particularly those that have a commercial impact, and represent an externally validated measure of technological novelty … [and] used the number of patent applications as a proxy for innovation."

However, there have always been critics regarding using patents to measure and reflect innovative activity. For example, one famous study warns about using the number of patented inventions as a measure of innovation:

It has long been known that patents do not work in practice as they do in theory. Rarely, if ever, do patents confer perfect appropriability, although they do afford considerable protection on new chemical products and rather simple mechanical inventions. Many patents can be "invented around" at modest costs. They are especially ineffective at protecting process innovations. Often patents provide little protection because the legal requirements for upholding their validity or for proving their infringement are high. In some industries, particularly where the innovation is embedded in processes, trade secrets are a viable alternative to patents. Trade secret protection is possible, however, only if a firm can put its product before the public and still keep the underlying technology secret. Usually only chemical formulas and industrial-commercial processes (e.g., cosmetics and recipes) can be protected as trade secrets after they're "out." (Teece, 1986, p. 287)

Although innovation measures still rely on patents in the private sector, patents do not necessarily lead to positive impacts, so governments may not support R&D and patents in the future (Gold, 2021). Thus, when it comes to the measurement of public sector innovation, metrics from the private sector is important but not sufficient due to structural differences between public and private organizations. As discussed in Chapter 5, most innovations in the public sector are process and service innovations, in contrast to the product innovations of the private sector. Kelly (2005, p. 77) distinguishes the public and private sectors:

Unlike private providers, public providers may not target the most affluent segment of the market for their efforts; our professional ethics make that impossible. Managers make a reasonable choice, then, to focus their attention on internal measures of service delivery and not on external measures of value creation from consumers. Theoretically, the relevant question for public managers is whether external measures of value creation – citizen satisfaction – are enhanced by efforts to improve performance. Practically, it is whether the performance goal is achieved.

Thus, public organizations do not aim to profit, and efficiency is only one criterion of success (as mentioned in Chapter 3). Equity, accountability, and justice are core values in the public sector.

Additionally, the main purpose of public organizations is creating public value: making public organizations more successful, innovative, and sustainable (without aiming to make profits), aiming for a good governance, and increasing happiness of service users (Chen et al., 2021; Jørgensen & Bozeman, 2007; Moore, 1995). For example,

Chen et al. (2021) provide the following examples of how public value can be created through innovations in the public sector:

[W]hen a municipality works with its citizens and service providers to develop innovative approaches to curb-side recycling, it is combining user convenience and concern with sustainability in a way that is integrated with its preexisting capacity to offer sanitation services. When an education authority innovates in its curriculum, it is implementing new strategies for student success. When a government offers innovative pathways for communication and transparency to its citizens, it promotes the foundational values of democratic governance. (Chen et al., 2021, p. 1677)

These examples suggest that public organizations are distinct from the private sector and must adhere to greater values while providing services. Not only the inputs but also the expected outcomes of innovation differ in public organizations.

Furthermore, the outcomes of public sector innovation focus on long-term outcomes such as dealing with grand challenges or wicked problems, including global warming, sustainability, integrating migrations, and aging demographics. Therefore, the government's approach to solving those problems may not have an immediate impact, although some regulations may change individual behavior (such as small fees for plastic use). Nevertheless, most outcomes of these policies represent long-term impacts, such as moving to electric vehicles and reducing the consumption of oil. While governments aim to bring about positive outcomes through innovations or policy changes, they also aim to correct market failures (mentioned in Chapter 10) and implement large-scale social changes. These grand challenges require public organizations and policymakers to implement more comprehensive or radical innovations as well as more collaborative innovations. For example, as Chindarkar et al. (2017, p. 8) point out:

[I]ncreasing complexity of social problems and concerns has led many governments to attempt to adopt a more systematic and integrated approach to social policy rather than the bandaid approach of incremental changes or the siloed policy patchwork that existed in the past. For example, social problems such as elderly care require coordination between the health sector, labor market, and the pension system, among others. Such an integrated design approach, with a systematic mixing of policy instruments rather than ad hoc layering, is more likely to result in optimal outcomes.

In this regard, as public organizations aim to solve grand challenges and wicked problems, they rely more on external actors (mentioned in Chapter 8) and government actions to promote innovation. In contrast, private organizations are typically less concerned with the long-term outcomes of innovations or the grand challenges confronting society.

Understanding Innovation Outputs and Outcomes

It is challenging enough to understand and apply innovation as a concept. To measure it presents an even greater challenge. As innovative activity has grown in importance and relevance to society, more resources and effort have been devoted to the measurement of innovation. One of the greatest impediments to unraveling the links between standards of living and economic development on the one hand, and innovation on the other, has been the challenge of moving from concept to measurement. It is challenging enough to conceptualize innovation. Measurement presents an additional set of hurdles for a concept that is as elusive as innovation (Kuznets, 1962). There have been three general approaches to the measurement of innovation. The first is to measure inputs in the innovation process, the second is to measure intermediate outputs, and the third is to measure of actual innovations. All three have their inherent limitations and are fraught with important qualifications.

Inputs into the innovation process generally involve measures of R&D, such as expenditures on R&D or the share of workers accounted by workers devoted to R&D. The advantage of this input measure is its ease and low cost of measurement. The disadvantage is the large gap between what is being measured (R&D) and the concept (innovation). Not all innovation comes from R&D, and certainly not from formal R&D laboratories. Similarly, not all R&D results in innovation (Scherer, 1983). The intermediate measure of innovation generally involves patented inventions (Jaffe, 1986; Pakes & Griliches, 1980). The advantage of patents as a measure of innovation over R&D is that an invention has taken place. In addition, patents have become easy to measure, in that their collection and availability has become prioritized by most governments. However, the disadvantage is that most patents reflect invention and not innovation. Not all innovations are the result of inventions applying for and receiving legal patent protection. Similarly, most patented inventions never become actual innovations, in that they are never commercialized (Pakes, 1985).

Direct measures of innovation generally involve objective assessments of significant new product and process introductions (Acs & Audretsch, 1988, 1990), or subjective measures based on self-assessments of the share of sales accounted for by new products. While the latter is easier to measure through surveys, the former is more reliable, albeit considerably more expensive.

Several outputs or outcomes may result from the same innovation. For instance, the benefits of innovation may include programmatic outcomes (e.g., effectiveness and efficiency), prestige (e.g., recognition and approval), and internal or structural benefits (e.g., increasing employee satisfaction and employee relationship) (Downs & Mohr, 1979). Thus, policymakers may aim to bring about more benefits to their organizations, society, and employees through innovation. There are several reasons why we should measure and understand innovation outputs and outcomes.

First of all, if we measure something (such as a performance), then we can also manage and lead it (Hatry, 2006). In addition, as Daft (1978, p. 195) argues, the innovation process has four steps: "starting with the conception of an idea, which is proposed, then a decision is made to adopt, and finally the innovation is implemented." However, an important limitation of the existing research is that it does not identify the effects after implementing the innovation (see van Acker & Bouckaert, 2018). In fact, as Arundel et al. (2015) state, because there are only a few studies on the relationship between sources and types of innovation and the outcomes of innovation, we still do not know how the sources of innovation affect the outcomes of innovation. Likewise, one study finds that "many have come to consider innovation as a goal in itself, missing out on issues around innovation's impact on public service outcomes, particularly where such outcomes could be negative" (Dudau et al., 2018, p. 255).

As Cinar (2020, p. 95) argues: "Innovation must produce a positive value. In the private sector, this can be sales, profit, growth or return on investment. However, in the case of public sector innovation, the measurement of this value is not as simple because most of the public services are provided for free." Thus, the benefits of innovation in the public sector are not straightforward, as there are multiple goals, strategies, and conflicting interests among public organizations and stakeholders (Rainey, 2009). Thus, public sector innovations typically compromise some values such as efficiency, effectiveness, equity, justice, accountability, and transparency, which may lead to less than ideal innovations. Still, as scholars argue: "If we transform public governance in the right ways, public innovation may be boosted to the benefit of users, citizens, public employees, private stakeholders and society at large" (Torfing & Triantafillou, 2016, p. 3). For example, as Gault and Soete (2022, p. 1) point out: "Policymakers are not just interested in the occurrence of innovation but in the outcome. Does it result in more jobs and economic growth? Is it expected to reduce carbon emissions, to advance renewable energy production and energy storage? How does innovation support the Sustainable Development Goals?" Likewise, policy and government documents suggest that innovations should positively impact governments, society, and individuals (OECD, 2015, 2017). Thus, analyzing innovation outcomes has not only academic but, more importantly, practical implications.

Specifically, Guenduez and Mettler (2022) find that when governments innovate, it improves citizens' daily lives as well as the competitiveness of countries. Thus, innovation benefits public sector employees, citizens, public organizations, private organizations (e.g., via spillover effects), society, and nations. For instance, imagine that the department (ministry) of education in one country has implemented an innovation, which positively and significantly affects the quality of education (e.g., student learning). Or imagine that the department of health in a specific country has implemented a product innovation, finding a cure for a specific disease. Or imagine that a public organization has invented a process innovation, making organizational activities more efficient and effective. These particular innovations not only have organizational outcomes but also social, national, and even global outcomes.

Analyzing innovations in hospitals in Sweden, Svensson and Hartmann (2018) find that most innovations in hospitals have positive effects on the productivity of hospitals, and many of the innovations reduce expenditures. Additionally, several innovations have positive effects on patients' life quality. Another study finds that public sector employees interacting and collaborating with universities report positive benefits to innovation, as ideas emanating from universities can increase the quality of products and services of public organizations

(Demircioglu & Audretsch, 2019). Studies also find that bottom-up innovations lead to positive outcomes such as improving the administrative processes of organizations (Arundel et al., 2015; Borins, 2001, 2014). Another study finds that bottom-up innovations can enhance employee job satisfaction in public organizations (Demircioglu, 2021). Thus, these examples show that there are multiple benefits of innovation in the public sector.

An OECD report (2017, p. 14) provides several examples from different countries of innovation outcomes:

Public sector innovation uses new approaches to create public value for individuals and society. It is changing how the public sector operates to deliver better outcomes. In Finland, socially excluded people get free medical checks in bars or on the street through a new mobile health check system. It is developing effective collaborations with other actors to target public resources where they are needed. In Mexico, people living in rural areas do not need to travel long distances to get public services, a social transfer, and other payment services at the nearest gas station or village store. It is helping to build more inclusive, open, and caring societies, enhancing trust among citizens. In France, families are helping older people with no family connections to live autonomously in a caring environment by sharing housing facilities and shared space.

These are clear examples of how innovation can benefit individuals and society.

Additionally, the contexts, sources, and benefits of innovations may be directly connected. For example, bottom-up innovations may generate more prominent and positive benefits to organizations in some contexts than other types of innovation. Although innovations are expected to reduce costs, improve processes, increase quality, and make citizens happier, not all innovations have a positive impact. As Torfing and Triantafillou (2016, p. 3) argue: "If we transform public governance in the right ways, public innovation may be boasted to the benefit of users, citizens, public employees, private stakeholders and society at large." Thus, policymakers should focus on the benefits of innovation although in some cases, there will be unexpected consequences (Peters, 2010).

According to the Innobarometer 2010 (European Commission, 2011, p. 192), the positive outcomes of innovations including the following: "enabling your organisation to offer services to more or new types of users," "enabling your organisation to better target its services," "improving user satisfaction," "improving user access to information, "enabling faster delivery of services," "simplifying administrative procedures," "reducing costs for providing services," and "improving employee satisfaction or working conditions." Thus, all these factors are typical outputs and outcomes of innovation. Therefore, policymakers can measure the effects of innovation by asking these or similar questions.

Levels of Analysis and Innovation Outcomes

Innovations may impact different outcomes at different levels of analysis, such as at the national, organizational, and individual levels. For instance, innovative countries are typically economically more advanced. Innovative countries are also more dynamic and flexible in terms of the regulatory environment that can further improve their competitiveness, development, and FDI. We are not making a causal statement here that innovation directly increases economic growth and development, although we believe that innovation can enhance macroeconomic outcomes such as government and national growth. Nevertheless, our point is that innovative activities are highly, significantly, and positively correlated with desirable macro-level outcomes.

At the organizational level, as innovation can be used as a performance criterion, innovative organizations can be seen performing better and more successfully than noninnovative organizations. These organizations can also hire more talented and promising people, further impacting their innovativeness. Meanwhile, innovative organizations can seek higher budgets (so that they may receive more personnel and resources) and appear more legitimate than less innovative organizations.

At the individual level, innovative employees may feel accomplished and satisfied by the practice of innovation. They may also feel that they have more knowledge, mastery, and competence (e.g., by knowing and sharing how to innovate). Self-determination theory states that when an individual's competence increases, they have higher motivation and satisfaction (Deci et al., 1989; Demircioglu, 2021; Ryan & Deci, 2017). Therefore, innovation can also positively affect employee satisfaction and motivation through competence and mastery. Innovation can also positively impact employee well-being, motivation, and job satisfaction. Employees will have higher self-efficacy and motivation when the organizational environment supports individuals and increases their creativity and innovation (White, 1959).

As mentioned earlier in this chapter, we should focus on the outcomes of innovations. Our focus could be on national-level outcomes (e.g., how innovation impacts economic growth, development, and trust in society); the organizational outcomes of innovation in the public sector, such as reducing costs, improving administrative procedures, and improving the quality of work; and individual-level outcomes, such as how innovation impacts employee job satisfaction and citizens' satisfaction with public services.

Negative Outcomes of Innovation

Innovations are typically expected to reduce costs and increase the quality of services. However, there are also unexpected consequences of innovations. Not all innovations have positive effects because innovation is a risky and open-ended process that includes exploration and trial and error. Not only science and knowledge but also intuition are involved in the process of innovation (Sørensen & Torfing, 2018).

By nature, innovation requires some risk-taking, so although there may be benefits to a particular innovation, there may also be negative outputs or outcomes. As argued by Hartley and Knell (2022, p. 40):

When it comes to innovation, failure is – or at least should be – a given. By its very nature, innovation involves risk and unpredictability, in both processes and outcomes. Whether occurring in the private, public or voluntary sector (or in hybrid organizations), innovation can involve the creation, testing, implementation and diffusing of new ideas, concepts and solutions. At any stage along this innovation pathway things can go wrong. Public services in particular may have to contend with additional risks of failure, because services which are under state governance are often inherently contested and controversial, must cater for a range of citizens and users rather than just a limited set of "customers," and often face greater scrutiny of their innovations and the associated risk-taking from the media, citizens and communities.

In addition, not everyone agrees that the same innovation has had a positive impact. Thus, as Serrat (2017) argues, there are many unintended and desirable outputs and outcomes of innovation. However, as pro-innovation bias exists, the negative consequences of innovations do not attract as much academic attention and are usually not reported (Cinar et al., 2022a; Hartley & Knell, 2022; Serrat, 2017). For instance, although innovation can increase competitive advantage and organizational growth, it may also have negative outcomes such as increasing costs and disrupting strategies, power structures, and the control of managers and employees (C. Jung & G. Lee, 2016). As Salge and Vera (2012, p. 550) claim, "costly innovative activity in the public sector cannot constitute a virtue in itself, but needs to contribute to the provision of better public services ... rigorous research is required to examine whether and – perhaps more important – under which conditions innovative activity contributes to tangible improvements in the quality of public services."

A negative outcome of innovation could be that some innovations have less value to organizations or are less practical. Additionally, some innovations may be too costly to implement. Furthermore, we can also claim that organizations do not always need to implement innovations if a system already works well. For instance, if an IT system works well, is secure, and its users are satisfied with it, there is less rationale for the organization to change the system. Other negative aspects of innovation could be that countries may focus too much on the Innovation Index, leading to a "gamed" system in which countries increase the number of patents but the patents themselves have little practical benefit.

Innovation may not only affect organizations but also employees. Negative effects of innovation at the individual level could be that as some innovations are risky, there is uncertainty about which innovations will be successful. Innovations take time to develop and implement, so employees may feel that they are exhausted from the innovation process, and stress and burnout can increase. In other words, innovation may affect employees' attitudes and behaviors. For instance, in the British private sector, Bryson et al. (2009) found that implementing many innovations reduced employees' job satisfaction. Even if innovations increase efficiency, they may have other negative effects or outputs such as reducing employees' job satisfaction. In a public sector setting, Yang and Kassakert (2010) similarly found that many innovations in the United States government reduce employee job satisfaction. In this regard, multiple outputs or outcomes may conflict with each other, and policymakers should find the right balance among these outcomes.

When it comes to measuring the negative aspects of innovation, the Innobarometer has measured the negative effects of innovation with the following survey items: "Creating additional administrative costs," "reducing the types or flexibility of your services," "leading to slower delivery of services," and "creating user resistance or dissatisfaction" (European Commission, 2011, p. 192). Thus, all these factors (e.g., increasing costs and user dissatisfaction) are common factors indicating the negative impacts of an innovation. Therefore, policymakers can measure the effects of innovation by asking these or similar questions.

In this regard, we reject the claim that all organizations must be constantly innovative. Instead, we argue that governments, organizations, organizational leaders, and employees need to be strategic about how and when to innovate while expecting that innovations may have unexpected negative outcomes. Even with negative outcomes, though, innovations can still contribute to organizational learning and development as well as creating a more entrepreneurial and innovative organizational climate.

Conclusion

This chapter has demonstrated that analyzing the outputs and outcomes of innovation are vital. Innovations should yield positive outcomes, such as reducing costs and improving service quality (Demircioglu, 2017; Demircioglu & Audretsch, 2019; Kattel et al., 2013; Sandor, 2018). Without analysis of the impact of innovative activity, we cannot assess whether a particular innovation is helpful in terms of enhanced organizational performance. Innovation for the sake of innovation provides few benefits. Instead, the benefits accruing from innovative activity need to be explicitly identified and analyzed. Thus, organizational leaders and policymakers should focus on the benefits of innovation, as doing so has benefits, including positive spillover effects. Nevertheless, not all innovations are breakthroughs or need to be breakthroughs in order to bring about benefits. In fact, as mentioned earlier, most innovations in the public sector are incremental innovations, yet they can still significantly benefit individuals, organizations, societies, and nations.

Organizational leaders and policymakers should also focus on improving the innovation culture or climate. An important aspect of an innovation climate is support for innovative activities, including whether employees are encouraged to come up with new ideas and whether organizational leaders encourage employees to be creative. Nevertheless, policymakers should also keep in mind that many innovations fail or lead to negative impacts. Thus, measuring the outputs and outcomes of innovation is vital, as measuring the outcomes of innovations helps public organizations and organizational leaders to evaluate which innovations truly benefit individuals, organizations, and nations.

12 | *Ethics and Public Sector Innovation*

Introduction

To the best of our knowledge, we have seen a few articles and books about how ethics affect innovative activities in the public sector (c.f. van der Wal & Demircioglu, 2020) and the private sector (c.f. Yidong & Xinxin, 2013). This gap is unfortunate because, like each policy implementation, innovations have unexpected consequences (Hood & Peters, 2004). In his famous book on the diffusion of innovations, Rogers (2003, p. 14) argues that "the innovation-decision process is essentially an information-seeking and information-processing activity in which an individual is motivated to reduce uncertainty about the advantages and disadvantages of the innovation." However, as mentioned in Chapter 11, it is difficult (if not impossible) to predict the outcomes or potential harms of an innovation before its implementation. For instance, Jordan (2014, p. 68) argues:

In making sweeping claims for innovation as integral to public performance, proponents of innovation, often unwittingly, make the subsidiary claim that an obligation to innovate ought to override other considerations, such as protecting citizens from the consequences of policy failures. If innovation is a scientific (or even pseudo-scientific) process of experimentation and evaluation to fulfill an objective, particularly an objective with myriad causal paths, then failure is a likely outcome of many experiments. And failures are risky and costly.

In other words, even if a failure or unethical issues are not desired while innovating, these are not avoidable. Therefore, ethical issues appear mostly after the implementation of an innovation.

In addition, as mentioned in Chapter 11, a pro-innovation bias exists in the literature. As Feller and Menzel (1977, p. 51) warned, most literature on innovation "suffers from a pro-innovation bias," which is an assumption that innovation is beneficial to organizations and that early adopters of innovations will be at an advantage. Another problem of the literature on innovation is selection bias (Perry & Kraemer, 1978). According to Perry and Kraemer (1978, p. 181):

Selection bias poses two major problems for unraveling the nature of diffusion processes. First, it ignores the possible contingent conditions that differentiate between the "take-off" and spread of a successful innovation and a similar, but non-diffusing, innovation. For policy-makers interested in intervening in technological change processes, these contingencies are frequently the most crucial information for successful policy development. Second, the selection bias of diffusion research also ignores "flops" that do diffuse.

Thus, due to these biases, the negative outcomes of innovations are typically not reported. There are also other reasons for not paying much attention to ethical issues. Perhaps one of the main reason why almost no studies link innovation activities and ethics is that innovation and ethics are different areas of scholarship or subfields of two fields (e.g., management versus ethics and philosophy), and thus there is almost no interaction among these two subfields.

We believe that this lack of studies on the ethics of innovation is unfortunate because in many ways, ethics are a vital element of public administration: Many decisions are based on ethics, ethical dilemmas exist for many policies, and codes of ethics determine many public policies (Gueras & Garofalo, 2010; Lewis & Gilman, 2005). In fact, as Lewis and Gilman (2005, p. 21) argue: "Public managers' morale, identity, and capacity for decision making and innovation are entangled in ethics, and rightly so, because public service is our society's instrument for managing complexity and interdependency." They continue that "[p]ublic expectations and formal standards today demand that managers undertake sophisticated ethical reasoning and apply rigorous ethical standards to decisions and behavior" (Lewis & Gilman, 2005, p. 21)

Ethics: What and Why

The first question that we need to answer is: What is ethics? The Britannica dictionary defines ethics as "the discipline concerned with what is morally good and bad and morally right and wrong" (britannica.com). In ethics, "values have been defined as a set of beliefs and principles that influence or guide people's actions." Historically, ethics have been understood as morality, values increasing individual happiness, and – at the society level – as values, principles, and actions that are based on justice and fairness.

Let's imagine that public organizations do not innovate or fail to innovate in public services. Or imagine a particular organization, say a department for tax collection, an agency that regulates the market, or a department of education. Lack of innovation in these organizations may cause an inability to provide better education, tax collection, and security, eventually hindering trust and resulting in ethical issues. If obtaining a work visa for foreigners is too slow of a process, the country may not be able to attract human talent because talented employees will not spend months or even years waiting for visa decisions. The 9/11 terrorist attacks and Hurricane Katrina were disasters that revealed a lack of responsiveness and innovation in government agencies (Kapucu & van Wart, 2006; Kettl, 2008). In this regard, we believe that it is also an ethical responsibility for public organizations to innovate.

Although public sector innovations can be highly successful in any dimension (such as increasing the performance of organizations and individuals, reducing costs, and increasing the quality of public services), innovations always have a potentially negative side. Although ethics can be primarily associated with innovation failures, some successful innovations can also have negative or unethical aspects. More specifically, as mentioned earlier, some innovations are expected to reduce costs, increase quality, improve processes, and increase organizational or individual performance. Thus, a particular innovation increasing the quality of public services or reducing costs can be positively associated with ethics as these can improve human lives. However, a particular innovation may change organizational dynamics. So, for instance, technological innovation may result in fewer employees being needed for a particular job. In this regard, layoffs would be caused by a particular innovation. Thus, the lack of innovation suggests that public agencies are not as compatible as private organizations. For example, particular public services may be slow, not reflect the citizens' demand, or not able to save money. However, the same innovation may increase the unemployment rate. Thus, this issue represents an ethical dilemma.

Additionally, when evaluating policies, we need to go beyond typical evaluations focusing solely on efficiency and economic impacts and analyze the social and policy impacts of innovations (Bozeman & Sarewitz, 2011; Ribeiro & Shapira, 2020). Studies argue that from an ethical viewpoint, innovations should impact citizens' lives positively (Vigoda-Gadot et al., 2005), which is consistent with ethical principles. However, populist attitudes (particularly radical populism) reduce innovations and lead to unethical outcomes (Borins, 2018). Populism reduces innovations and leads to the unfair treatment of citizens, as seen in many Trump-era policies that led to the politicization and polarization of society (Bauer & Becker, 2020; Borins, 2018). Furthermore, in Switzerland, populism "towards 'common sense' treatment of crime and criminals successfully delegitimized a potentially effective juvenile justice innovation" (Borins, 2018, p. 1867). Borins (2018, p. 1867) also reports his colleague's findings from Turkey after 2016:

The number of applications from Turkey to the UN's public innovation award competition dropped from 21 in 2014 to 2 in 2017. Alarmingly, the correspondent reports from personal knowledge that civil servants involved in IT innovations and those who as part of their work visited western countries are now being jailed on charges of anti-state sympathies. It is a stark reminder that when populism becomes a pretext for dictatorship, public servants whose professional values will not align with an increasingly illegitimate regime will likely be among its first targets.

In this regard, dictatorial rulers not only undermine institutions and justice but also undermine public sector innovation and its potential ethical impacts.

Meanwhile, many management reform practices such as NPM reforms, cutback management, and businesslike government pose ethical issues, as increased efficiency often entails employee layoffs and the dissolving of unions. Vigoda-Gadot et al. (2005, p. 75) explain:

NPM … neglects certain moral principles that are at risk when powerful market mechanisms are infused into government thinking. Safety nets for the weaker segments of the population and care for the less able may fall by the wayside when market concerns enter into bureaucratic thought. The encouragement of market forces through competition according to the dictates of a liberal, ideological economy and the quest for greater efficiency and cost saving measures may thus result in a dangerous moral indifference on the part of public administration. Hence, the post-managerial approach is to rely on a third way of governance and on a more ambitious, long-term ideology of global human progress, transnational policy learning, and a more equal distribution of knowledge, practices, and goods across nations and societies.

There are also conflicting rationalities among policies and decision making, causing such ethical dilemmas as, "between political rationality (focusing on the question 'who gets what, how and when?')," "legal rationality (stressing the importance of the 'rule of law')," "economic rationality (stressing the importance of an efficient allocation of costs and benefits)," and "professional/scientific/technological rationality (putting forward the values that relate to professional and scientifically acquired knowledge, based on professional standards and professional theories of action)" (Bekkers et al., 2011b, p. 21). Thus, if a particular innovation focuses on economic rationality such as the NPM reforms, there may be ethical dilemmas or unexpected consequences when other rationalities, such as the political or professional reasons, are considered. Furthermore, Hodgson (2002) observes that even a seemingly practical innovation, no matter how clever and relevant, can be so risky (by disregarding long-standing experience) that it becomes irrational because prioritizing efficiency while disregarding ethics and human values is likely to result in an irrational nightmare and failure.

However, as mentioned in Chapter 10, the government's intervention or role in innovation may not work for several reasons (Breznitz & Ornston, 2018). The government's intervention to correct market failure may lead to corruption and bribery (Acemoglu & Verdier, 2000) "because government intervention designed to correct market failures requires the use of bureaucrats to make decisions, it will create opportunities for these employees to be corrupt and demand bribes" (Acemoglu & Verdier, 2000, p. 195). Thus, government failure could become highly unethical. Government failure in general – and failing to provide public services to citizens in particular – results in declining trust in governments and public organizations (Baniamin, 2019), leading to ethical issues. Furthermore, democratic regimes prioritize pluralism, so minority parties or opposition groups may not allow some projects (e.g., healthcare reform) to correct market failure, and polarization may occur during the policy process. As Breznitz and Ornston (2018, p. 723) argue, "the formidable fiscal resources and coordinating capacities that enable policymakers to achieve immediate economies of scale in established industries can be a liability when targeting unknown industries with yet-to-be-determined business models."

Ethical Lessons from Different Organizations

Many studies find that ethics do not necessarily reduce efficiency or innovations (Stensöta, 2010). Indeed, emphasizing ethics can further increase public organizations' innovativeness. Two types of ethos exist for public organizations. The first one is the bureaucratic ethos, which is "a set of core values that includes accountability, neutral and professional competence, efficiency, effectiveness, economy, impartiality, objectivity, loyalty and obedience to elected officials and superiors, honesty and integrity, consistency and predictability, reliability, diligence and prudence, avoidance of partisanship, and respect and courtesy to both the public and elected officials" (Goss, 1996, p. 581). The second one is the democratic ethos, which is "a set of core values like obligation to use administrative discretion to advance certain social values, political principles, and the public interest" (Goss, 1996, p. 581). When employees aim to balance these two value systems, they need to be not only ethical but also innovative as they consider how to achieve public interest with efficiency, consistency, impartiality, and predictability. In this regard, relying on ethics and ethical principles can force public organizations and public sector employees to become more innovative.

There are differences between public and private organizations in terms of ethical practices. On this matter, Gueras and Garofalo (2010, pp. xiv–xv) give the following two examples. First, "a private company may recognize a moral responsibility to donate some of its profits to charity, but a public agency may be ethically prohibited from such largesse with public funds." Second, a "public agency may be ethically bound by the will of the general public to hire employees at union wage scales, but a small private company with very little capital may be unable to afford such salaries without firing people or risking bankruptcy." These examples support the findings from Chapter 3 about the difference between public and private organizations. Additionally, there are shorter- and longer-term effects of the same innovation, so it may take time to understand the ethical consequences of innovations.

As there are limited examples from the public sector, we provide some examples from private organizations (particularly from the service industry) that have faced ethical issues. Rogers (2003) gives several examples from society, including smoking and using chemical fertilizers in agriculture. For example, most airlines used to distribute a packet of cigarettes for free after meals or coffee until the 1960s to allow, or even encourage, people to smoke (Rogers, 2003). This example could be considered a service or marketing innovation, as other companies did not use this innovation and it aimed to increase customer satisfaction. However, when medical reports consistently found strong evidence that smoking (including second-hand smoke) was harmful to individual health, governments started banning smoking in certain places (including flights) while also significantly taxing sales of cigarettes. This example demonstrates the government's role in innovation (e.g., regulating the market and using instruments such as taxes). The same example demonstrates how values have changed over the years, which is also related to ethics. For instance, today it would be considered unethical for a company to use innovative tools to encourage smoking. On the contrary, activities such as restricting smoking, using different tools to discourage smoking, and even banning smoking could also be considered innovations.

Rogers's (2003) other example is about chemical innovations in the United States. In the 1950s, chemicals (e.g., DDT and DES) were recommended by universities to increase the productivity of crops. Using these new chemical products was certainly an innovation (e.g., product innovation) in the 1950s because it was novel, implemented, and positively affected outcomes. However, the US Environmental Protection Agency banned the use of DDT and DES in the 1970s, as it was later revealed that these chemicals were incredibly harmful to people's health. This example also illustrates the government's role in innovation (e.g., regulation and banning) and the ethical side of innovation (e.g., governments took action in response to negative impacts on citizens' health).

Third, even if an innovation yields positive benefits, ethical issues or concerns may exist if these benefits are not widely distributed or if a company charges far more than what is deemed necessary based on costs. A typical example of these issues concerns patents, which are protected by law; some drug companies are then able to charge extortionate fees for a particular medicine (e.g., some drugs, such as Zynteglo and Hemgenix, have cost over US$2.5 million to users in recent years). Ribeiro and Shapira (2020, p. 3) provide some historical background on patents:

The public dimension of patents has been an object of scrutiny for a long time, arguably since governments around the world started to implement and regulate their patent systems. As early as 1813, Thomas Jefferson, the first patent examiner of the US patent system, voiced concerns over the power of monopolies and how they could be detrimental to society … In countries such as Germany and France, compulsory public interest licensing laws were passed in the early decades of the 20th century. This was fueled by concerns over the accessibility to basic goods enjoying private protection, such as technologies and pharmaceuticals needed in wartime, which motivated public interest clauses in patent law.

Additionally, analyzing the US patent documents in the area of synthetic biology, Ribeiro and Shapira (2020) find that there are differences in terms of private and public value propositions. Accordingly, while "market and industrial opportunities," "cost and efficiency," "increasing compound yields," and "upscaling production" are the main private value propositions, "scientific advancements," "environmental sustainability," "human health," "food security," "animal health," and "job creation" are the main public value propositions. Therefore, there are not only differences between private and public value based on novel innovations (patents), but public sector innovations have expected positive outcomes for society.

Our fourth example is more recent and comes from the company Amazon. An ethical dilemma may occur not because of the outputs or outcomes but because of the process, such as working hours or work–life balance. There may be psychological costs for constant innovation not only in the private sector but also in the public sector. Kantor and Streitfeld (2015) find that Amazon encourages innovations in the workplace and primarily bottom-up innovations. However, although employees are well-paid, increasing pressure for innovation can increase employee stress and potential mistakes because innovation requires taking risks. They describe one employee in the company:

Jason Merkoski, 42, an engineer, worked on the team developing the first Kindle e-reader and served as a technology evangelist for Amazon, traveling the world to learn how people used the technology so it could be improved. He left Amazon in 2010 and then returned briefly in 2014. "The sheer number of innovations means things go wrong, you need to rectify, and then explain, and heaven help if you got an email from Jeff," he said. "It's as if you've got the C.E.O. of the company in bed with you at 3 a.m. breathing down your neck." (Kantor & Streitfeld, 2015, p. 8)

Even if these examples are from private settings, they are also highly relevant to public organizations and citizens. Such examples also show the government's role in innovation, including business innovation, which we can call marketing and service innovation as in the case of encouraging smoking in airlines in the 1950s. Thus, these examples are also relevant to Chapter 10. Furthermore, these examples demonstrate the complex and interrelated nature of public and private organizations (e.g., private organizations innovate and public organizations respond to ethical issues such as health concerns by using different innovative tools). In sum, to understand ethical issues and dilemmas, we can learn from the private sector and the interactions among public and private organizations and service users.

Examples of Ethical Issues

Several studies have demonstrated the ethical dimensions of innovations, especially concerning technological innovations in the public sector. Recent studies have analyzed the role and importance of open innovations and suggest that public organizations should encourage citizens to participate in policy processes or even decisions through some innovative and democratic tools, such as online government platforms (Heimstädt & Reischauer, 2018; Mergel & Desouza, 2013; Yuan & Gascó-Hernandez, 2021). For instance, Mergel and Desouza (2013, p. 889) state that citizens' participation "will contribute to the advancement of democracy and the vitality of public institution." However, some ethical issues may arise with citizens' participation, such as misleading information (Taeihagh, 2017) that may lead to ethical concerns.

Another example is telework, which is widely recognized as constituting an innovative work practice, mostly adopted during COVID-19 by almost all organizations (Raghavan et al., 2021). With telework, employees do not always need to be present in their offices. However, not all employees are allowed to use telework, and some work descriptions (such as street-level bureaucrats or service workers) cannot telework. For instance, many police officers are still needed in the streets, and doctors and nurses are still needed in hospitals. Therefore, although the option of teleworking benefits organizations and employees, because not everyone can use this option, there may be an issue of equity and thus of ethics.

Keeping and using personal biometric data in order to deal with crime and terrorism provides another compelling example:

When assessing this innovation from the logic of consequence, the following questions would be asked. How reliable are the technologies that are used? What are the costs of a central databases, and how accessible is this database? ... However, innovations in the public sector are also judged on their appropriateness ... Hence, in the example of assessing biometric data, not only should costs and benefits be taken into account, but also the effects that this innovation has on other values privacy ... This suggests the need to take into account the balancing between more economic and other values that lie behind innovations, while trying to meet the needs and challenges of specific groups or of society as a whole (in terms of responsiveness). (Bekkers et al., 2011b, pp. 17–18)

Governments are using big data and AI to become more innovative and serve citizens better. Still, big data could be seen as posing a threat to citizen privacy, could decrease civil freedoms, and could increase government control, as occurred in China's Social Credit System (Guenduez et al., 2020). Additionally, using big data in government operations is not objective. It could increase inequality, especially for the vulnerable populations. For example, disabled people may be left out as they may not be able to use technologies effectively (Guenduez et al., 2020).

Another concern is that employees can be displaced as a result of innovation. As Schot and Steinmueller (2018, p. 1562) warn, innovation can potentially cause "unemployment in sectors experiencing rapid technical change; however, in the long term, everyone will benefit since new high quality jobs will be generated." They further caution that innovation can also cause "destructive creation, benefiting the few at the expense of the many, leading to low-quality jobs, and creating more problems than it solves ... Innovation contributes massively to the current resource-intensive, wasteful and fossil fuel-based paradigm of mass production and mass consumption" (Schot and Steinmueller, 2018, p. 1562).

Inequality and thus ethical problems may increase because of increasing adoption of technologies in the public sector. According to

Schot and Steinmueller (2018, p. 1562), innovation can lead "directly to inequality because current innovation trajectories favour high tech solutions which assume high quality and pervasive infrastructure, and produces mass-produced products aimed mainly for consumers with substantial purchasing power" (Schot & Steinmueller, 2018, p. 1562). In fact, there is at least some evidence suggesting that public sector innovation displaces employment in the public sector, or at least results in elevated employee turnover rates (Cinar et al., 2019). For example, one study finds that about 40 percent of top managers left their organizations when Baltimore (a city in the US state of Maryland) implemented innovations (Sanger, 2008).

Another example of ethical issues of innovation comes from public health. As Sanger and Levin (1992, p. 102) explain:

In the 1960s the synthetic chemical, methadone, was developed in Holland to block heroin craving and was used there and in Hong Kong for heroin treatment. Later it was used in a small-scale methadone maintenance program at a New York hospital. HSA's [New York's Health Service Administration] developing methadone maintenance program was, therefore, tinkering with an both established idea and established program. The innovation lay in placing the idea in two contexts: first, by making the city the sponsor of a chemical treatment program (the city's previous programs had been "talking therapies") second, by defining a new target population-all addicts-and using aggressive outreach program to reach it. Previous successful drug treatment programs had focused on a small group of stable, highly motivated addicts.

However, though methadone is used to save lives, it has many harmful effects, including mental alteration and breathing problems. Furthermore, the availability of this drug may encourage people to use drugs excessively. Therefore, it was not surprising that some countries such as Singapore strictly control methadone (Singhealth, 2021, para. 15). This example also shows that a medical innovation developed by public hospitals and research centers may have hidden costs, negative spillover effects, or simply unethical aspects.

Last but not least, innovations can also have a deleterious societal impact. Gault and Soete (2022, p. 7) point to the devastation wreaked by financial innovation: "As an example of destructive innovation, consider some of the new financial product innovations, based on sub-prime mortgages, packaged as 'collateralized debt obligations' of 'asset-backed securities' which were made available in the years prior to the financial crisis in 2008. They all fitted the definition of innovation."

Conclusion

Unfortunately, there are few studies linking ethics and innovation. Exceptions include the work by van der Wal and Demircioglu (2020) and Yidong and Xinxin (2013) on the effects of ethical leadership on employees' innovative work behavior in the public and private sectors. An important reason why almost no studies have connected innovation and ethics may be that the field or scholarship of innovation and the field or scholarship of ethics are distinct, reflecting minimal interaction between these two subfields. Ethics is closely related to the quality of bureaucracy, good governance, and even performance in the public sector, but it is understudied by scholars of public administration and management (Drechsler, 2015). More specifically, we believe that ignoring the role of ethics is unfortunate because ethics is an essential priority for public sector innovation in many ways. For example: (1) A product innovation may increase efficiency but at the cost of laying off employees; (2) installing cameras on streets may reduce crimes but at the cost of reducing privacy; (3) collecting data on citizens' preferences and behavior may help to serve them better, but these data may be used unethically; and (4) a lack of innovation in government may result in a lack of responsiveness and thus may undermine trust.

As mentioned at the beginning of this chapter, there are many unknowns about the relationship between innovation and ethics, particularly in the public sector context. Thus, there are many limitations that run through the existing research, which may point the way toward promising directions for future studies. One issue is that sustainability has become a popular and relevant topic for ethics. The focus on sustainability can impact innovations because sustainable solutions, such as shared cars, facilitate collaboration, and sharing underutilized items forces individuals and organizations to be more innovative. As Foss and Saebi (2017, p. 221) argue, "the question of how managers can innovate their BMs [business models] toward greater sustainability has not been addressed sufficiently to date. Thus, a more explicit and systematic use of the BMI [business model innovation] construct is warranted to further this research field." Thus, public organizations can also focus on more sustainable solutions for public policy and public administration problems.

Second, we still have limited knowledge of how different types of innovation affect ethics. For example, are there any differences among product, service, process, and marketing innovations in terms of ethical principles? Product and service innovations may lead to more unemployment, while marketing innovations may lead to government failure. Which types of innovations can enhance the legitimacy of an organization and in what contexts? These are some questions that future studies may investigate further. Finally, during COVID-19, governments worldwide implemented many innovations, including service and process innovations. However, we still do not know the long-term effects and consequences of these policies for governments, societies, and individuals. Thus, future studies may look into the ethical consequences of these policies.

13 | Conclusions

An important insight is that context matters for innovation. Some contexts are characterized by low-innovation opportunities because they offer few opportunities for innovative activity. By contrast, high-innovation opportunities are replete with opportunities for innovative activity. One reason for the heterogeneity in the innovation opportunity of the context is the inherent risk and uncertainty about the outcomes emanating from innovation. A vital academic and practical question is how to enhance innovative activities in all contexts (e.g., different public organizations in different countries) regardless of barriers to innovation and contextual limitations.

Within the span of a generation, innovation has become interwoven in the fabric of modern society. Germany and Singapore refer to themselves as the countries of "ideas and innovation." Switzerland and Sweden celebrates its ranking as the most innovative country in Europe. Chile shares that it is "the most innovative country in Latin America." Milan champions MIND: the Milano Innovation District. Korea boasts its "Innovation Center." When it comes to the new societal challenges of sustainability, fueled by the need for environmental sustainability, income equity, and social inclusion, we all agree that innovation will be at the heart of paving the way forward.

What fuels the emergence of innovation as the driving force for economic and societal progress? Scholars have subjected innovation to the analytical lens of a broad spectrum of academic disciplines and fields to come up with a broad spectrum of answers and insights, ranging from companies to entrepreneurs, workers, institutions, finance, and culture – pretty much everything except for government.

Government is the last place anyone would look for innovation. As the founder of Intel, Gordon Moore, famously observed: "Combine liberal amounts of technology, capital and sunshine. Add one (1) university. Stir vigorously" (Moore & Davis, 2004, p. 9). According to the master of innovation, Moore, the government is not a necessary ingredient for innovation at all. Even the weather apparently contributes more to innovation than does the government. In much of the public discourse, the view of government was cemented by President Ronald Reagan, who, at a press conference on August 12, 1986, warned: "The nine most terrifying words in the English language are 'I'm from the government and I'm here to help.'" The best way that the government could help innovation was to stand down.

The point of this book is to dispute this conventional wisdom that, at best, the government has no role in innovation and, at worst, the more it tries to help the worse the actual innovative performance will be. This book makes it clear that there are two important ways that governments can enhance innovation. The first draws on a long tradition of research focusing on the role of government in providing key resources or aligning incentives for their provision, which are conducive to innovation. To the extent that new knowledge and ideas are catalysts for innovative activity, governments can, do, and should play an active role in both the provision of knowledge and human capital and also aligning incentives for private investments in knowledge and human capital. In particular, the academic discipline of economics has been consistent and adamant about the promise of the government to address the market failure inherent in the provision of knowledge and new ideas. Pathbreaking research by Link (2013), Leyden and Link (1999, 2015), Link and Link (2009), Link and Siegel (2007), Link and Scott (2019), and Rossini and Bozeman (1977) make it clear that the government can shift the winds of innovation and technological change from impeding the investment decisions of private actors to uplifting them. This rich literature is replete with compelling examples of government programs that have unleashed a torrent of innovative activity, ranging from the SBIR Program to the Bayh–Dole Act, federal research laboratories, and the massive funding of technology by federal agencies, such as the Department of Defense and Department of Energy.

However, this book also highlights a less analyzed role for the government in innovation, and that is in its public management. The management practices and organization within the public sector can also provide a rich source of innovation. This book has provided a blueprint for how public management can be conducive to innovation by being innovative itself. It is one thing to say that government can and should be supportive of innovation. It goes a step further to suggest that government can and should be innovative in its own management.

The reluctance to view innovation more as a promise than a problem may have its roots in the incipience of modern management theory. Well over a century ago, Frederick Taylor (1911), in *The Principles of Scientific Management*, posited that a scientific approach to the management of organizations would result in a superior and more predictable organizational performance. The key to organizational scientific management lies in replacing autonomous decision making with structure, organization, hierarchy, and control. The inevitable result of scientific management was a commodification and standardization of management, where the structure, organization, and process mattered more and the manager mattered less – that what mattered more were the overall managerial processes and tasks. The great achievement of Taylor (1911) was to take the manager out of management. Rather, processes could replace the hand of the manager. Fueled by a scientific explosion of quantification throughout the social sciences, the incipient field of management prospered by shifting the lens from the human side of the manager to the managerial process. Through the formalization of modern management research, the focus on the manager herself was replaced by a concern for the management system, with a priority on efficiency. Innovation in management was relegated to an afterthought. This was nowhere more true than in the context of management in the public sector.

However, ignoring innovation in the public sector imposes a punishing cost on society in at least two ways. The first is that even as the priority and race for innovation pervades society, a substantial portion of the workforce employed in the public sector is simply written off. In the United States, this accounts for about one-fifth of all jobs, in the ballpark of 120 million workers. In Sweden, the share of workers employed in the public sector is considerably greater at 30 percent. It is just slightly lower in other Scandinavian countries, such as Denmark and Finland. Discounting the potential of the public sector to innovate simply writes off a major part of society, ultimately eroding the promise of innovation. The same urgency and logic underlying social inclusion and increasing the breadth of society participating in the economy applies to sectors as well. Including marginalized and previously excluded groups in the innovation process has generally been found to enhance innovative activity. This holds for the public sector as well.

A mistake made by both the incipient research community as well as thought leaders in public policy and business as the priority of innovation in society surged in the late 1980s and early 1990s was the assumption that it involved only a restricted part of the economy: the large corporation. Theory, measurement, and policy all revolved around and remained focused on the largest companies. For example, the highly visible MIT Commission on Industrial Productivity, in *Made in America: Regaining the Productive Edge* (Dertouzos et al., 1989), focused exclusively on practices and policies to restore the innovative advantage of America's largest manufacturing corporations. In fact, by the end of the century, the United States found itself prospering from a wave of innovative activity that would have been unimaginable just a few years earlier, in what Stiglitz (2004) called *The Roaring Nineties: A New History of the World's Most Prosperous Decade.* However, the new era of innovation was not ushered in from the part of the economy assumed to be the sole source of innovation – the large corporations – but rather from a source hardly noticed and analyzed in the scholarly literature: new and small firms. Scholarly literature missed the mark by writing off large parts of the economy deemed to be excluded from innovation. This may have contributed to the policy fallacy made throughout the developed countries of neglecting the development of a highly innovative part of the economy. As the great philosopher George Santanyan warned: "Those who do not learn history are doomed to repeat it." Ignoring the promise of public sector innovation comes at its own peril.

The second way in which ignoring public sector innovation costs society is by reducing innovative activity in the private sector. More recent theories and frameworks of innovation focus on the interconnectedness of the actors, in that they form a coherent ecosystem. This interdependence means that a paucity of innovation emanating from a key component of the innovation ecosystem can ultimately deplete the innovation activity of other components. This view suggests that the propensity of the private sector to generate innovative activity is linked to public sector innovation.

On January 28, 1986, after just seventy-three seconds into its flight trajectory, the Space Shuttle *Challenger* exploded, killing all seven crew members, including a commander, a pilot, mission specialists, and a teacher. No one would have ever said that the o-ring, which seals a joint in the right solid rocket booster, powered the Space Shuttle.

However, as Kremer (1993) showed, the ability of the overall system to attain its goal was undermined by its weakest link: the o-ring. To the extent that innovation with the public management of the public sector enables innovation in the private sector, ignoring public sector innovation will result not just in less innovation in the public sector but also in the private sector.

An anxious world is besieged with anxieties about the future. The environment is endangered. Social unrest and political divisiveness cripple society. Innovation holds the promise for solutions. Innovation in the future will involve the public sector, either directly or indirectly. Innovation is simply too important and crucial to be left in the hands of the few. A new era of public sector innovation, working in tandem with its private sector counterpart, holds the promise for a secure and viable future.

References

Acemoglu, D., & Restrepo, P. (2020). The wrong kind of AI? Artificial intelligence and the future of labour demand. *Cambridge Journal of Regions, Economy and Society, 13*(1), 25–35.

Acemoglu, D., & Robinson, J. A. (2013). *Why nations fail: The origins of power, prosperity, and poverty.* New York, NY: Crown Business.

Acemoglu, D., & Verdier, T. (2000). The choice between market failures and corruption. *American Economic Review, 90*(1), 194–211.

Acs, Z. J., & Audretsch, D. B. (1988). Innovation in large and small firms: An empirical analysis. *The American Economic Review, 78*(4), 678–690.

Acs, Z. J., & Audretsch, D. B. (1990). *Innovation and small firms.* Boston, MA: MIT Press.

Acs, Z. J., & Audretsch, D. B. (2003). Innovation and technological change. In Z. J. Acs, & D. B. Audretsch (Eds.), *Handbook of entrepreneurship research* (pp. 55–79). Norwell, MA: Kluwer Academic Publishers.

Acs, Z. J., Audretsch, D. B., & Lehmann, E. E. (2013). The knowledge spillover theory of entrepreneurship. *Small Business Economics, 41*(4), 757–774.

Acs, Z. J., Audretsch, D. B., Lehmann, E. E., & Licht, G. (2017). National systems of innovation. *The Journal of Technology Transfer, 42*(5), 997–1008.

Acs, Z. J., Braunerhjelm, P., Audretsch, D. B., & Carlsson, B. (2009). The knowledge spillover theory of entrepreneurship. *Small Business Economics, 32*(1), 15–30.

Afsar, B., & Masood, M. (2018). Transformational leadership, creative self-efficacy, trust in supervisor, uncertainty avoidance, and innovative work behavior of nurses. *The Journal of Applied Behavioral Science, 54*(1), 36–61.

Agranoff, R. (1991). Human services integration: Past and present challenges in public administration. *Public Administration Review, 51*(6), 533–542.

Agranoff, R., & McGuire, M. (2004). *Collaborative public management: New strategies for local governments.* Washington, DC: Georgetown University Press.

Aiken, M., & Hage, J. (1971). The organic organization and innovation. *Sociology, 5*(1), 63–82.

Alatas, S. F. (2021). Deparochialising the Canon: The case of sociological theory. *Journal of Historical Sociology, 34*(1), 13–27.

Albury, D. (2005). Fostering innovation in public services. *Public Money and Management, 25*(1), 51–56.

Albury, D. (2011). Creating the conditions for radical public service innovation. *Australian Journal of Public Administration, 70*(3), 227–235.

Ali, M., Shujahat, M., Ali, Z., Kianto, A., Wang, M., & Bontis, N. (2022). The neglected role of knowledge assets interplay in the pursuit of organisational ambidexterity. *Technovation, 114*, 102452. www.sciencedirect.com/science/article/abs/pii/S0166497221002339? via%3Dihub

Allison, G. T. (1980). *Public and private management: Are they fundamentally alike in all unimportant respects?* Cambridge, MA: John F. Kennedy School of Government, Harvard University.

Alsos, G. A., Clausen, T. H., & Isaksen, E. J. (2016). Innovation among public-sector organisations: Push and pull factors. In J. L. H. Alves (Ed.), *Entrepreneurial and innovative practices in public institutions: A quality of life approach* (pp. 81–98). Switzerland: Springer.

Altshuler, A. A., & Behn, R. D. (1997). *Innovation in American government: Challenges, opportunities, and dilemmas.* Washington, DC: Brookings Institution Press.

Altshuler, A. A., & Zegans, M. D. (1997). Innovation and public management: Notes from the state house and city hall. In A. A. Altshuler, & R. D. Bchn (Eds.), *Innovation in American government: Challenges, opportunities, and dilemmas* (pp. 68–80). Washington, DC: The Brookings Institution Press.

Amabile, T. M., Conti, R., Coon, H., Lazenby, J., & Herron, M. (1996). Assessing the work environment for creativity. *Academy of Management Journal, 39*(5), 1154–1184.

Andersen, J. A. (2010). Public versus private managers: How public and private managers differ in leadership behavior. *Public Administration Review, 70*(1), 131–141.

Anderson, N., Potočnik, K., & Zhou, J. (2014). Innovation and creativity in organizations: A state-of-the-science review, prospective commentary, and guiding framework. *Journal of Management, 40*(5), 1297–1333.

Anderson, N. R., & West, M. A. (1998). Measuring climate for work group innovation: Development and validation of the team climate inventory. *Journal of Organizational Behavior, 19*(3), 235–258.

Angle, H. L. (2000). Psychology and organizational innovation. In H. L. Angle, A. H. Van de Ven, & M. S. Poole (Eds.), *Research on the management of innovation: The Minnesota studies* (pp. 135–170). New York: Oxford University Press.

Anseel, F., Beatty, A. S., Shen, W., Lievens, F., & Sackett, P. R. (2015). How are we doing after 30 years? A meta-analytic review of the antecedents and outcomes of feedback-seeking behavior. *Journal of Management, 41*(1), 318–348. Retrieved from http://jom.sagepub.com/content/41/1/318.full.pdf

Ansell, C., & Gash, A. (2008). Collaborative governance in theory and practice. *Journal of Public Administration Research and Theory, 18*(4), 543–571.

Ansell, C., Sørensen, E., & Torfing, J. (2021). The COVID-19 pandemic as a game changer for public administration and leadership? The need for robust governance responses to turbulent problems. *Public Management Review, 23*(7), 949–960.

Arrow, K. J. (1962). The economic implications of learning by doing. *The Review of Economic Studies, 29*(3), 155–173.

Arundel, A., Bloch, C., & Ferguson, B. (2019). Advancing innovation in the public sector: Aligning innovation measurement with policy goals. *Research Policy, 48*(3), 789–798.

Arundel, A., Casali, L., & Hollanders, H. (2015). How European public sector agencies innovate: The use of bottom-up, policy-dependent and knowledge-scanning innovation methods. *Research Policy, 44*(7), 1271–1282.

Arundel, A., & Huber, D. (2013). From too little to too much innovation? Issues in measuring innovation in the public sector. *Structural Change and Economic Dynamics, 27*, 146–159.

Arundel, A., Lorenz, E., Lundvall, B.-Å., & Valeyre, A. (2007). How Europe's economies learn: A comparison of work organization and innovation mode for the EU-15. *Industrial and Corporate Change, 16*(6), 1175–1210.

Aryal, G., Mann, J., Loveridge, S., & Joshi, S. (2018). Exploring innovation creation across rural and urban firms: Analysis of the national survey of business competitiveness. *Journal of Entrepreneurship and Public Policy, 7*(4), 357–376.

Audretsch, D., Colombelli, A., Grilli, L., Minola, T., & Rasmussen, E. (2020). Innovative start-ups and policy initiatives. *Research Policy, 49*(10), 104027.

Audretsch, D. B. (1991). *The market and the state: Government policy towards business in Europe, Japan and the United States.* New York: New York University Press.

Audretsch, D. B., Belitski, M., Caiazza, R., Günther, C., & Menter, M. (2022). From latent to emergent entrepreneurship: The importance of context. *Technological Forecasting & Social Change, 175*, 121356.

Audretsch, D. B., & Feldman, M. P. (1996). R&D spillovers and the geography of innovation and production. *The American Economic Review, 86*(3), 630–640.

Audretsch, D. B., & Feldman, M. P. (2004). Knowledge spillovers and the geography of innovation. *Handbook of Regional and Urban Economics*, 4, 2713–2739.

Audretsch, D. B., & Fiedler, A. (2023). Does the entrepreneurial state crowd out entrepreneurship? *Small Business Economics*, 60(2), 573–589.

Audretsch, D. B., Siegel, D. S., & Terjesen, S. (2020). Entrepreneurship in the public and nonprofit sectors. *Public Administration Review*, 80(3), 468–472.

Australian Government. (2010). *Ahead of the game: Blueprint for reform of Australian government administration*. Barton, ACT, Australia: Advisory Group on Reform of Australian Government Administration.

Australian National Audit Office (ANAO). (2009). *Innovation in the public sector: Enabling better performance, driving new directions*. Barton, ACT, Australia: Australian National Audit Office.

Australian Public Service Commission (APSC). (2011). *State of the service report 2010–2011: Australian public service employee survey results*. Canberra: Australian Public Service Commission.

Australian Public Service Commission (APSC). (2013). *State of the service report: State of the service series 2012–2013*. Canberra, Australia: Australian Public Service Commission. Retrieved from www.apsc.gov.au/__data/assets/pdf_file/0018/29223/SOSR-2012_13-final-tagged2.pdf

Australian Public Service Commission (APSC). (2020). *State of the service report 2019–2020*. Canberra: Commonwealth of Australia.

Autio, E., Kenney, M., Mustar, P., Siegel, D., & Wright, M. (2014). Entrepreneurial innovation: The importance of context. *Research Policy*, 43(7), 1097–1108.

Baker, R. (1994). Comparative public management: Coming in from the cold. In R. Baker (Ed.), *Comparative public management: Putting US public policy and implementation in context* (pp. 1–8). Westport, CT: Praeger.

Baldridge, J. V., & Burnham, R. A. (1975). Organizational innovation: Individual, organizational, and environmental impacts. *Administrative Science Quarterly*, 20(2), 165–176.

Baldwin, C., & Von Hippel, E. (2011). Modeling a paradigm shift: From producer innovation to user and open collaborative innovation. *Organization Science*, 22(6), 1399–1417.

Balven, R., Fenters, V., Siegel, D. S., & Waldman, D. (2018). Academic entrepreneurship: The roles of identity, motivation, championing, education, work-life balance, and organizational justice. *Academy of Management Perspectives*, 32(1), 21–42.

Bamberger, P. (2008). From the editors beyond contextualization: Using context theories to narrow the micro-macro gap in management research. *Academy of Management Journal*, 51(5), 839–846.

Baniamin, H. M. (2019). Linking socio-economic performance, quality of governance, and trust in the civil service: Does culture intercede in the perceived relationships? Evidence from and beyond Bangladesh, Nepal and Sri Lanka. *Asia Pacific Journal of Public Administration*, *41*(3), 127–141.

Barrutia, J. M., & Echebarria, C. (2019). Drivers of exploitative and explorative innovation in a collaborative public-sector context. *Public Management Review*, *21*(3), 446–472.

Bartlett, D., & Dibben, P. (2002). Public sector innovation and entrepreneurship: Case studies from local government. *Local Government Studies*, *28*(4), 107–121.

Bartos, S. (2003). Creating and sustaining innovation. *Australian Journal of Public Administration*, *62*(1), 09–14.

Barzelay, M. (2000). The new public management: A bibliographical essay for Latin American (and other) scholars. *International Public Management Journal*, *3*(2), 229–265.

Barzelay, M. (2001). *The new public management: Improving research and policy dialogue*. Berkeley: University of California Press.

Bason, C. (2010). *Leading public sector innovation: Co-creating for a better society*. Bristol: Policy Press.

Bauer, M. W. (2008). Diffuse anxieties, deprived entrepreneurs: Commission reform and middle management. *Journal of European Public Policy*, *15*(5), 691–707.

Bauer, M. W. (2012). Tolerant, if personal goals remain unharmed: Explaining supranational bureaucrats' attitudes to organizational change. *Governance*, *25*(3), 485–510.

Bauer, M. W., & Becker, S. (2020). Democratic backsliding, populism, and public administration. *Perspectives on Public Management and Governance*, *3*(1), 19–31.

Becker, S. W., & Whisler, T. L. (1967). The innovative organization: A selective view of current theory and research. *Journal of Business*, *40*(4), 462–469.

Bekkers, V., Edelenbos, J., & Steijn, B. (2011a). *Innovation in the public sector: Linking capacity and leadership*. Basingstoke, Hampshire, GBR: Palgrave Macmillan.

Bekkers, V., Edelenbos, J., & Steijn, B. (2011b). Linking innovation to the public sector: Contexts, concepts and challenges. In V. Bekkers, J. Edelenbos, & B. Steijn (Eds.), *Innovation in the public sector: Linking capacity and leadership* (pp. 3–32). Basingstoke, Hampshire, GBR: Palgrave Macmillan.

Bekkers, V., & Noordegraaf, M. (2016). Public managers and professionals in collaborative innovation. In J. Torfing, & P. Triantafillou (Eds.), *Enhancing public innovation by transforming public governance* (pp. 139–159). New York: Cambridge University Press.

Bentley, D., & Bentley, C. (2022). *Winning the week: How to plan a successful week, every week.* Fayetteville, AR: Houndstooth Press.

Berman, E. M., Chen, D.-Y., Wang, X., & Liu, I. (2019). Executive entrepreneurship in national departments. *Administration & Society, 51*(6), 855–884.

Berman, E. M., & Kim, C.-G. (2010). Creativity management in public organizations: Jump-starting innovation. *Public Performance & Management Review, 33*(4), 619–652.

Bernier, L. (2001). Developing the public service of tomorrow: Imaginative government. *Public Sector Management, 12*(2), 17–20.

Bernier, L., & Hafsi, T. (2007). The changing nature of public entrepreneurship. *Public Administration Review, 67*(3), 488–503.

Bezes, P., & Jeannot, G. (2018). Autonomy and managerial reforms in Europe: Let or make public managers manage? *Public Administration, 96*(1), 3–22.

Birkland, T. A. (2004). "The World Changed Today": Agenda-setting and policy change in the wake of the September 11 terrorist attacks. *Review of Policy Research, 21*(2), 179–200.

Bloch, C. (2011). *Measuring public innovation in the Nordic countries (MEPIN).* Nordic Council of Ministers.

Bloch, C., & Bugge, M. M. (2013). Public sector innovation – From theory to measurement. *Structural Change and Economic Dynamics, 27*, 133–145. Retrieved from www.sciencedirect.com/science/article/pii/S0954349X13000477

Bogers, M., Chesbrough, H., & Moedas, C. (2018). Open innovation: Research, practices, and policies. *California Management Review, 60*(2), 5–16.

Bommert, B. (2010). Collaborative innovation in the public sector. *International Public Management Review, 11*(1), 15–33.

Boon, J., Wynen, J., & Callens, C. (2023). A stakeholder perspective on public sector innovation: Linking the target groups of innovations to the inclusion of stakeholder ideas. *International Review of Administrative Sciences, 89*(2), 330–345.

Borins, S. F. (1998). *Innovating with integrity: How local heroes are transforming American government.* Washington, DC: Georgetown University Press.

Borins, S. F. (2000). Loose cannons and rule breakers, or enterprising leaders? Some evidence about innovative public managers. *Public Administration Review, 60*(6), 498–507.

Borins, S. F. (2001). *The challenge of innovating in government.* Arlington, VA: PricewaterhouseCoopers Endowment for the Business of Government.

Borins, S. F. (2002). Leadership and innovation in the public sector. *Leadership & Organization Development Journal*, 23(8), 467–476.

Borins, S. F. (2009). *Innovations in government: Research, recognition, and replication*. Washington, DC: Brookings Institution Press.

Borins, S. F. (2010). *Innovation as narrative*. Cambridge, MA: Ash Center for Democratic Governance and Innovation, Harvard Kennedy School.

Borins, S. F. (2014). *The persistence of innovation in government*. Washington, DC: Brookings Institution Press with Ash Center for Democratic Governance and Innovation.

Borins, S. F. (2018). Public sector innovation in a context of radical populism. *Public Management Review*, 20(12), 1858–1871.

Boukamel, O., & Emery, Y. (2017). Evolution of organizational ambidexterity in the public sector and current challenges of innovation capabilities. *The Innovation Journal: The Public Sector Innovation Journal*, 2(22), 1–26.

Boyer, E. J., Kolpakov, A., & Schmitz, H. P. (2019). Do executives approach leadership differently when they are involved in collaborative partnerships? A perspective from international Nongovernmental Organizations (INGOs). *Public Performance & Management Review*, 42(1), 213–240.

Boyne, G. A. (2002). Public and private management: What's the difference? *Journal of Management Studies*, 39(1), 97–122.

Bozeman, B. (2004). *All organizations are public: Comparing public and private organizations*. Washington, DC: Beard Books.

Bozeman, B., & Crow, M. (1991). Technology transfer from US government and university R&D laboratories. *Technovation*, 11(4), 231–246.

Bozeman, B., & Kingsley, G. (1998). Risk culture in public and private organizations. *Public Administration Review*, 58(2), 109–118.

Bozeman, B., & Sarewitz, D. (2011). Public value mapping and science policy evaluation. *Minerva*, 49(1), 1–23.

Breul, J. D., & Kamensky, J. M. (2008). Federal government reform: Lessons from Clinton's "reinventing government" and Bush's "management agenda" initiatives. *Public Administration Review*, 68(6), 1009–1026.

Breznitz, D., & Ornston, D. (2018). The politics of partial success: Fostering innovation in innovation policy in an era of heightened public scrutiny. *Socio-Economic Review*, 16(4), 721–741. https://doi.org/10.1093/ser/mww018

Brown, K., & Osborne, S. P. (2012). *Managing change and innovation in public service organizations*. New York, NY: Routledge.

Bryson, A., Dale-Olsen, H., & Barth, E. (2009). *How does innovation affect worker well-being?* London: School of Business and Political Science, Centre for Economic Performance (London)

Bugge, M., Mortensen, P. S., & Bloch, C. (2011). *Measuring public innovation in Nordic Countries*. Report on the Nordic Pilot Studies – Analyses of methodology and results.

Bugge, M. M., & Bloch, C. W. (2016). Between bricolage and break-throughs – Framing the many faces of public sector innovation. *Public Money & Management, 36*(4), 281–288.

Burns, T. E., & Stalker, G. M. (1961). *The management of innovation*. London: Tavistock.

Bysted, R., & Hansen, J. R. (2015). Comparing public and private sector employees' innovative behaviour: Understanding the role of job and organizational characteristics, job types, and subsectors. *Public Management Review, 17*(5), 698–717.

Callens, C. (2023). User involvement as a catalyst for collaborative public service innovation. *Journal of Public Administration Research and Theory, 33*(2), 329–341.

Cantwell, J. (2006). Innovation and competitiveness. In J. Fagerberg, & D. C. Mowery (Eds.), *Oxford handbook of innovation* (pp. 543–567). New York: Oxford University Press.

Capponi, G., Martinelli, A., & Nuvolari, A. (2022). Breakthrough innovations and where to find them. *Research Policy, 51*(1), 104376.

Carley, S. (2011). The era of state energy policy innovation: A review of policy instruments. *Review of Policy Research, 28*(3), 265–294.

Carlino, G. A. (2001). Knowledge spillovers: Cities' role in the new economy. *Business Review Q, 4*, 17–24.

Carney, R. W., & Zheng, L. Y. (2009). Institutional (Dis)incentives to innovate: An explanation for Singapore's innovation gap. *Journal of East Asian Studies, 9*(2), 291–319. https://doi.org/10.1017/s1598240800003015

Carr, K. (2009). *Powering ideas: An innovation agenda for the 21st century*. Australia: Department of Innovation, Industry, Science and Research.

Chan, H. S., & Gao, J. (2008). Old wine in new bottles: A county-level case study of anti-corruption reform in the People's Republic of China. *Crime, Law and Social Change, 49*(2), 97–117.

Cheah, S. (2016). Framework for measuring research and innovation impact. *Innovation, 18*(2), 212–232.

Chen, J., Walker, R. M., & Sawhney, M. (2021). Public service innovation: A typology. *Public Management Review, 22*(11), 1674–1695.

Chen, Y. (2006). Marketing innovation. *Journal of Economics & Management Strategy, 15*(1), 101–123.

Chenok, D. J., Kamensky, J. M., Keegan, M. J., & Ben-Yehuda, G. (2013). *Six trends driving change in government*. Washington, DC: IBM Center for The Business of Government.

Chesbrough, H. (2007). Business model innovation: It's not just about technology anymore. *Strategy & Leadership, 35*(6), 12–17.

Chicot, J., & Matt, M. (2018). Public procurement of innovation: A review of rationales, designs, and contributions to grand challenges. *Science and Public Policy, 45*(4), 480–492.

Chindarkar, N., Howlett, M., & Ramesh, M. (2017). Introduction to the special issue: "Conceptualizing Effective Social Policy Design: Design Spaces and Capacity Challenges." *Public Administration and Development, 37*(1), 3–14.

Cho, Y. J., & Song, H. J. (2021). How to facilitate innovative behavior and organizational citizenship behavior: Evidence from public employees in Korea. *Public Personnel Management, 50*(4), 509–537.

Christensen, C., Anthony, S., & Roth, E. A. (2004). *Seeing what's next: Using the theories of innovation to predict industry change.* Boston, MA: Harvard Business Press.

Christensen, T., Lægreid, P., Roness, P. G., & Røvik, K. A. (2007). *Organization theory and the public sector: Instrument, culture and myth.* New York: Routledge.

Chung, S. (2002). Building a national innovation system through regional innovation systems. *Technovation, 22*(8), 485–491.

Cinar, E. (2020). Chapter 3: Public sector innovation. In P. Trott (Ed.), *Innovation management and new product development* (pp. 80–102). London: Pearson.

Cinar, E., Demircioglu, M. A., Acik, A. C., & Simms, C. (2024). Public sector innovation in a city state: exploring innovation types and national context in Singapore. *Research Policy, 53*(2), 104915.

Cinar, E., Simms, C., & Trott, P. (2022a). Collaborative public sector innovation: An analysis of Italy, Japan, and Turkey. *Governance.*

Cinar, E., Simms, C., Trott, P., & Demircioglu, M. A. (2022b). Public sector innovation in context: A comparative study of innovation types. *Public Management Review*, 1–29.

Cinar, E., Trott, P., & Simms, C. (2019). A systematic review of barriers to public sector innovation process. *Public Management Review, 21*(2), 264–290.

Cinar, E., Trott, P., & Simms, C. (2021). An international exploration of barriers and tactics in the public sector innovation process. *Public Management Review, 23*(3), 326–353.

Clausen, T. H., Demircioglu, M. A., & Alsos, G. A. (2020). Intensity of innovation in public sector organizations: The role of push and pull factors. *Public Administration, 98*(1), 159–176.

Cohen, W. M., & Levinthal, D. A. (1990). Absorptive capacity: A new perspective on learning and innovation. *Administrative Science Quarterly, 35*(1), 128–152.

Corwin, R. G. (1972). Strategies for organizational innovation: An empirical comparison. *American Sociological Review, 37*(4), 441–454.

Crow, M., & Bozeman, B. (1998). *Limited by design: R&D laboratories in the US national innovation system.* New York: Columbia University Press.

Cunningham, J. B., & Kempling, J. S. (2009). Implementing change in public sector organizations. *Management Decision, 47*(2), 330–344.

D'Attoma, I., & Ieva, M. (2020). Determinants of technological innovation success and failure: Does marketing innovation matter? *Industrial Marketing Management, 91*, 64–81.

D'Este, P., Iammarino, S., Savona, M., & von Tunzelmann, N. (2008). What hampers innovation? Evidence from the UK CIS4. *SEWPS, SPRU Electronic Working Paper Series, Paper* (168).

D'Este, P., Iammarino, S., Savona, M., & von Tunzelmann, N. (2012). What hampers innovation? Revealed barriers versus deterring barriers. *Research Policy, 41*(2), 482–488.

Daft, R. L. (1978). A dual-core model of organizational innovation. *Academy of Management Journal, 21*(2), 193–210.

Daft, R. L., & Marcic, D. (2019). *Understanding management*. Boston, MA: Cengage Learning.

Damanpour, F. (1991). Organizational innovation: A meta-analysis of effects of determinants and moderators. *Academy of Management Journal, 34*(3), 555–590.

Damanpour, F., Sanchez-Henriquez, F., & Avellaneda, C. N. (2022). Environmental and organizational antecedents of plural sourcing of public services. *Public Administration Review, 82*(2), 325–337.

Damanpour, F., & Schneider, M. (2009). Characteristics of innovation and innovation adoption in public organizations: Assessing the role of managers. *Journal of Public Administration Research and Theory, 19*(3), 495–522.

Damanpour, F., Walker, R. M., & Avellaneda, C. N. (2009). Combinative effects of innovation types and organizational performance: A longitudinal study of service organizations. *Journal of Management Studies, 46*(4), 650–675.

Dawson, G. S., & Denford, J. S. (2015). *A playbook for CIO-enabled innovation in the federal government*. Retrieved from Washington, DC: www.businessofgovernment.org/sites/default/files/A%20Playbook%20 for%20CIO-Enabled%20Innovation%20in%20the%20Federal%20 Government.pdf

De Coninck, B., Gascó-Hernández, M., Viaene, S., & Leysen, J. (2021). Determinants of open innovation adoption in public organizations: A systematic review. *Public Management Review*, 1–25. https://doi.org/10.108 0/14719037.2021.2003106

De Dreu, C. K. (2006). When too little or too much hurts: Evidence for a curvilinear relationship between task conflict and innovation in teams. *Journal of Management, 32*(1), 83–107.

de Lancer Julnes, P., & Gibson, E. (2016). *Innovation in the public and nonprofit sectors: A public solutions handbook*. New York, NY: Routledge.

de Vries, H., Bekkers, V., & Tummers, L. (2016). Innovations in the public sector: A systematic review and future research agenda. *Public Administration*, 94(1), 146–166.

De Vries, H., Tummers, L., & Bekkers, V. (2018). The diffusion and adoption of public sector innovations: A meta-synthesis of the literature. *Perspectives on Public Management and Governance*, 1(3), 159–176.

Deci, E. L., Connell, J. P., & Ryan, R. M. (1989). Self-determination in a work organization. *Journal of Applied Psychology*, 74(4), 580–590.

Demircioglu, M. A. (2017). Reinventing the wheel? Public sector innovation in the age of governance. *Public Administration Review*, 77(5), 800–805.

Demircioglu, M. A. (2017b). *Three essays on public sector innovation*. (Ph.D. Dissertation). Indiana University, Bloomington, IN.

Demircioglu, M. A. (2018). The effects of empowerment practices on perceived barriers to innovation: Evidence from public organizations. *International Journal of Public Administration*, 41(15), 1302–1313.

Demircioglu, M. A. (2018). Organizational innovation. In A. Farazmand (Ed.), *Global encyclopedia of public administration, public policy, and governance* (pp. 4356–4360). Cham, Switzerland: Springer International Publishing.

Demircioglu, M. A. (2019). Why does innovation in government occur and persist? Evidence from the Australian government. *Asia Pacific Journal of Public Administration*, 41(4), 217–229.

Demircioglu, M. A. (2020). The effects of organizational and demographic context for innovation implementation in public organizations. *Public Management Review*, 22(12), 1852–1875.

Demircioglu, M. A. (2021). Sources of innovation, autonomy, and employee job satisfaction in public organizations. *Public Performance & Management Review*, 44(1), 155–186.

Demircioglu, M. A., & Audretsch, D. B. (2017). Conditions for innovation in public sector organizations. *Research Policy*, 46(9), 1681–1691. Retrieved from www.sciencedirect.com/science/article/pii/S0048733317301385

Demircioglu, M. A., & Audretsch, D. B. (2019). Public sector innovation: The effect of universities. *The Journal of Technology Transfer*, 44(2), 596–614.

Demircioglu, M. A., & Audretsch, D. B. (2020). Conditions for complex innovations: Evidence from public organizations. *The Journal of Technology Transfer*, 45(3), 820–843.

Demircioglu, M. A., Audretsch, D. B., & Slaper, T. F. (2019). Sources of innovation and innovation type: Firm-level evidence from the United States. *Industrial and Corporate Change*, 28(6), 1365–1379.

Demircioglu, M. A., & Berman, E. (2019). Effects of the innovation climate on turnover intention in the Australian public service. *The American Review of Public Administration*, 49(5), 614–628.

Demircioglu, M. A., & Chen, C.-A. (2019). Public employees' use of social media: Its impact on need satisfaction and intrinsic work motivation. *Government Information Quarterly*, *36*(1), 51–60.

Demircioglu, M. A., & Chowdhury, F. (2021). Entrepreneurship in public organizations: The role of leadership behavior. *Small Business Economics*, *57*(3), 1107–1123.

Demircioglu, M. A., Chowdhury, F., & Vivona, R. (2020). Public sector entrepreneurship. In Ali Farazmand (Ed.), *Global encyclopedia of public administration and public policy*. Cham, Switzerland. https://doi .org/10.1007/978-3-319-31816-5_4002-1

Demircioglu, M. A., Hameduddin, T., & Knox, C. (2023). Innovative work behaviors and networking across government. *International Review of Administrative Sciences*, *89*(1), 145–164.

Demircioglu, M. A., & Van der Wal, Z. (2022). Leadership and innovation: What's the story? The relationship between leadership support level and innovation target. *Public Management Review*, *24*(8), 1289–1311.

Demircioglu, M. A., & Vivona, R. (2021). Depoliticizing the European immigration debate: How to employ public sector innovation to integrate migrants. *Research Policy*, *50*(2), 104150.

Denhardt, J. V., & Denhardt, R. B. (2015). *The new public service: Serving, not steering*. New York, NY: Routledge.

Dertouzos, M. L., Lester, R. K., & Solow, R. M. (1989). *Made in America: Regaining the productive edge*. Cambridge, MA: The MIT Press.

Donges, A., Meier, J.-M., & Silva, R. C. (2023). The impact of institutions on innovation. *Management Science*, *69*(4), 1951–1974.

Dosi, G. (1988). The nature of the innovative process. In C. Freeman, R. Nelson, G. Silverberg, G. Dosi, & L. Soete (Eds.), *Technical change and economic theory* (pp. 221–238). London: Pinter.

Downs Jr, G. W., & Mohr, L. B. (1979). Toward a theory of innovation. *Administration & Society*, *10*(4), 379–408.

Drechsler, W. (2009). The rise and demise of the new public management: Lessons and opportunities for South East Europe. *International Public Administration Review*, *7*(3), 7–27.

Drechsler, W. (2015). Paradigms of non-Western public administration and governance. In A. Massey, & K. Johnston (Eds.), *The international handbook of public administration and governance* (pp. 104–131). Cheltenham: Edward Elgar.

Drechsler, W. (2020). Good bureaucracy: Max Weber and public administration today. *Max Weber Studies*, *20*(2), 219–224.

Drechsler, W., & Randma-Liiv, T. (2016). In some Central and Eastern European countries, some NPM tools may sometimes work: A reply to Dan and Pollitt's 'NPM can work'. *Public Management Review*, *18*(10), 1559–1565.

Dudau, A., Kominis, G., & Szocs, M. (2018). Innovation failure in the eye of the beholder: Towards a theory of innovation shaped by competing agendas within higher education. *Public Management Review, 20*(2), 254–272.

Dunleavy, P. (2014). *Democracy, bureaucracy and public choice: Economic approaches in political science.* London: Routledge.

Durant, R. F. (2008). Sharpening a knife cleverly: Organizational change, policy paradox, and the "weaponizing" of administrative reforms. *Public Administration Review, 68*(2), 282–294.

Dutta, S., Lanvin, B., León, L. R., & Wunsch-Vincent, S. (2022). *Global innovation index 2022: What is the future of innovation-driven growth.* Geneva: WIPO.

(E&Y), Ernst & Young. (2017). *Public sector innovation: From ideas to actions.* Canada: Ernst & Young LLP (E&Y).

Earl, L. (2003). Innovation and change in the public sector: A seeming oxymoron. *Statistics Canada SIEID Working Paper Series* (2002–01).

Edler, J., & Georghiou, L. (2007). Public procurement and innovation – Resurrecting the demand side. *Research Policy, 36*(7), 949–963.

Edquist, C., & Zabala-Iturriagagoitia, J. M. (2012). Public procurement for innovation as mission-oriented innovation policy. *Research Policy, 41*(10), 1757–1769.

Efrat, K. (2014). The direct and indirect impact of culture on innovation. *Technovation, 34*(1), 12–20.

Ek Österberg, E., & Qvist, M. (2020). Public sector innovation as governance reform: A comparative analysis of competitive and collaborative strategies in the Swedish transport sector. *Administration & Society, 52*(2), 292–318.

Emerson, K., Nabatchi, T., & Balogh, S. (2012). An integrative framework for collaborative governance. *Journal of Public Administration Research and Theory, 22*(1), 1–29.

Engelen, A., Gupta, V., Strenger, L., & Brettel, M. (2015). Entrepreneurial orientation, firm performance, and the moderating role of transformational leadership behaviors. *Journal of Management, 41*(4), 1069–1097.

Ettlie, J. E., Bridges, W. P., & O'keefe, R. D. (1984). Organization strategy and structural differences for radical versus incremental innovation. *Management Science, 30*(6), 682–695.

European Commission. (2011). *Innobarometer 2010. Analytical report: Innovation in public organization.* Brussels: Directorate General Communication, The European Commission.

Evans, P., & Rauch, J. E. (1999). Bureaucracy and growth: A cross-national analysis of the effects of "Weberian" state structures on economic growth. *American Sociological Review, 64*(5), 748–765.

Fagerberg, J., Mowery, D. C., & Nelson, R. R. (2006). *The Oxford handbook of innovation.* New York: Oxford University Press.

Fayol, H. (2013). *General and industrial management*. Eastford, CT: Martino Fine Books.

Feldman, M. P. (1994). *The geography of innovation*. Boston: Kluwer.

Feldman, M. P., & Audretsch, D. B. (1999). Innovation in cities: Science-based diversity, specialization and localized competition. *European Economic Review*, *43*(2), 409–429.

Feller, I., & Menzel, D. C. (1977). Diffusion milieus as a focus of research on innovation in the public sector. *Policy Sciences*, *8*(1), 49–68.

Fernandez, S., & Moldogaziev, T. (2013). Using employee empowerment to encourage innovative behavior in the public sector. *Journal of Public Administration Research and Theory*, *23*(1), 155–187.

Fernandez, S., & Pitts, D. W. (2011). Understanding employee motivation to innovate: Evidence from front line employees in United States federal agencies. *Australian Journal of Public Administration*, *70*(2), 202–222.

Fernandez, S., & Rainey, H. G. (2006). Managing successful organizational change in the public sector. *Public Administration Review*, *66*(2), 168–176.

Fernandez, S., & Wise, L. R. (2010). An exploration of why public organizations 'Ingest' innovations. *Public Administration*, *88*(4), 979–998.

Flanagan, K., Uyarra, E., & Laranja, M. (2011). Reconceptualising the 'policy mix' for innovation. *Research Policy*, *40*(5), 702–713.

Foss, N. J., & Saebi, T. (2017). Fifteen years of research on business model innovation: How far have we come, and where should we go? *Journal of Management*, *43*(1), 200–227.

Fromhold-Eisebith, M., & Eisebith, G. (2005). How to institutionalize innovative clusters? Comparing explicit top-down and implicit bottom-up approaches. *Research Policy 34*(8), 1250–1268.

Fuglsang, L., & Pedersen, J. S. (2011). How common is public sector innovation and how similar is it to private sector innovation? In V. Bekkers, J. Edelenbos, & B. Steijn (Eds.), *Innovation in the public sector* (pp. 44–60). London: Palgrave Macmillan.

Galli, R., & Teubal, M. (2005). Paradigmatic shifts in national innovation systems. In C. Edquist (Ed.), *Systems of innovation: Technologies, institutions and organizations* (pp. 342–370). Oxon: Routledge.

Gault, F. (2018). Defining and measuring innovation in all sectors of the economy. *Research Policy*, *47*(3), 617–622.

Gault, F., & Soete, L. (2022). Innovation indicators. In *Oxford research encyclopedia of business and management* (pp. 1–26). New York: Oxford University Press. https://oxfordre.com/business/display/10.1093/acrefore/9780190224851.001.0001/acrefore-9780190224851-e-331

Gaynor, G. H. (2013). Innovation: Top down or bottom up. *IEEE Engineering Management Review*, *41*(3), 5–6.

Geels, F. W., & Schot, J. (2007). Typology of sociotechnical transition pathways. *Research Policy*, 36(3), 399–417.

Gertner, J. (2012). *The idea factory: Bell labs and the great age of American innovation*. New York, NY: Penguin.

Giest, S. (2017). The challenges of enhancing collaboration in life science clusters: Lessons from Chicago, Copenhagen and Singapore. *Science and Public Policy*, 44(2), 163–173. https://doi.org/10.1093/scipol/scw046

Gintova, M. (2019). Use of social media in Canadian public administration: Opportunities and barriers. *Canadian Public Administration*, 2019(1), 7–26.

Glaeser, E. L., Kallal, H. D., Scheinkman, J. A., & Shleifer, A. (1992). Growth in cities. *Journal of Political Economy*, 100(6), 1126–1152.

Glor, E. (2001). Innovation patterns. *The Innovation Journal: The Public Sector Innovation Journal*, 6(3), 1–46.

Goffin, K., & Mitchell, R. (2010). *Innovation management: Strategy and implementation using the pentathlon framework*. Basingstoke: Palgrave Macmillan.

Gold, E. R. (2021). The fall of the innovation empire and its possible rise through open science. *Research Policy*, 50(5), 104226.

Goodsell, C. T. (1985). *The case for bureaucracy: A public administration polemic*. Chatham, NJ: Chatham House.

Goss, R. P. (1996). A distinct public administration ethics? *Journal of Public Administration Research and Theory*, 6(4), 573–597.

Greenhalgh, T., Robert, G., Macfarlane, F., Bate, P., & Kyriakidou, O. (2004). Diffusion of innovations in service organizations: Systematic review and recommendations. *Milbank Quarterly*, 82(4), 581–629. https://doi.org/10.1111/j.0887-378X.2004.00325.x

Gregory, R. G. (1993). The Australian innovation system. In R. R. Nelson (Ed.), *National innovation systems: A comparative analysis* (pp. 324–352). New York: Oxford University Press.

Griffith, R., Huergo, E., Mairesse, J., & Peters, B. (2006). Innovation and productivity across four European countries. *Oxford Review of Economic Policy*, 22(4), 483–498. https://doi.org/10.1093/oxrep/grj028

Griliches, Z. (1979). Issues in assessing the contribution of research and development to productivity growth. *Bell Journal of Economics*, 10(1), 92–116.

Griliches, Z. (1987). *R&D, patents and productivity*. Chicago, IL: University of Chicago Press.

Guenduez, A. A., & Mettler, T. (2023). Strategically constructed narratives on artificial intelligence: What stories are told in governmental artificial intelligence policies? *Government Information Quarterly*, 40(1), 101719.

Guenduez, A. A., Mettler, T., & Schedler, K. (2020). Technological frames in public administration: What do public managers think of big data? *Government Information Quarterly*, *37*(1), 101406.

Gueras, D., & Garofalo, C. (2010). *Practical ethics in public administration*. Vienna, VA: Berrett-Koehler Publishers.

Guerzoni, M., Aldridge, T. T., Audretsch, D. B., & Desai, S. (2014). A new industry creation and originality: Insight from the funding sources of university patents. *Research Policy*, *43*(10), 1697–1706.

Gulick, L. (2015). Notes on the theory of organization. In J. M. Shafritz, & P. H. Whitbeck (Eds.), *Classics of organization theory* (pp. 52–61). Boston, MA: Cengage Learning.

Gumusluoglu, L., & Ilsev, A. (2009). Transformational leadership, creativity, and organizational innovation. *Journal of Business Research*, *62*(4), 461–473.

Hackman, J. R., & Oldham, G. R. (1980). *Work redesign*. Reading, MA: Addison-Wesley.

Hage, J. T. (1999). Organizational innovation and organizational change. *Annual Review of Sociology*, *25*, 597–622.

Hall, P. A. (1983). Policy innovation and the structure of the State: The politics-administration nexus in France and Britain. *The ANNALS of the American Academy of Political and Social Science*, *466*(1), 43–59.

Hall, P. A., & Thelen, K. (2009). Institutional change in varieties of capitalism. *Socio-Economic Review*, *7*(1), 7–34.

Hameduddin, T., Fernandez, S., & Demircioglu, M. A. (2020). Conditions for open innovation in public organizations: Evidence from Challenge. gov. *Asia Pacific Journal of Public Administration*, *42*(2), 111–131.

Han, H. (2019). Governance for green urbanisation: Lessons from Singapore's green building certification scheme. *Environment and Planning C-Politics and Space*, *37*(1), 137–156. https://doi.org/10.1177/2399654418778596

Hannan, M. T., & Freeman, J. (1984). Structural inertia and organizational change. *American Sociological Review*, *49*(2), 149–164.

Hansen, J. A., & Pihl-Thingvad, S. (2019). Managing employee innovative behaviour through transformational and transactional leadership styles. *Public Management Review*, *21*(6), 918–944.

Hansen, S.-O., & Wakonen, J. (1997). Innovation, a winning solution? *International Journal of Technology Management*, *13*(4), 345–358.

Haque, M. S. (1996). The contextless nature of public administration in Third World countries. *International Review of Administrative Sciences*, *62*(3), 315–329.

Hargadon, A. B., & Douglas, Y. (2001). When innovations meet institutions: Edison and the design of the electric light. *Administrative Science Quarterly*, *46*(3), 476–501.

Hart, N. (1996). Marshall's theory of value: The role of external economies. *Cambridge Journal of Economics*, 20(3), 353–369.

Hartley, J. (2005). Innovation in governance and public services: Past and present. *Public Money and Management*, 25(1), 27–34.

Hartley, J. (2014). New development: Eight and a half propositions to stimulate frugal innovation. *Public Money & Management*, 34(3), 227–232.

Hartley, J., Alford, J., Hughes, O., & Yates, S. (2013). *Leading with political astuteness – A white paper: A study of public managers in Australia, New Zealand and the United Kingdom.* Canberra: Australia and New Zealand School of Government, Chartered Institute of Management & The Open University Business School.

Hartley, J., & Knell, L. (2022). Innovation, exnovation and intelligent failure. *Public Money & Management*, 42(1), 40–48.

Hartley, J., Sørensen, E., & Torfing, J. (2013). Collaborative innovation: A viable alternative to market competition and organizational entrepreneurship. *Public Administration Review*, 73(6), 821–830.

Hashi, I., & Stojčič, N. (2013). The impact of innovation activities on firm performance using a multi-stage model: Evidence from the community innovation survey 4. *Research Policy*, 42(2), 353–366.

Hatry, H. P. (2006). *Performance measurement: Getting results.* Washington, DC: The Urban Institute.

Hayter, C. S., Link, A. N., & Scott, J. T. (2018). Public-sector entrepreneurship. *Oxford Review of Economic Policy*, 34(4), 676–694.

Heimstädt, M., & Reischauer, G. (2019). Framing innovation practices in interstitial issue fields: open innovation in the NYC administration. *Innovation*, 21(1), 128–150. https://doi.org/10.1080/14479338.2018.1514259

Heper, M., & Berkman, U. (1979). Administrative studies in Turkey: A general perspective. *International Social Science Journal*, 31(2), 305–327.

Heracleous, L., & Johnston, R. (2009). Can business learn from the public sector? *European Business Review*, 21(4), 373–379. https://doi.org/10.1108/09555340910970454

Herrmann, A. M., & Peine, A. (2011). When 'national innovation system' meet 'varieties of capitalism' arguments on labour qualifications: On the skill types and scientific knowledge needed for radical and incremental product innovations. *Research Policy*, 40(5), 687–701.

Hijal-Moghrabi, I., Sabharwal, M., & Ramanathan, K. (2020). Innovation in public organizations: Do government reforms matter? *International Journal of Public Sector Management*, 33(6/7), 731–749.

Hirst, G., Van Knippenberg, D., Chen, C.-H., & Sacramento, C. A. (2011). How does bureaucracy impact individual creativity? A cross-level investigation of team contextual influences on goal orientation–creativity relationships. *Academy of Management Journal*, 54(3), 624–641.

Ho, P. (2015). Reasonable men adapt, unreasonable men change the World. In S. Jayakumar, & R. Sagar (Eds.), *The big ideas of Lee Kuan Yew* (pp. 88–101). Singapore: Straits Times Press.

Ho, Y.-P., Ruan, Y., Hang, C.-C., & Wong, P.-K. (2016). Technology upgrading of small-and-medium-sized enterprises (SMEs) through a manpower secondment strategy – A mixed-methods study of Singapore's T-Up program. *Technovation, 57–58*, 21–29.

Hochberg, Y. V., Serrano, C., & Ziedonis, R. (2015). Intangible but bankable. *Science, 348*(6240), 1202.

Hodgson, M. G. (2002). *Rethinking world history: Essays on Europe, Islam and world history*. Cambridge, UK: Cambridge University Press.

Hofstede, G. (1998). Identifying organizational subcultures: An empirical approach. *Journal of Management Studies, 35*(1), 1–12.

Hofstede, G., Hofstede, G., & Minkov, M. (2010). *Cultures and organizations: Software of the mind*. New York, NY: McGraw-Hill.

Hofstede, G., Neuijen, B., Ohayv, D. D., & Sanders, G. (1990). Measuring organizational cultures: A qualitative and quantitative study across twenty cases. *Administrative Science Quarterly, 35*(2), 286–316.

Hood, C. (1991). A public management for all seasons? *Public Administration, 69*(1), 3–19.

Hood, C., & Dixon, R. (2013). A model of cost-cutting in government? The great management revolution In UK central government reconsidered. *Public Administration, 91*(1), 114–134.

Hood, C., & Dixon, R. (2015). *A government that worked better and cost less?: Evaluating three decades of reform and change in UK central Government*. Oxford: Oxford University Press.

Hood, C., & Peters, G. (2004). The middle aging of new public management: Into the age of paradox? *Journal of Public Administration Research and Theory, 14*(3), 267–282.

Howlett, M., & Ramesh, M. (2014). The two orders of governance failure: Design mismatches and policy capacity issues in modern governance. *Policy and Society, 33*(4), 317–327.

Howlett, M., Ramesh, M., & Perl, A. (2009). *Studying public policy: Policy cycles and policy subsystems*. New York: Oxford University Press.

Huang, B., & Yu, J. (2019). Leading digital technologies for coproduction: The case of "Visit Once" administrative service reform in Zhejiang Province, China. *Journal of Chinese Political Science, 24*(3), 513–532.

Hultman, N., Sierra, K., & Shapiro, A. (2012). *Innovation and technology for green growth*. Washington, DC: The Brookings Institution.

Hüsig, S., & Mann, H.-G. (2010). The role of promoters in effecting innovation in higher education institutions. *Innovation, 12*(2), 180–191.

Hyytinen, A., & Toivanen, O. (2005). Do financial constraints hold back innovation and growth? Evidence on the role of public policy. *Research Policy, 34*(9), 1385–1403.

Intarakumnerd, P., Chairatana, P.-A., & Tangchitpiboon, T. (2002). National innovation system in less successful developing countries: the case of Thailand. *Research Policy, 31*(8), 1445–1457.

Irvine, K., Chua, L., & Eikass, H. S. (2014). The four national taps of Singapore: A holistic approach to water resources management from drainage to drinking water. *Journal of Water Management Modeling*, 1–11. https://doi.org/10.14796/jwmm.C375

Jaffe, A. B. (1986). *Technological opportunity and spillovers of R&D: Evidence from firms' patents, profits and market value.* Cambridge, MA: National Bureau of Economic Research. Working Paper No. 1815.

Janenova, S., & Kim, P. S. (2016). Innovating public service delivery in transitional countries: The case of one stop shops in Kazakhstan. *International Journal of Public Administration, 39*(4), 323–333.

Jia, N., Huang, K. G., & Man Zhang, C. (2019). Public governance, corporate governance, and firm innovation: An examination of state-owned enterprises. *Academy of Management Journal, 62*(1), 220–247.

Jones, G. R. (1983). Transaction costs, property rights, and organizational culture: An exchange perspective. *Administrative Science Quarterly, 28*(3), 454–467.

Jordan, S. R. (2014). The innovation imperative: An analysis of the ethics of the imperative to innovate in public sector service delivery. *Public Management Review, 16*(1), 67–89.

Jørgensen, T. B., & Bozeman, B. (2007). Public values: An inventory. *Administration & Society, 39*(3), 354–381.

Judge, T. A., & Bono, J. E. (2001). Relationship of core self-evaluations traits – self-esteem, generalized self-efficacy, locus of control, and emotional stability – with job satisfaction and job performance: A meta-analysis. *Journal of Applied Psychology, 86*(1), 80.

Jung, C. S., & Lee, G. (2016). Organizational climate, leadership, organization size, and aspiration for innovation in government agencies. *Public Performance & Management Review, 39*(4), 757–782.

Jung, H. J., & Lee, J. (2016). The quest for originality: A new typology of knowledge search and breakthrough inventions. *Academy of Management Journal, 59*(5), 1725–1753.

Kaasa, A. (2013). *Culture as a possible factor of innovation: Evidence from the European Union and neighbouring countries.* Retrieved from www.ub.edu/searchproject/wp-content/uploads/2013/01/WP-5.5.pdf

Kamensky, J. M. (1996). Role of the "reinventing government" movement in federal management reform. *Public Administration Review, 56*(3), 247–255.

Kanter, R. M. (1983). *The change masters: Innovation and productivity in American corporations*. New York: Simon & Schuster.

Kantor, J., & Streitfeld, D. (2015). Inside Amazon: Wrestling big ideas in a bruising workplace. *The New York Times*, 2015, 1–9. www.nytimes .com/2015/08/16/technology/inside-amazon-wrestling-big-ideas-in-a-bruising-workplace.html

Kapucu, N., & Boin, A. (2017). *Disaster and crisis management: Public management perspectives*. New York, NY: Routledge.

Kapucu, N., & Ustun, Y. (2018). Collaborative crisis management and leadership in the public sector. *International Journal of Public Administration, 41*(7), 548–561.

Kapucu, N., & Van Wart, M. (2006). The evolving role of the public sector in managing catastrophic disasters: Lessons learned. *Administration & Society, 38*(3), 279–308.

Kassim, H., Peterson, J., Bauer, M. W., Connolly, S., Dehousse, R., Hooghe, L., & Thompson, A. (2013). *The European commission of the twenty-first century*. Oxford: Oxford University Press.

Kattel, R., Cepilovs, A., Drechsler, W., Kalvet, T., Lember, V., & Tõnurist, P. (2013). Can we measure public sector innovation? A literature review. *LIPSE Working papers (no. 2)*. Rotterdam: Erasmus University Rotterdam.

Kattel, R., & Mazzucato, M. (2018). Mission-oriented innovation policy and dynamic capabilities in the public sector. *Industrial and Corporate Change, 27*(5), 787–801.

Kattel, R., Randma-Liiv, T., & Kalvet, T. (2011). Small states, innovation and administrative capacity. In V. Bekkers, J. Edelenbos, & B. Steijn (Eds.), *Innovation in the public sector* (pp. 61–81). London: Palgrave Macmillan.

Kaufman, H. (1981). *The administrative behavior of federal bureau chiefs*. Washington, DC: Brookings Institution.

Kearney, C., Hisrich, R., & Roche, F. (2008). A conceptual model of public sector corporate entrepreneurship. *International Entrepreneurship and Management Journal, 4*(3), 295–313.

Kelly, J. M. (2005). The dilemma of the unsatisfied customer in a market model of public administration. *Public Administration Review, 65*(1), 76–84.

Kelman, S. (2005). *Unleashing change: A study of organizational renewal in government*. Washington, DC: Brookings Institution Press.

Kelman, S. (2021). *Bureaucracies as innovative organizations*. Faculty Research Working Paper Series RWP21-017. Boston, MA: Harvard Kennedy School.

Kettl, D. F. (2005). *The global public management revolution*. Washington, DC: Brookings Institution Press.

Kettl, D. F. (2008). *The next government of the United States: Why our institutions fail us and how to fix them*. New York City: WW Norton & Company.

Kim, Y. (2010). Stimulating entrepreneurial practices in the public sector: The roles of organizational characteristics. *Administration & Society*, 42(7), 780–814.

Kimberly, J. R. (1979). Issues in the creation of organizations: Initiation, innovation, and institutionalization. *Academy of Management Journal*, 22(3), 437–457.

Kleiman, M. A., & Teles, S. M. (2008). Market and non-market failures. In M. Moran, M. Rein, & R. E. Goodin (Eds.), *The Oxford handbook of public policy* (pp. 624–650). Oxford: Oxford University Press.

Klein, K. J., & Sorra, J. S. (1996). The challenge of innovation implementation. *Academy of Management Review*, 21(4), 1055–1080.

Knill, C. (1999). Explaining cross-national variance in administrative reform: Autonomous versus instrumental bureaucracies. *Journal of Public Policy*, 19(2), 113–139.

Knox, S., & Marin-Cadavid, C. (2022). A practice approach to fostering employee engagement in innovation initiatives in public service organisations. *Public Management Review*, 1–26.

Kobarg, S., Stumpf-Wollersheim, J., & Welpe, I. M. (2019). More is not always better: Effects of collaboration breadth and depth on radical and incremental innovation performance at the project level. *Research Policy*, 48(1), 1–10.

Kremer, M. (1993). The O-ring theory of economic development. *The Quarterly Journal of Economics*, 108(3), 551–575.

Kuhlmann, S. (2001). Future governance of innovation policy in Europe – Three scenarios. *Research Policy*, 30(6), 953–976.

Kuhlmann, S., & Rip, A. (2014). *The challenge of addressing Grand Challenges: A think piece on how innovation can be driven towards the "Grand Challenges" as defined under the prospective European Union Framework Programme Horizon 2020*. University of Twente.

Kuznets, S. (1962). Inventive activity: Problems of definition and measurement. In *The rate and direction of inventive activity: Economic and social factors* (pp. 19–52). Princeton, NJ: Princeton University Press.

Lahat, L., & Ofek, D. (2022). Emotional well-being among public employees: A comparative perspective. *Review of Public Personnel Administration*, 42(1), 31–59. https://doi.org/10.1177/0734371X20939642

Lapuente, V., & Suzuki, K. (2020). Politicization, bureaucratic legalism, and innovative attitudes in the public sector. *Public Administration Review*, 80(3), 454–467.

Lapuente, V., & Suzuki, K. (2021). The prudent entrepreneurs: Women and public sector innovation. *Journal of European Public Policy*, 28(9), 1345–1371.

Lawrence, P. R., & Lorsch, J. W. (1967). *Organization and environment managing differentiation and integration.* Boston, MA: Graduate School of Business Administration, Harvard University.

Leckel, A., Veilleux, S., & Dana, L. P. (2020). Local open innovation: A means for public policy to increase collaboration for innovation in SMEs. *Technological Forecasting and Social Change, 153,* 119891.

Lee, C., & Ma, L. (2020). The role of policy labs in policy experiment and knowledge transfer: A comparison across the UK, Denmark, and Singapore. *Journal of Comparative Policy Analysis, 22*(4), 281–297. https://doi.org/10.1080/13876988.2019.1668657

Lee, S. (2022). When tensions become opportunities: Managing accountability demands in collaborative governance. *Journal of Public Administration Research and Theory, 32*(4), 641–655.

Lee, S. M., Hwang, T., & Choi, D. (2012). Open innovation in the public sector of leading countries. *Management Decision, 50*(1), 147–162.

Leman, C. K. (2002). Direct government. In L. M. Salamon (Ed.), *The tools of government: A guide to the new governance* (pp. 48–79). New York: Oxford University Press.

LePine, J. A., & Van Dyne, L. (2001). Peer responses to low performers: An attributional model of helping in the context of groups. *Academy of Management Review, 26*(1), 67–84.

Levitats, Z., Vigoda-Gadot, E., & Vashdi, D. R. (2019). Engage them through emotions: Exploring the role of emotional intelligence in public sector engagement. *Public Administration Review, 79*(6), 841–852.

Lewis, C. W., & Gilman, S. C. (2005). *The ethics challenge in public service: A problem-solving guide.* San Francisco, CA: John Wiley & Sons.

Lewis, E. (1988). *American politics in a bureaucratic age: Citizens, constituents, clients, and victims.* New York: University Press of America.

Lewis, J. M., Ricard, L. M., & Klijn, E. H. (2018). How innovation drivers, networking and leadership shape public sector innovation capacity. *International Review of Administrative Sciences, 84*(2), 288–307.

Leyden, D. P. (2016). Public-sector entrepreneurship and the creation of a sustainable innovative economy. *Small Business Economics, 46*(4), 553–564.

Leyden, D. P., & Link, A. N. (1992). *Government's role in innovation.* Norwell, MA: Springer Science & Business Media.

Leyden, D. P., & Link, A. N. (2015). *Public sector entrepreneurship: US technology and innovation policy.* New York, NY: Oxford University Press.

Light, P. C. (2014). *A cascade of failures: Why government fails, and how to stop it.* Retrieved from Washington, DC: www.brookings.edu/wp-content/uploads/2016/06/Light_Cascade-of-Failures_Why-Govt-Fails.pdf

Lim, S., & Prakash, A. (2014). Voluntary regulations and innovation: The case of ISO 14001. *Public Administration Review*, 74(2), 233–244.

Lindblom, C. (1959). The science of "muddling through." *Public Administration Review*, 19(2), 79–88.

Lindblom, C. E. (1979). Still muddling, not yet through. *Public Administration Review*, 39(6), 517–526.

Link, A. N. (2013). *Public support of innovation in entrepreneurial firms*. Northampton, MA: Edward Elgar Publishing.

Link, A. N. (2017). Ideation, entrepreneurship, and innovation. *Small Business Economics*, 48(2), 279–285.

Link, A. N., & Bozeman, B. (1991). Innovative behavior in small-sized firms. *Small Business Economics*, 3(3), 179–184.

Link, A. N., & Link, J. R. (2009). *Government as entrepreneur*. New York: Oxford University Press.

Link, A. N., & Rees, J. (1990). Firm size, university based research, and the returns to R&D. *Small Business Economics*, 2(1), 25–31.

Link, A. N., & Scott, J. T. (2019). The economic benefits of technology transfer from US federal laboratories. *The Journal of Technology Transfer*, 44(5), 1416–1426.

Link, A. N., & Siegel, D. S. (2007). *Innovation, entrepreneurship, and technological change*. New York: Oxford University Press.

Liu, H. K. (2017). Crowdsourcing government: Lessons from multiple disciplines. *Public Administration Review*, 77(5), 656–667.

Lodge, M., & Gill, D. (2011). Toward a new era of administrative reform? The myth of post-NPM in New Zealand. *Governance*, 24(1), 141–166.

Lœgreid, P., & Christensen, T. (2013). *Transcending new public management: The transformation of public sector reforms*. Burlington, VT: Ashgate Publishing, Ltd.

Lœgreid, P., Per, Roness, P. G., & Verhoest, K. (2011). Explaining the innovative culture and activities of state agencies. *Organization Studies*, 32(10), 1321–1347. https://doi.org/10.1177/0170840611416744

Loewe, P., & Dominiquini, J. (2006). Overcoming the barriers to effective innovation. *Strategy & Leadership*, 34(1), 24–31.

Lucas Jr, R. E. (1988). On the mechanics of economic development. *Journal of Monetary Economics*, 22(1), 3–42.

Lucas Jr, R. E. (1993). Making a miracle. *Econometrica: Journal of the Econometric Society*, 61(2), 251–272.

Lundvall, B.-Å. (2010). *National systems of innovation: Toward a theory of innovation and interactive learning*. London: Anthem press.

Lynn Jr, L. E. (2006). *Public management: Old and new*. New York, NY: Routledge.

Mann, J., & Loveridge, S. (2022). Measuring urban and rural establishment innovation in the United States. *Economics of Innovation and New Technology*, 31(7), 650–667.

Mansfield, E. (1968). *Industrial research and technological innovation: An econometric analysis*. New York: Norton.

March, J. G. (1991). Exploration and exploitation in organizational learning. *Organization Science*, 2(1), 71–87.

Marcum, J. W. (1999). Out with motivation, in with engagement. *National Productivity Review*, 18(4), 43–46. Retrieved from http://dx.doi.org/10.1002/npr.4040180409

Mazzucato, M. (2015). *The entrepreneurial state: Debunking public vs. private sector myths*. London: Anthem Press.

Mazzucato, M. (2016). An entrepreneurial society needs an entrepreneurial state. *Harvard Business Review*. https://hbr.org/2016/10/an-entrepreneurial-society-needs-an-entrepreneurial-state

Mazzucato, M. (2018). Mission-oriented innovation policies: Challenges and opportunities. *Industrial and Corporate Change*, 27(5), 803–815.

McLean, L. D. (2005). Organizational culture's influence on creativity and innovation: A review of the literature and implications for human resource development. *Advances in Developing Human Resources*, 7(2), 226–246.

Meier, K. J., Rutherford, A., & Avellaneda, C. N. (2017). *Comparative public management: Why national, environmental, and organizational context matters*. Washington, DC: Georgetown University Press.

Meijer, A. (2015). E-governance innovation: Barriers and strategies. *Government Information Quarterly*, 32(2), 198–206.

Meijer, A. (2019). Public innovation capacity: Developing and testing a self-assessment survey instrument. *International Journal of Public Administration*, 42(8), 617–627.

Meijer, A., & De Jong, J. (2020). Managing value conflicts in public innovation: Ostrich, chameleon, and dolphin strategies. *International Journal of Public Administration*, 43(11), 977–988.

Meissner, D., & Kergroach, S. (2021). Innovation policy mix: Mapping and measurement. *The Journal of Technology Transfer*, 46(1), 197–222.

Mergel, I., & Desouza, K. C. (2013). Implementing open innovation in the public sector: The case of Challenge.gov. *Public Administration Review*, 73(6), 882–890.

Merritt, C. C., Malatesta, D., Carboni, J. L., Wright, J. E., & Kennedy, S. S. (2021). What is public? Big questions emerging from the clash of legal and policy paradigms. *Perspectives on Public Management and Governance*, 4(2), 130–145.

Mitra, S. (2022). Innovations in Indian public administration. *Public Money & Management*, 43(8), 833–840.

Mohr, L. B. (1969). Determinants of innovation in organizations. *American Political Science Review*, 63(1), 111–126.

Montgomery, J. D. (1967). Sources of bureaucratic reform: Problems of power, purpose and politics. *Comparative Administrative Group Occasional Paper*.

Moon, M. J. (1999). The pursuit of managerial entrepreneurship: Does organization matter? *Public Administration Review*, 59(1), 31–43.

Moon, M. J., Khaltar, O., Lee, J., Hwang, C., & Yim, G. (2020). Public entrepreneurship and organizational performance in Asia: Do entrepreneurial leadership, ethical climate and Confucian values matter in Korea and China. *Australian Journal of Public Administration*, 79(3), 298–329.

Moore, G., & Davis, K. (2004). Learning the silicon valley way. In T. Bresnahan, & A. Gambardella (Eds.), *Building high-tech clusters: Silicon Valley and beyond* (pp. 7–39). New York: Cambridge University Press.

Moore, M., & Hartley, J. (2008). Innovations in governance. *Public Management Review*, 10(1), 3–20.

Moore, M. H. (1995). *Creating public value: Strategic management in government*. Boston, MA: Harvard University Press.

Moore, M. H. (2005). Break-through innovations and continuous improvement: Two different models of innovative processes in the public sector. *Public Money and Management*, 25(1), 43–50.

Moussa, M. (2021a). Barriers on innovation in Australian public sector organisations. In A. McMurray, N. Muenjohn, & C. Weerakoon (Eds.), *The Palgrave handbook of workplace innovation* (pp. 179–196). Cham, Switzerland: Palgrave Macmillan.

Moussa, M. (2021b). Examining and reviewing innovation strategies in Australian public sector organisations. In A. McMurray, N. Muenjohn, & C. Weerakoon (Eds.), *The Palgrave handbook of workplace innovation* (pp. 317–333). Cham, Switzerland: Palgrave Macmillan.

Mowery, D. C. (1992). The US national innovation system: Origins and prospects for change. *Research Policy*, 21(2), 125–144.

Mulgan, G. (2014). *Innovation in the public sector: How can public organisations better create, improve and adapt?* London: Nesta.

Nair, S. (2022). *Rethinking policy piloting: Insights from Indian agriculture*. India: Cambridge University Press.

Nakamura, L. (2000). Economics and the new economy: The invisible hand meets creative destruction. *Business Review*, 2000, 15–30.

Nasi, G., Cucciniello, M., Mele, V., Valotti, G., Bazurli, R., de Vries, H., … Monthuber, E. M. (2015). *Determinants and barriers of adoption, diffusion and upscaling of ICT-driven social innovation in the public sector: A comparative study across 6 EU countries.* LIPSE Research Report #5. Milan, Italy.

Nelson, R. R. (1993). *National innovation systems: A comparative analysis.* New York, NY: Oxford University Press.

Nelson, R. R., & Rosenberg, N. (1993). Technical innovation and national systems. In R. R. Nelson (Ed.), *National innovation systems: A comparative analysis* (pp. 3–21). New York, NY: Oxford University Press.

Nelson, R. R., & Winter, S. G. (1977). In search of a useful theory of innovation. *Research Policy, 6*(1), 36–76.

Neuroni, A. C., Marti, M. D., & Wüst, A. C. (2021). *"Ready to innovate?" Exploring the innovation capabilities of public agencies.* Paper presented at the Proceedings of Ongoing Research, Practitioners, Posters, Workshops, and Projects of the International Conference EGOV-CeDEM-ePart 2021, University of Granada, Spain (Hybrid) 7–9 September 2021.

Niskanen, W. A. (2017). *Bureaucracy & representative government.* New York: Routledge.

Noble, D., Charles, M. B., Keast, R., & Kivits, R. (2019). Desperately seeking innovation nirvana: Australia's cooperative research centres. *Policy Design and Practice, 2*(1), 15–34.

Noordegraaf, M., Douglas, S., Geuijen, K., & Van Der Steen, M. (2019). Weaknesses of wickedness: A critical perspective on wickedness theory. *Policy and Society, 38*(2), 278–297.

Noveck, B., & Glover, R. (2019). *Today's problems, yesterday's toolkit.* Australia and New Zealand School of Government (ANZSOG). https://apo.org.au/node/253231

Nowacki, C., & Monk, A. (2020). Ambidexterity in government: The influence of different types of legitimacy on innovation. *Research Policy, 49*(1), 103840.

O'Flynn, J. (2021). Confronting the big challenges of our time: Making a difference during and after COVID-19. *Public Management Review, 23*(7), 961–980.

O'Toole, L. J., & Meier, K. J. (2015). Public management, context, and performance: In quest of a more general theory. *Journal of Public Administration Research and Theory, 25*(1), 237–256.

OECD. (1999). *Managing national innovation systems.* Paris: Organisation for Economic Co-operation and Development.

OECD. (2015). *The innovation imperative in the public sector: Setting an agenda for action.* Paris: OECD Publishing.

OECD. (2017). *Fostering innovation in the public sector.* Paris: OECD Publishing.

OECD (2023). *Government at a glance 2023*. Paris: OECD Publishing. https://doi.org/10.1787/3d5c5d31-en.

OECD/Eurostat. (2005). *Oslo manual: Guidelines for collecting and interpreting innovation data* (3rd ed.). Paris: OECD Publishing.

OECD/Eurostat. (2018). *Oslo manual 2018: Guidelines for collecting, reporting, and using data on innovation*. Paris: OECD Publishing.

Oh, H., & Yi, C.-G. (2022). Development of innovation studies in Korea from the perspective of the national innovation system. *Sustainability*, *14*(3), 1752.

O'Leary, R. (2010). Guerrilla employees: Should managers nurture, tolerate, or terminate them? *Public Administration Review*, *70*(1), 8–19.

Osborne, D., & Gaebler, T. (1992). *Reinventing government: How the entrepreneurial spirit is transforming government*. Reading, MA: Adison Wesley Public Comp.

Osborne, D., & Plastrik, P. (1997). *Banishing bureaucracy: The five strategies for reinventing government*. New York, NY: Plume.

Osborne, S., & Brown, K. (2005). *Managing change and innovation in public sector organisations*. New York: Routledge.

Osborne, S. P., & Brown, L. (2011). Innovation, public policy and public services delivery in the UK. The word that would be king. *Public Administration*, *89*(4), 1335–1350. Retrieved from http://dx.doi.org/10.1111/j.1467-9299.2011.01932.x

Osborne, S. P., & Brown, L. (2013). *Handbook of innovation in public services*. Cheltenham: Edward Elgar Publishing.

Ostrom, E. (1965). *Public entrepreneurship: A case study in ground water basin management*. Los Angeles: University of California.

Ostrom, E. (2005). Doing institutional analysis digging deeper than markets and hierarchies. In C. Menard, & M. M. Shirley (Eds.), *Handbook of new institutional economics* (pp. 819–848). Dordrecht, The Netherlands: Springer.

Page, S. (2005). What's new about the new public management? Administrative change in the human services. *Public Administration Review*, *65*(6), 713–727.

Pakes, A. (1985). On patents, R & D, and the stock market rate of return. *Journal of Political Economy*, *93*(2), 390–409.

Pakes, A., & Griliches, Z. (1980). Patents and R&D at the firm level: A first report. *Economics Letters*, *5*(4), 377–381.

Palumbo, R. (2021). Engaging to innovate: An investigation into the implications of engagement at work on innovative behaviors in healthcare organizations. *Journal of Health Organization and Management*, *35*(8), 1025–1045.

Palumbo, R., Manesh, M. F., Pellegrini, M. M., & Flamini, G. (2022). Setting the conditions for open innovation in the food industry: Unravelling the human dimension of open innovation. *British Food Journal*, 124(6), 1786–1809.

Palumbo, R., & Manna, R. (2018). Innovation at the crossroads: An investigation of the link between inter-organizational relationships and innovation. *International Journal of Organizational Analysis*, 26(3), 432–449.

Park, C. H. (2018). Cross-sector collaboration for public innovation. *Journal of Public Administration Research and Theory*, 28(2), 293–295.

Park, C. H., & Johnston, E. W. (2017). A framework for analyzing digital volunteer contributions in emergent crisis response efforts. *New Media & Society*, 19(8), 1308–1327.

Pavitt, K. (1984). Sectoral patterns of technical change: Towards a taxonomy and a theory. *Research Policy*, 13(6), 343–373.

Perry, J. L. (2020). *Managing organizations to sustain passion for public service*. New York: Cambridge University Press.

Perry, J. L., & Danziger, J. N. (1980). The adoptability of innovations: An empirical assessment of computer applications in local governments. *Administration & Society*, 11(4), 461–492.

Perry, J. L., & Kraemer, K. L. (1978). Innovation attributes, policy intervention, and the diffusion of computer applications among local governments. *Policy Sciences*, 9(2), 179–205.

Perry, J. L, & Kraemer, K. L. (1980). Chief executive support and innovation adoption. *Administration & Society*, 12(2), 158–177.

Perry, J. L., & Rainey, H. G. (1988). The public-private distinction in organization theory: A critique and research strategy. *Academy of Management Review*, 13(2), 182–201.

Perry, J. L., & Wise, L. R. (1990). The motivational bases of public service. *Public Administration Review*, 50(3), 367–373.

Peters, B. G. (2015). *Advanced introduction to public policy*. Northampton, MA: Edward Elgar Publishing.

Peters, B. G. (2019). The politics of bureaucracy after 40 years. *The British Journal of Politics and International Relations*, 21(3), 468–479.

Peters, G. B. (2010). *The politics of bureaucracy*. New York, NY: Routledge.

Pfeffer, J. (1992). *Managing with power: Politics and influence in organizations*. Boston, MA: Harvard Business Press.

Pianta, M. (2006). Innovation and employment. In J. Fagerberg, & D. C. Mowery (Eds.), *Oxford handbook of innovation* (pp. 568–598). New York, NY: Oxford University Press.

Piatak, J. S., Sowa, J. E., Jacobson, W. S., & McGinnis Johnson, J. (2020). Infusing public service motivation (PSM) throughout the employment relationship: A review of PSM and the human resource management process. *International Public Management Journal*, 24(1), 86–105.

Pierce, J. L., & Delbecq, A. L. (1977). Organization structure, individual attitudes and innovation. *Academy of Management Review*, 2(1), 27–37.

Pillai, R., & Meindl, J. R. (1998). Context and charisma: A "meso" level examination of the relationship of organic structure, collectivism, and crisis to charismatic leadership. *Journal of Management*, 24(5), 643–671.

Pollitt, C. (2007). The new public management: An overview of its current status. *Administratie Si Management Public* (8), 110–115.

Pollitt, C. (2011). Innovation in the public sector: An introductory overview. In J. E. V. Bekkers, & B. Steijn (Eds.), *Innovation in the public sector: Linking capacity and leadership* (pp. 35–43). Basingstoke: Palgrave/Macmillan.

Pollitt, C. (2013). *The public service: Dissolution, revolution, evolution?* Paper presented at the IPAA National Conference, Canberra, Australia.

Pollitt, C., & Bouckaert, G. (2004). *Public management reform: A comparative analysis*. USA: Oxford University Press.

Pollitt, C., & Bouckaert, G. (2011). *Public management reform: A comparative analysis – New public management, governance, and the Neo-Weberian state*. New York, NY: Oxford University Press.

Pollitt, C., & Bouckaert, G. (2017). *Public management reform: A comparative analysis-into the age of austerity*. New York, NY: Oxford University Press.

Popa, S., Soto-Acosta, P., & Martinez-Conesa, I. (2017). Antecedents, moderators, and outcomes of innovation climate and open innovation: An empirical study in SMEs. *Technological Forecasting and Social Change*, 118, 134–142.

Potts, J., & Kastelle, T. (2010). Public sector innovation research: What's next? *Innovation*, 12(2), 122–137.

Prpić, J., Taeihagh, A., & Melton, J. (2015). The fundamentals of policy crowdsourcing. *Policy & Internet*, 7(3), 340–361.

Publicservice.gov.mt (n.d.). *The public service and the public sector*. https://publicservice.gov.mt/en/Pages/The%20Public%20Service/PublicService PublicSector.aspx

Public Utilities Board (PUB). (n.d.). *Four national taps*. Pub: Singapore's National Water Agency. www.pub.gov.sg/watersupply/fournationaltaps

Qiu, H., & Chreim, S. (2022). A tension lens for understanding public innovation diffusion processes. *Public Management Review*, 24(12), 1873–1893.

Quah, J. S. (2018). Why Singapore works: Five secrets of Singapore's success. *Public Administration and Policy*, 21(1), 5–21.

Raghavan, A., Demircioglu, M. A., & Taeihagh, A. (2021). Public health innovation through cloud adoption: A comparative analysis of drivers and barriers in Japan, South Korea, and Singapore. *International Journal of Environmental Research and Public Health*, 18(1). https://doi.org/10.3390/ijerph18010334

Rahm, D., Bozeman, B., & Crow, M. (1988). Domestic technology transfer and competitiveness: An empirical assessment of roles of university and governmental R&D laboratories. *Public Administration Review*, 48(6), 969–978.

Rainey, H. G. (2009). *Understanding and managing public organizations*. San Francisco, CA: John Wiley & Sons.

Rana, T., Hoque, Z., & Jacobs, K. (2019). Public sector reform implications for performance measurement and risk management practice: Insights from Australia. *Public Money & Management*, 39(1), 37–45.

Ranerup, A., & Henriksen, H. Z. (2019). Value positions viewed through the lens of automated decision-making: The case of social services. *Government Information Quarterly*, 36(4), 101377.

Rauch, J. E., & Evans, P. B. (2000). Bureaucratic structure and bureaucratic performance in less developed countries. *Journal of Public Economics*, 75(1), 49–71.

Ribeiro, B., & Shapira, P. (2020). Private and public values of innovation: A patent analysis of synthetic biology. *Research Policy*, 49(1), 103875.

Rinne, T., Steel, G. D., & Fairweather, J. (2012). Hofstede and Shane revisited: The role of power distance and individualism in national-level innovation success. *Cross-Cultural Research*, 46(2), 91–108.

Roessner, J. D. (1977). Incentives to innovate in public and private organizations. *Administration & Society*, 9(3), 341–365.

Rogers, E. M. (2003). *Diffusion of innovations*. New York: Free Press.

Romer, P. M. (1986). Increasing returns and long-run growth. *Journal of Political Economy*, 94(5), 1002–1037.

Romer, P. M. (1990). Endogenous technological change. *Journal of Political Economy*, 98(5, Part 2), S71–S102.

Romzek, B. S., & Dubnick, M. J. (1987). Accountability in the public sector: Lessons from the Challenger tragedy. *Public Administration Review*, 47(3), 227–238.

Rossini, F., & Bozeman, B. (1977). National strategies for technological innovation. *Administration & Society*, 9(1), 81–110.

Rowe, L. A., & Boise, W. B. (1974). Organizational innovation: Current research and evolving concepts. *Public Administration Review*, 34(3), 284–293.

Ryan, R. M., & Deci, E. L. (2000). Intrinsic and extrinsic motivations: Classic definitions and new directions. *Contemporary Educational Psychology*, 25(1), 54–67.

Ryan, R. M., & Deci, E. L. (2017). *Self-determination theory: Basic psychological needs in motivation, development, and wellness*. New York, NY: Guilford Publications.

Saari, E., Lehtonen, M., & Toivonen, M. (2015). Making bottom-up and top-down processes meet in public innovation. *The Service Industries Journal, 35*(6), 325–344.

Sadler, R. J. (2000). Corporate entrepreneurship in the public sector: The dance of the chameleon. *Australian Journal of Public Administration, 59*(2), 25–43.

Sahni, N. R., Wessel, M., & Christensen, C. (2013). Unleashing breakthrough innovation in government. *Stanford Social Innovation Review, 2013*(Summer), 27–31.

Salge, T. O., & Vera, A. (2012). Benefiting from public sector innovation: The moderating role of customer and learning orientation. *Public Administration Review, 72*(4), 550–559.

Sally, R. (2013). *States and firms: Multinational enterprises in institutional competition*. New York: Routledge.

Şandor, S. D. (2018). Measuring public sector innovation. *Transylvanian Review of Administrative Sciences, 14*(54), 125–137.

Sanger, M. B. (2008). From measurement to management: Breaking through the barriers to state and local performance. *Public Administration Review, 68*(S1), 70–85.

Sanger, M. B., & Levin, M. A. (1992). Using old stuff in new ways: Innovation as a case of evolutionary tinkering. *Journal of Policy Analysis and Management, 11*(1), 88–115.

Sapat, A. (2004). Devolution and innovation: The adoption of state environmental policy innovations by administrative agencies. *Public Administration Review, 64*(2), 141–151.

Sapprasert, K., & Clausen, T. H. (2012). Organizational innovation and its effects. *Industrial and Corporate Change, 21*(5), 1283–1305.

Sarkar, S. (2021). Breaking the chain: Governmental frugal innovation in Kerala to combat the COVID-19 pandemic. *Government Information Quarterly, 38*(1), 101549.

Sarros, J. C., Cooper, B. K., & Santora, J. C. (2008). Building a climate for innovation through transformational leadership and organizational culture. *Journal of Leadership & Organizational Studies, 15*(2), 145–158.

Scherer, F. M. (1983). The propensity to patent. *International Journal of Industrial Organization, 1*(1), 107–128.

Schot, J., & Steinmueller, W. E. (2018). Three frames for innovation policy: R&D, systems of innovation and transformative change. *Research Policy, 47*(9), 1554–1567.

Schumpeter, J. A. (1942). *Capitalism, socialism and democracy*. New York: Harper Brothers.

Scott, W. R., & Davis, G. F. (2015). *Organizations and organizing: Rational, natural and open systems perspectives*. Upper Saddle River, NJ: Routledge.

Serrat, O. (2017). *Knowledge solutions: Tools, methods, and approaches to drive organizational performance*. Mandaluyong, Philippines: Springer.

Shane, S. (1993). Cultural influences on national rates of innovation. *Journal of Business Venturing, 8*(1), 59–73.

Sherraden, M. (2017). Fifty years of social innovation: Reflections on social policy in Singapore. In N. T. Tan, S. Chan, K. Mehta, & D. Androff (Eds.), *Transforming society: Strategies for social development from Singapore, Asia and around the world* (pp. 31–43). London: Routledge.

Shim, D. C., Park, H. H., & Chung, K. H. (2023). Workgroup innovative behaviours in the public sector workplace: The influence of servant leadership and workgroup climates. *Public Management Review, 25*(5), 901–925.

Siegel, D. S., & Wright, M. (2015). Academic entrepreneurship: Time for a rethink? *British Journal of Management, 26*(4), 582–595.

Simon, H. A. (1976). *Administrative behavior*. New York: Free Press.

Simon, H. A. (1986). Rationality in psychology and economics. *Journal of Business, 59*(4), S209–S224.

Simon, H. A. (1998). Why public administration? *Journal of Public Administration Research and Theory: J-PART, 8*(1), 1–11.

Singhealth. (2021). *Methadone*. www.singhealth.com.sg/patient-care/medicine/methadone

Smith, K. (2005). Economic infrastructures and innovation systems. In C. Edquist (Ed.), *Systems of innovation: Technologies, institutions and organisations* (pp. 86–106). New York, NY: Routledge.

Smits, R., & Kuhlmann, S. (2004). The rise of systemic instruments in innovation policy. *International Journal of Foresight and Innovation Policy, 1*(1–2), 4–32.

Sørensen, E., & Torfing, J. (2011). Enhancing collaborative innovation in the public sector. *Administration & Society, 43*(8), 842–868.

Sørensen, E., & Torfing, J. (2018). Co-initiation of collaborative innovation in urban spaces. *Urban Affairs Review, 54*(2), 388–418.

Stensöta, H. O. (2010). The conditions of care: Reframing the debate about public sector ethic. *Public Administration Review, 70*(2), 295–303.

Stewart-Weeks, M., & Kastelle, T. (2015). Innovation in the public sector. *Australian Journal of Public Administration, 74*(1), 63–72.

Stiglitz, J. E. (2004). *The roaring nineties: A new history of the world's most prosperous decade*. New York, NY: WW Norton & Company.

Stojčič, N. (2021). Collaborative innovation in emerging innovation systems: Evidence from Central and Eastern Europe. *The Journal of Technology Transfer, 46*(2), 531–562.

Suchitwarasan, C., Cinar, E., Simms, C., & Kim, J. (2023) Public sector innovation for sustainable development goals: A comparative study of innovation types in Thailand and Korea. Australian Journal of Public Administration, doi.org/10.1111/1467-8500.12619

Suddaby, R., & Foster, W. M. (2017). History and organizational change. *Journal of Management, 43*, 19–38.

Suseno, Y., Standing, C., Gengatharen, D., & Nguyen, D. (2020). Innovative work behaviour in the public sector: The roles of task characteristics, social support, and proactivity. *Australian Journal of Public Administration, 79*(1), 41–59.

Sutton, R. I., & Staw, B. M. (1995). What theory is not. *Administrative Science Quarterly, 40*(3), 371–384.

Suzuki, K., & Avellaneda, C. N. (2018). Women and risk-taking behaviour in local public finance. *Public Management Review, 20*(12), 1741–1767.

Suzuki, K., & Demircioglu, M. A. (2019). The association between administrative characteristics and national level innovative activity: Findings from a cross-national study. *Public Performance & Management Review, 42*(4), 755–782.

Suzuki, K., & Demircioglu, M. A. (2021). Is impartiality enough? Government impartiality and citizens' perceptions of public service quality. *Governance, 34*(3), 727–764.

Suzuki, K., Ha, H., & Avellaneda, C. N. (2020). Direct and non-linear innovation effects of demographic shifts. *Australian Journal of Public Administration, 79*(3), 351–369. https://doi.org/10.1111/1467-8500.12424

Svensson, P. O., & Hartmann, R. K. (2018). Policies to promote user innovation: Makerspaces and clinician innovation in Swedish hospitals. *Research Policy, 47*(1), 277–288.

Taeihagh, A. (2017). Crowdsourcing: A new tool for policy-making? *Policy Sciences, 50*(4), 629–647.

Tan, J., & Cha, V. (2021). Innovation for circular economy. In L. Liu, & S. Ramakrishna (Eds.), *An introduction to circular economy* (pp. 369–395). Singapore: Springer.

Tan, K. P. (2008). Meritocracy and elitism in a global city: Ideological shifts in Singapore. *International Political Science Review, 29*(1), 7–27.

Taques, F. H., López, M. G., Basso, L. F., & Areal, N. (2021). Indicators used to measure service innovation and manufacturing innovation. *Journal of Innovation & Knowledge, 6*(1), 11–26.

Taylor, F. W. (1911). *The principles of scientific management.* New York: Harper & Brothers.

Teece, D. J. (1986). Profiting from technological innovation: Implications for integration, collaboration, licensing and public policy. *Research Policy, 15*(6), 285–305.

Terjesen, S., & Patel, P. C. (2017). In search of process innovations: The role of search depth, search breadth, and the industry environment. *Journal of Management, 43*(5), 1421–1446.

Thelen, K. (2009). Institutional change in advanced political economies. *British Journal of Industrial Relations, 47*(3), 471–498.

Thompson, V. A. (1965). Bureaucracy and innovation. *Administrative Science Quarterly, 10*(1), 1–20.

Tõnurist, P., Kattel, R., & Lember, V. (2017). Innovation labs in the public sector: What they are and what they do? *Public Management Review, 19*(10), 1455–1479.

Torfing, J., & Triantafillou, P. (2016). Public innovations around the World. In J. Torfing, & P. Triantafillou (Eds.), *Enhancing public innovation by transforming public governance* (pp. 71–94). New York, NY: Cambridge University Press.

Torfing, J., & Triantafillou, P. (2016). *Enhancing public innovation by transforming public governance.* New York, NY: Cambridge University Press.

Torregrosa-Hetland, S., Pelkonen, A., Oksanen, J., & Kander, A. (2019). The prevalence of publicly stimulated innovations – A comparison of Finland and Sweden, 1970–2013. *Research Policy, 48*(6), 1373–1384.

Torugsa, N., & Arundel, A. (2016a). Complexity of innovation in the public sector: A workgroup-level analysis of related factors and outcomes. *Public Management Review, 18*(3), 392–416.

Torugsa, N. A., & Arundel, A. (2016b). The nature and incidence of workgroup innovation in the Australian public sector: Evidence from the Australian 2011 state of the service survey. *Australian Journal of Public Administration, 75*(2), 202–221.

Tullock, G., Brady, G. L., & Seldon, A. (2002). *Government failure: A primer in public choice.* Washington, DC: Cato Institute.

van Acker, W., & Bouckaert, G. (2018). What makes public sector innovations survive? An exploratory study of the influence of feedback, accountability and learning. *International Review of Administrative Sciences, 84*(2), 249–268.

Van de Ven, A. H. (1986). Central problems in the management of innovation. *Management Science, 32*(5), 590–607.

Van de Ven, A. H., Polley, D. E., Garud, R., & Venkataraman, S. (1999). *The innovation journey.* New York: Oxford University Press.

van der Voet, J. (2019). Organizational decline and innovation in public organizations: A contextual framework of cutback management. *Perspectives on Public Management and Governance, 2*(2), 139–154.

Van der Voet, J., & Steijn, B. (2021). Team innovation through collaboration: How visionary leadership spurs innovation via team cohesion. *Public Management Review, 23*(9), 1275–1294.

van der Wal, Z. (2017). *The 21st century public manager*. London: Macmillan Education UK.

Van der Wal, Z., De Graaf, G., & Lasthuizen, K. (2008). What's valued most? Similarities and differences between the organizational values of the public and private sector. *Public Administration, 86*(2), 465–482.

Van der Wal, Z., & Demircioglu, M. A. (2020). More ethical, more innovative? The effects of ethical culture and ethical leadership on realized innovation. *Australian Journal of Public Administration, 79*(3), 271–278.

Van Dooren, W., Bouckaert, G., & Halligan, J. (2015). *Performance management in the public sector*. New York: Routledge.

Verhoest, K., Verschuere, B., & Bouckaert, G. (2007). Pressure, legitimacy, and innovative behavior by public organizations. *Governance, 20*(3), 469–497.

Verspagen, B. (2006). Innovation and economic growth. In J. Fagerberg, & D. C. Mowery (Eds.), *Oxford handbook of innovation* (pp. 487–513). New York, NY: Oxford University Press.

Vigoda-Gadot, E., Shoham, A., Schwabsky, N., & Ruvio, A. (2005). Public sector innovation for the managerial and the post-managerial era: Promises and realities in a globalizing public administration. *International Public Management Journal, 8*(1), 57–81.

Vivona, R. (2023). The new era leadership for the public sector? Entrepreneurship, effectiveness, and democracy. *Public Management Review*, 1–17.

Vivona, R., Demircioglu, M. A., & Audretsch, D. B. (2023). The costs of collaborative innovation. *The Journal of Technology Transfer, 48*(3), 873–899.

Vivona, R., Demircioglu, M. A., & Raghavan, A. (2021). Innovation and innovativeness for the public servant of the future: What, why, how, where, and when. In H. Sullivan, & H. Dickinson (Eds.), *The Palgrave handbook of the public servant* (pp. 1643–1664). Switzerland: Springer.

Von Hippel, E. (1986). Lead users: A source of novel product concepts. *Management Science, 32*(7), 791–805.

Von Hippel, E. (1988). *The sources of innovation*. New York: Oxford University Press.

Von Hippel, E. (2005). *Democratizing innovation*. Boston, MA: MIT Press.

Von Hippel, E. (2017). *Free innovation*. Boston, MA: The MIT Press.

Von Mises, L. (1944). *Bureaucracy*. New Haven: Yale University Press.

Waarts, E., & Van Everdingen, Y. (2005). The influence of national culture on the adoption status of innovations: An empirical study of firms across Europe. *European Management Journal, 23*(6), 601–610.

Walker, R. M. (2008). An empirical evaluation of innovation types and organizational and environmental characteristics: Towards a configuration framework. *Journal of Public Administration Research and Theory*, *18*(4), 591–615. Retrieved from http://jpart.oxfordjournals.org/content/18/4/591.abstract

Walker, R. M. (2014). Internal and external antecedents of process innovation: A review and extension. *Public Management Review*, *16*(1), 21–44.

Walsh, J. P., Lee, Y.-N., & Nagaoka, S. (2016). Openness and innovation in the US: Collaboration form, idea generation and implementation. *Research Policy*, *45*(8), 1660–1671.

Wamsley, G. L., & Zald, M. N. (1973). The political economy of public organizations. *Public Administration Review*, *33*(1), 62–73.

Wang, J., & Hooi, R. (2019). The moderation effect of workplace experience on innovation motivation: A study of STEM faculty in Singapore. *Technology Analysis & Strategic Management*, *31*(7), 862–874.

Weber, M. (1968). *The theory of social and economic organization*. New York: The Free Press.

Wegrich, K. (2019). The blind spots of collaborative innovation. *Public Management Review*, *21*(1), 12–20.

Weimer, D. L., & Vining, A. R. (2005). *Policy analysis: Concepts and practice*. Upper Saddle River: Pearson.

Wettenhall, R. (1988). Local government as innovators. *Australian Journal of Public Administration*, *47*(4), 351–375.

Weyland, K. (2008). Toward a new theory of institutional change. *World Politics*, *60*(2), 281–314.

White, R. W. (1959). Motivation reconsidered: The concept of competence. *Psychological Review*, *66*(5), 297–333.

Williamson, O. E. (1999). Public and private bureaucracies: A transaction cost economics perspectives. *The Journal of Law, Economics, and Organization*, *15*(1), 306–342.

Wilson, J. Q. (1966). Innovation in organization: Notes toward a theory. In J. D. Thompson (Ed.), *Approaches to organizational design* (pp. 193–218). Pittsburgh, PA: University of Pittsburgh Press.

Wilson, J. Q. (2000). *Bureaucracy: What government agencies do and why they do it*. New York, NY: Basic Books.

Wilson, W. (1887). The study of administration. *Political Science Quarterly*, *2*(2), 197–222.

Windrum, P. (2008). Innovation and entrepreneurship in public services. In P. Windrom, & P. Koch (Eds.), *Innovation in public sector services: Entrepreneurship, creativity and management* (pp. 3–22). Cheltenham, UK: Edward Elgar Publishing, Inc.

Windrum, P., & Koch, P. M. (2008). *Innovation in public sector services: Entrepreneurship, creativity and management*. Northampton, MA: Edward Elgar Publishing.

WIPO. (2021). *Global innovation index 2021: Tracking innovation through the COVID-19 crisis*. Geneva: World Intellectual Property Organization (WIPO).

Wirtz, B. W., Kubin, P. R., & Weyerer, J. C. (2023). Business model innovation in the public sector: An integrative framework. *Public Management Review*, 25(2), 340–375.

Wise, C. R. (2006). Organizing for homeland security after Katrina: Is adaptive management what's missing? *Public Administration Review*, 66(3), 302–318.

Wise, L. R. (1999). The use of innovative practices in the public and private sectors. *Public Productivity & Management Review*, 23(2), 150–168.

Wise, L. R. (2002). Public management reform: Competing drivers of change. *Public Administration Review*, 62(5), 556–567.

Wise, L. R., & Szucs, S. (1996). The public/private cleavage in a welfare state: Attitudes toward public management reform. *Governance*, 9(1), 43–70.

Wittmer, D. (1991). Serving the people or serving for pay: Reward preferences among government, hybrid sector, and business managers. *Public Productivity & Management Review*, 14(4), 369–383.

Word, J. K., & Sowa, J. E. (2017). *The nonprofit human resource management handbook: From theory to practice*. New York: Taylor & Francis.

Wu, X., & Ramesh, M. (2014). Market imperfections, government imperfections, and policy mixes: Policy innovations in Singapore. *Policy Sciences*, 47(3), 305–320. https://doi.org/10.1007/s11077-013-9186-x

Wynen, J., Verhoest, K., Ongaro, E., Van Thiel, S., & in cooperation with the COBRA network. (2014). Innovation-oriented culture in the public sector: Do managerial autonomy and result control lead to innovation? *Public Management Review*, 16(1), 45–66.

Wynn, D. E. Jr., Pratt, R. M. E., & Bradley, R. V. (2015). *Making open innovation ecosystems work: Case studies in healthcare*. Washington, DC: The IBM Center for The Business of Government.

Xie, X., Wu, Y., & Devece, C. (2022). Is collaborative innovation a double-edged sword for firms? The contingent role of ambidextrous learning and TMT shared vision. *Technological Forecasting and Social Change*, 175, 121340.

Yang, K., & Kassekert, A. (2010). Linking management reform with employee job satisfaction: Evidence from federal agencies. *Journal of Public Administration Research and Theory*, 20(2), 413–436. Retrieved from www.jstor.org/stable/40732517

Yidong, T., & Xinxin, L. (2013). How ethical leadership influence employees' innovative work behavior: A perspective of intrinsic motivation. *Journal of Business Ethics*, 116(2), 441–455.

Yoshida, D. T., Sendjaya, S., Hirst, G., & Cooper, B. (2014). Does servant leadership foster creativity and innovation? A multi-level mediation study of identification and prototypicality. *Journal of Business Research*, *67*(7), 1395–1404.

Yuan, Q., & Gasco-Hernandez, M. (2021). Open innovation in the public sector: Creating public value through civic hackathons. *Public Management Review*, *23*(4), 523–544.

Yuriev, A., Boiral, O., & Talbot, D. (2022). Is there a place for employee-driven pro-environmental innovations? The case of public organizations. *Public Management Review*, *24*(9), 1383–1410.

Zahoor, N., & Al-Tabbaa, O. (2020). Inter-organizational collaboration and SMEs' innovation: A systematic review and future research directions. *Scandinavian Journal of Management*, *36*(2), 101109.

Zambrano-Gutiérrez, J. C., & Puppim de Oliveira, J. A. (2022). The dynamics of sources of knowledge on the nature of innovation in the public sector: Understanding incremental and transformative innovations in local governments. *Journal of Public Administration Research and Theory*, *32*(4), 656–670.

Zhang, Y., & Zhu, X. (2020). The moderating role of top-down supports in horizontal innovation diffusion. *Public Administration Review*, *80*(2), 209–221.

Zhou, J., & Rouse, E. D. (2021). Introduction: Shared foundations and diverse inquiries for advancing creativity and innovation research. In J. Zhou, & E. D. Rouse (Eds.), *Handbook of research on creativity and innovation* (pp. 1–10). Northampton, MA: Edward Elgar Publishing.

Index

Printed in the United States
by Baker & Taylor Publisher Services